The Folklore of the British Isles
General Editor: Venetia J. Newall

The Folklore

of

Devon

The Folklore of Devon

RALPH WHITLOCK

Illustrations by Gay John Galsworthy

ROWMAN AND LITTLEFIELD
TOTOWA, NEW JERSEY

Library of Congress Cataloging in Publication Data
Whitlock, Ralph.
    The Folklore of Devon.

    (The Folklore of the British Isles)
    Bibliography: p.201
    Includes indexes.
        1. Folk-lore—England—Devon. 2. Devon, Eng.—
Social life and customs. I. Title.
GR142.D5W35   390'.09423'5   76-30400
ISBN 0-87471-954-2

First published in the United States 1977
by Rowman and Littlefield, Totowa, N.J.
Printed in Great Britain.

Contents

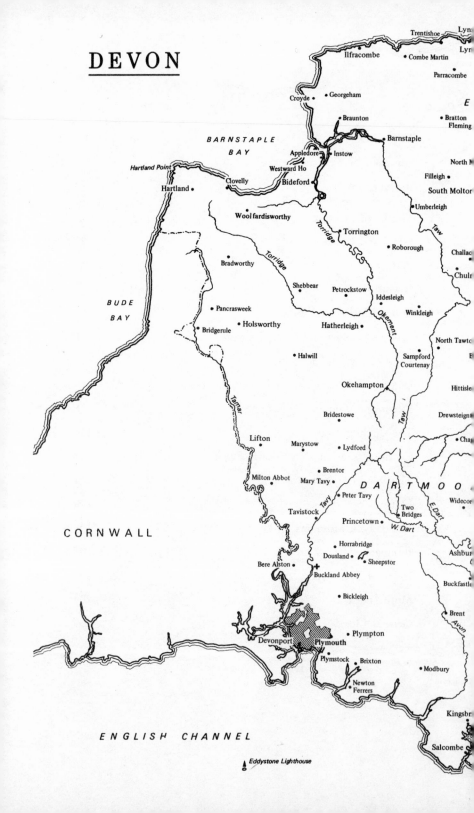

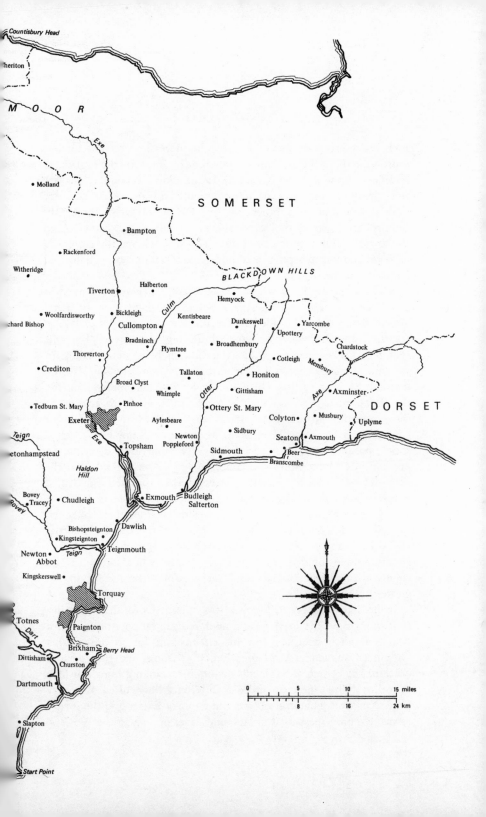

Foreword

Each year nearly a quarter of Britain's holidaymakers set out for our south-western peninsula, mostly making Devonshire their goal, or travelling through Devon towards Land's End. 'Peaceful', 'quaint', and 'charming' are favourite adjectives used by the West Country Tourist Board in their brochures, yet Defoe, an early eighteenth-century visitor, spoke of Devonshire as 'so full of great towns, and the towns so full of people, and these people so universally employed in trade and manufacture, that not only it cannot be equalled in England, but perhaps not in Europe'.

William III, the King whom Defoe championed and defended in *The True Born Englishman,* still a potent condemnation of racial prejudice, had himself landed in Devonshire two decades earlier. A tale from Brixham, where he came ashore, suggests that he chose the spot mistakenly, imagining that the Church bells were pealing in welcome. Actually they were celebrating 5 November, Guy Fawkes' downfall 83 years earlier. The Gunpowder Plot fell midway during the period considered in Wallace MacCaffrey's study of Exeter. In this prosperous, urban society, 'status was measured not by birth but by commercial success. Here rapid ascent from humble to exalted social position was not only an acceptable but a common phenomenon.' John Hooker, Chamberlain of Exeter, who died at the very end of Elizabeth I's reign, stressed that the well-established monied classes also had easy social access to the old landed gentry. Though questioning the equation of wealth with merit, Hooker felt that all was for the best in the best of counties – 'this little corner of this land can live better of itself without the rest of the land than all the residue can live without it. . . . The whole province and county within these boundaries is in greatness the second to the greatest in this land . . .'.

In his territorial boast, Hooker was wrong. Devonshire remains, as it was before the local government reorganisation, third in area among English counties, but his enthusiasm for so beautiful a 'province' was understandable. Exeter, throughout this period, continued to be one of England's major cities, ranking fourth or fifth in wealth. While the coast relied mainly on fishing, often on a very large scale, cloth manufacture was the staple of Exeter and the inland towns. Honiton specialised in lace, and Tiverton, where the Wesleys' elder brother, Samuel, had been headmaster of the famous school under George ɪ, followed suit late in the Georgian period. This resulted from the enterprise of John Heathcott, a refugee from Luddism in the Midlands.

Professor Thompson points out that, in a rare commendation of violence, John Wesley approved a hungry Irish 'mob' commandeering corn hoarded by profiteering merchants. In 1766, early in a wave of similar actions across the country, the Honiton lace workers moved against greedy local farmers, selling the corn communally on their behalf, but at the customary price. Like Wesley's Irish, they returned the proceeds to the owners, notable examples of the effectiveness of customary morality in a period before the manipulation of supply and demand aspired to quasi-legal status. From epithet, to customary term, to 'law' – here supply and demand, subjected to the whims of the profit motive, is transformed into economic folklore, a misuse of traditional thought patterns for adverse social engineering. The pretensions of the eighteenth-century merchant class, forerunners of these ideas, provoked outbreaks like that at Honiton. The rebel banner was often a loaf of bread, held aloft on a pole like a flag and decorated with a strip of black crape. In a particularly detailed account (1812), the loaf was also streaked with red ochre, the whole symbolising 'bleeding famine decked in Sackecloth.'

The standard country diet in west Devon was described by William Marshall at the end of the eighteenth century. It consisted of barley bread, skim-milk cheese and potatoes, with cider as the main drink. 'Not a few of the country labourers', he added, 'may be said to be honestly dishonest, declaring that a poor man cannot bring up a family on six shillings and honesty.' A rung or two up the economic ladder, John Tom was born into this world in the winter of 1799. Son of an innkeeper in mid-Cornwall, he spent his formative years at Launceston, under the care of the Reverend Richard Cope, a London Minister who ran the Congregational school there.

Dr Cope was headmaster at Launceston from 1800 to 1820, and apparently instilled into his pupils feelings of godly devotion bordering on fanaticism. The West Country environment probably increased his sense of mission, for in 1811 the *Taunton Courier* wrote: 'The belief in supernatural agency is universally prevalent in the Western Counties, and very few villages there are who cannot reckon at least one who is versed in "Hell's Black Grammar". This was a year or two before Tom arrived at Launceston. Writing from Tavistock nearly 25 years later, just two years before Tom's death, Anna Bray regarded the local country-folk as a people apart – 'in no part of England has the march of intellect marched at a slower pace than on the moor'. Her husband was Vicar of Tavistock, which bordered on Dartmoor. Thirty-three years after this, the Werrington Witch, probably a contemporary of Tom's at the time of his youthful days at Dr Cope's school, was an unwelcome *habituée* of Launceston market. A correspondent writing to *Notes and Queries* late in 1870, described the uncouth and sinister local attitude towards her, and added this comment: 'Superstition still prevails to a great extent' in the area, 'not only among the very poor and ignorant but among those who . . . would be supposed to have received . . . such an education as would dispel from their minds in some degree the idle fears of their ancestors' – farmers and landowners, for example.

Werrington and Sampford Courtenay, about 15 miles to the east, both lie in Black Torrington Hundred, the part of the county in which the Courtenay family acquired property in the thirteenth century. Later Powderham Castle, south of Exeter, became their seat, and it was to this distinguished residence that John Tom laid claim after he began, late in 1832, to style himself 'Sir William Percy Honeywood Courtenay, Knight of Malta, Rightful Heir to the Earldom of Devon, and of the Kentish estates of Sir Edward Hales, King of the Gypsies and King of Jerusalem'. In December 1832, when he stood for Parliament for Canterbury and received 375 votes – nearly 19 per cent of the votes cast – he wrote: 'I am the Heir of that family which none in Europe can excel, neither in ancient pedigree or illustrious actions.'

If Hooker only slightly exaggerated Devon's territorial importance, the same may be said of Tom's claims for the doyen of Devonshire families. It was true, in the first place, that they had a most distinguished continental past. And, as Leslie Pine, then Editor of *Burke's*, pointed out, the Courtenay Earldom of Devon, by surviving the Wars of the Roses with its influence intact, represented a rare exception among major British families. Henry Courtenay, whose son John was for a time the favourite of Queen Mary, was executed in 1539, and it was then that the family's local power waned rapidly. Ten years later the peasants of Sampford Courtenay were up in arms, but they were fighting for the Latin Prayer Book, not for the honour of the Earldom, although the Courtenays were still Catholics. Their bloody but futile gesture typifies attachment to pure symbolism, a characteristic not harmful in itself, but which is unduly open to exploitation. The mentally unbalanced John Tom, as Sir William Courtenay, was sane enough to be well aware of this.

Tom, or Courtenay, as he is more generally remembered, showed, in the same demagogic manner as Hitler, but without the accompanying zeal, a seemingly natural political flair. The background of this is unknown, but the seeds can perhaps be sought in the area where he grew up. Though calling himself Courtenay, his banner in later years was probably based on the Bedford lion. Lord Russell, created first Earl of Bedford in 1550 after his suppression of the Sampford Courtenay rising, came from a Dorset family. But in 1539, during the suppression of the monasteries, he had received the extensive properties of Tavistock Abbey. Werrington, with North Petherwin – parishes just outside Launceston on the Cornish side of the Tamar – probably became part of Devon because of their association with Tavistock. This was land which was much fought over during the Civil War, when Francis Russell, the fourth Earl, was among the mentors of the parliamentary side. John Pym, virtually Chief Executive of the Parliamentarians during his last years, was closely associated with Bedford, and was M.P. for Tavistock from 1625 until his death (1643). He lived to see the Roundhead triumph in April 1643 over a royalist army based at Launceston, a success attributed by parliamentary propagandists to a miraculous thunderstorm. This so dispirited the larger royalist forces that they withdrew towards Launceston, abandoning much of their equipment. For almost three years the Tamar was effectively the border between royalist Cornwall and the Parliamentarians.

Courtenay's political views were, according to the manner of his period, distinctly radical. On the other hand, like Launceston in which he grew up, he stood on the borderline where allegiance to the Crown was concerned. 'Justice for the poor! Justice for the rich!', a slogan he first used in 1833, has an ambivalent meaning, and by the final year of his life a favourite biblical quotation had become: 'Go to now, ye rich men, weep and howl for your miseries that shall come upon you.' But, at least at the period of his parliamentary campaign, his speeches often included a loyal toast.

Less than a year after appropriating the Courtenay title, he was certified insane, but four years later, following a distinguished career in the asylum's cricket team, he was set free. Handed into the care of friends near Faversham – he had been in Maidstone asylum – he rapidly recruited a retinue among local labourers and small farmers, and, on 29 May 1838, the bread-loaf banner of rural poverty and unrest was raised again. 'The Health of the Poor' was the toast on this occasion, and before proposing it Courtenay had removed his usual imposing attire – he sometimes dressed as an eastern potentate – and donned the smock of an ordinary labourer. That this was Royal Oak Day seems to have been coincidental, and there is no indication that the occasion was recognised by any of his followers.

The loaf banner evidently had no crape adornment, but beside it was carried another flag, a rampant lion in red, on a pale blue field. Courtenay's biographer, Philip Rogers, thinks that this was the lion of England, already seen as badge of *The Lion*, a journal which Sir William had published periodically during Spring 1833. But here the beast resembles the traditional lion of England, gazing morosely forth, but with all its feet on the ground. Courtenay's banner, which has been preserved, shows a more inspiring emblem, and its heraldic background, as already suggested, might have been the Bedford lion.

It seems possible that he may also have had in mind the lion of *Genesis* 49.9 ('Judah is a lion's welp . . .'), an obscure portion of the Old Testament which, when he was still at Launceston, inspired a 64-year-old Devonshire visionary to an impressive phantom pregnancy. Joanna Southcott – 'such wondrous woman never was before,' she said of herself – was to give birth to the Shiloh of *Genesis* 49.10, and her disillusionment following the collapse of her pregnancy was rapidly cut short by death (1814).

By 1829, three years before John Tom transformed himself into Courtenay, another eccentric named Zion Ward had begun to enrapture reforming and anti-clerical audiences by asserting that he was Miss Southcott's Shiloh. Tom, who had joined the radical Spencean Society eight years earlier, would almost certainly have heard about this. It is even more clear that he knew of John Wroe, a Yorkshireman who claimed to have inherited the Southcottean mantle and to be called to a special mission towards the Jews. Courtenay's original appearance in Kent, before his Canterbury parliamentary campaign, was under the name of Count Moses

Rothschild, and like Miss Southcott's followers, elements of Jewish tradition seem to have influenced his appearance. Moreover, he aped Wroe in renaming the months – 1st Moon, for example, and so on.

Zion Ward interpreted the baffling prophecy in *Genesis* 49 to identify Shiloh with Christ, and himself with both. In January 1838, coincidentally a few months after Ward's death, Courtenay too conferred Christhood upon himself, a boast which he spelled out still more esoterically at the outset of his little rebellion. He had descended from the clouds and, not being a mortal man, would vanish without trace at the onset of a threatening enemy. When he and seven of his supporters met their ends in pitched battle with the authorities two days later, this claim was disproved, though some among his followers persisted for a time in expecting a resurrection.

Garbled as it is, the idea of descent from the clouds probably derived from *Revelation* 12. In this, the 'woman clothed with the sun, and with the moon under her feet' is mentioned, and this was a role in which Joanna Southcott had seen herself. Courtenay was fond of quoting *Revelation* 6.13, which speaks of the stars falling to earth. He would then draw his two pistols and fire skywards to bring this about, a proof of his supernatural power which greatly impressed his audience. The same Chapter in *Revelation* refers to a conquering hero on a white horse, a description which, as he liked to point out, fitted Courtenay's steed.

Courtenay's rebellion, local and ill-supported though it was, caused enough interest for the Central Society of Education to commission a report. This was put in the hands of a barrister named Liardet, and his comments included the following:

> During my stay in the district, I did not once observe the peasantry engaged in any games or sports, notwithstanding the weather was unusually favourable for such exercises. . . . For them there appeared to be no recreation of either an active or a quiet character, unless they resorted to the beershop, the only place open to them for enjoyment of any kind. . . .
>
> It is the absence of all lively and innocent amusements which has stamped on our peasantry the heavy clownish air which all foreigners remark. . . . but besides rendering men dull and heavy, it tends to make them brutal and savage, and incapable of deriving any pleasurable excitement, except from debauchery or fanaticism.

In these matters, not unimportant points in civilisation, we have positively receded since the days of Elizabeth.

Poverty, though widespread, was not universally abject, and certainly not among Courtenay's rebels. Boredom, coupled with a pseudo-religious fervour based on a very little biblical knowledge, drove them to follow him. Pope, 120 years earlier, described the plight of Teresa Blount, a member of the privileged classes, 'on her Leaving the Town after Coronation':

> She went, to plain-work and to purling brooks,
> Old-fashion'd halls, dull Aunts, and croaking rooks:
> She went from Op'ra, Park, Assembly, Play,
> To morning-walks, and pray'rs three hours a day.

To the wealthy it was, of course, open to recreate, on a small scale, the pleasures of town, the 'Op'ra, Park, Assembly, Play'. The empty social gatherings, polite musical soirées and amateur dramatics of country house life would seem boring today. But what a contrast to the opportunities available to the agricultural working class. Liardet posed the situation in extreme terms, but it was not an uncommon picture. It was often thanks to the intervention of an enlightened intelligentsia that rural culture was revivified, and while patronage is not an endearing system, is it really to be regretted in these circumstances?

The fact that, in some cases, popular culture found its genesis or resurrection in mimicry of the educated classes, does not imply that it was unreal, or fulfilled no genuine need. The country gentry, as well as migrants from the city merchant classes, could provide entertainments in which the common folk participated, either as audience or – in the case of country house cricket, for example – as performers. Imitation was not only the finest form of flattery; better still if it appealed to the antiquarian fashions of the day, or contributed to the sentimental upper-class view of country life.

Ralph Whitlock has been farming and writing on country matters for the last 40 years. As a result of his own personal experience and memories, and of his many contacts, he has produced a picture of traditional Devonshire beliefs and customs that is evocative and entertaining as well as authoritative.

London University, August 1976 Venetia Newell

Introduction

DEVON, EVEN till the present century, was a county of isolated communities. Partly this was due to its geology and topography, partly to its history. The county, the third largest in England, has as its nucleus the huge, austere and almost uninhabited massif of Dartmoor, around which the more fertile countryside is arranged as a frame. On the north it is fenced in by another bleak plateau of almost equal altitude, though Exmoor itself is two-thirds in Somerset. Another maze of steep-sided hills serves as a barrier between Devon and south Somerset and west Dorset. Nor are the intervening vales flat plains but rather a tangle of lesser hills, many of them buried in woods. It is a secretive, half-tamed countryside.

Although the geological measures of Devon range from volcanic granite to red sandstone and soft Cretaceous strata in east Devon, all have the common attribute of lending themselves to the formation of mud. Devon in winter, and in much of the other seasons as well, for the county has a high rainfall, is decidedly muddy. In the centuries before railroads and turnpikes a journey of twenty miles, such as would occupy a man galloping over the turf of the chalk country only a few hours, was a major expedition, not to be lightly undertaken. Until the eighteenth century there were few, if any, wheeled vehicles in Devon, the normal mode of transport being by pack-ponies and sledges. The latter, of course, did nothing to improve the deep sunken lanes which are a feature of the Devon countryside. The ruts grew deeper, year by year, and the high banks on either side prevented the lanes from drying out.

Fortunately the county has a long, indented coastline with numerous good anchorages, as well as several rivers offering access to the interior. Probably the existence of sea highways was at least partly responsible for the late development of land ones. The fact that Devon has two coasts has, however, some significance. The Taw and Torridge empty themselves into Bideford Bay, which faces northwestwards, and for the men of Bideford and Barnstaple to travel by sea to Exeter and Plymouth necessitates a voyage through the stormy waters around Land's End. Yet the worst mud and some of the most inhospitable hills in the county are interposed between the valleys of the Bideford rivers and that of the Exe. Small wonder that they turned their backs on each other and developed independently – as indeed, to some extent, did every other valley in the entire county.

When Vespasian, the Roman general, came to Devon during his campaign of conquest in AD 47-48 he found the country inhabited by the Dumnonii, a Celtic tribe. Thereafter, throughout the Roman era, it seems likely that the Dumnonii were left largely to govern themselves, though doubtless through the agency of Roman-educated native gentry. Very few villas have been discovered in Devon, and these have been in the southeast corner, within easy distance of the Fosse Way, which had its terminus at a port near the mouth of the Axe.

The last Roman legions left Britain about the year AD 410. The Saxon conquest of Dyvnaint, as the British state of the south-western peninsula was called, began in earnest more than two hundred years later. During that long period only one outstanding event is recorded, and that was a wholesale migration of Britons across the Channel to Armorica, which, largely because of that influx of population, became known as Britanny. The reason for the exodus is thought to have been plague, famine and despair of any settled future, owing to harassment by Saxon raiders. The migration was so large that, in conjunction with other disasters, it must have left large areas of Devon more or less vacant. In the years that followed, small parties of Saxons apparently came by sea to settle in the little river valleys of east Devon. They were not numerous enough to undertake any campaign of extermination against the remaining Britons, even if they had wished. When the kings of Wessex eventually determined on annexation, the Saxons had become Christian, so the war followed the normal pattern of conflict between Christian states. The Saxons evidently parcelled out the best lands into estates for their most powerful lords, but left the Celtic peasants in occupation of many of their holdings, particularly on the poorer soils.

So Briton and Saxon lived on, side by side, in the combes and vales of Devon, and the countryside was so thinly populated that there was room for both. Gradually more and more Saxon settlers drifted, splitting up the great fiefs into smaller estates and farms and carving new holdings out of the waste. But still much of the countryside remained empty, and when the worst of the Danish raids were over, pockets of Danish settlement had also been established in remote corners of the shire, without apparently interfering overmuch with any previous occupants. Even as late as the seventeenth century there was still much land to spare. Hence the latest theory about the Doone family, that they originated from Scottish freebooters who settled in the Doone valley of Exmoor at about that time.

The folklore of Devon is therefore a rich mixture of Celtic, Saxon, Danish and goodness knows what other elements, including quite possibly some that are pre-Celtic. The Devon moors are still the alleged haunt of pixies. We are not surprised to hear much about giants, bogeymen and witches, and the Devil has here a richer heritage than in most English counties. Customs such as the wassailing of apple-trees lingered long on Devonshire farms, and tales of smugglers, fairs and tin-miners abound. There is a good collection of legends about that still popular Devon hero, Sir Francis Drake. And the Devon dialect remains unique.

1 The Devil in Devon

THE DEVIL is prominent in the folklore of Devon. As in other counties, edifices and rock formations for which no other explanation was readily forthcoming were popularly attributed to the devil, and Devon is well stocked with such features.

At the southern end of the Isle of Lundy is an awe-inspiring chasm, 370 feet deep and 250 feet wide at the top, its perpendicular walls dropping down to two sea-caves. To crawl on hands and knees to the edge and peer into its depths is a test for the strongest nerves. Its name is The Devil's Limekiln. The fissure was blasted out by the devil, who dumped the surplus rock offshore in the form of the Shutter Rock, as a trap for mariners.

On the coast of north Devon, between Clovelly and Bucks Mills, a ridge of rocks runs for about a quarter of a mile into the sea, orientated towards Lundy. This, says local tradition, is the beginning of a causeway which the devil started to build out to the island. He abandoned the project when the handle of his shovel broke.

Dunkery Hill, the highest point of Exmoor, is also the work of the devil. It is made of rock and soil which he dumped there when digging the Punchbowl, a depression on Winsford Hill, over the border in Somerset.

The devil has another Exmoor memorial in the Valley of Rocks, near Lynton, where he caught a character named Ragged Dick and several of his friends dancing on Sunday. He turned them into slate, and there they remain, still bearing the name of Ragged Dick.

On Dartmoor the Devil's Frying-pan is a natural rock-basin near Mis Tor; and the devil has a tor of his own, Devil Tor. Near this peak is a menhir, or tall standing-stone, known as Beardown Man. On the top of another peak near Moretonhampstead, with the suggestive name of Hel Tor, is a circular stone, said to be a quoit thrown by the devil in the course of a fight with King Arthur. The devil lost and crept, sulking, back to Northlew, where he died of cold. One senses here a local joke at the expense of Northlew, as a place cold enough to freeze the devil!

The devil had another battle, this time with St Michael, on Brent Tor, near Tavistock. Again he lost and was kicked down the hill by the victorious saint, who tossed a great rock after him; it can still be seen lying there. The battle occurred after the local people had built a little church to St Michael on the summit of Brent Tor. They had originally planned for the church to be erected at the foot of the hill, but every night the devil moved the building stones to the top, so the villagers decided to let him have his way. St Michael, appearing belatedly, did not approve; hence the fracas. Similar legends are attached to churches at Plympton St Mary, Braunton, Honiton and Buckfastleigh. The site, originally intended for the church of St Mary at Plympton, before the devil interfered, is said to have been at Crownhill Castle, a mile to the east. At Honiton the devil left a souvenir of his clash with the local inhabitants in the Devil's Stone, which lies by the roadside on Church Hill.

At the foot of an oak near the church at Shebbear, in north Devon, is a massive stone known as the Devil's Boulder. Every year, on the evening of 5 November, the villagers perform the ceremony of 'Turning the Boulder'. First the church bells are rung – a prolonged jangle. Then men with crowbars undertake the formidable task of turning the stone over. Calamity will fall on Shebbear if they fail to perform the feat annually. It is said that, when the ceremony was discontinued, during the first world war, the following year was one of disaster for the village and neighbouring farms. There are several versions of the story which accounts for the presence of the stone. All introduce the Devil, who, according to perhaps the most popular version, dropped the stone when he was fleeing from heaven, after having been expelled. The purpose of the bell-ringing is said to be to drive away evil spirits. The juxtaposition of the stone and the church suggests that probably the stone was there first and that the ceremony has very ancient origins.

In the broad vale between Dartmoor and Exmoor the village of East Worlington has a standing stone dedicated to the devil, though now it bears four inscribed crosses. It is a shaped stone, with four faces and a flat top, standing about seven feet out of the ground. The devil dropped it on hearing the sound of East Worlington church bells. The legend says that he was carrying it from Okehampton to the sea, but does not suggest why.

A legend associated with the building of Bideford Bridge is very like those which tell of the devil moving church building-stones to a new site. The devil and the Virgin Mary were in this instance at variance over the site of the new bridge, and every night the devil came and destroyed the work done by the followers of Mary during the day. Eventually the builders decided to use woolpacks instead of stone for the foundations of the piers. In consequence they got so much work done in a day, and the bulky foundations attracted so much silt and debris when the tide went out, that the devil was unable to demolish them in a night, and so the bridge was built.

The devil similarly attempted to interfere with Sir Francis Drake when he was converting Buckland Abbey into a spendid private mansion. Drake himself outwitted his adversary. Keeping watch from a tree, he crowed like a cock when he saw the devil and his gang of demons starting their demolition work. The demons thought it was a real cock, heralding the dawn. When Drake lit his pipe, they were convinced that it was the sun rising and fled.

Once the devil threatened to demolish Lustleigh Church unless he were given a sacrifice. He selected a villager in the congregation who happened to have a pack of playing-cards in his pocket and hence was vulnerable. The alarmed man grabbed an unfortunate cat which happened to be passing and swung it against the church wall; this provided a substitute sacrifice and he escaped.

At Torquay the devil appears in the guise of 'Daddy', a chasm in the cliffs being known as 'Daddy's Hole'. Attached to it is the legend of a local girl who fell in love, but the young man's interest lay elsewhere. Try as she would, she could not entice him away from the other girl. She took to wandering forlornly by the sea-shore, and one evening was nearly bowled over by the Wild Hunt. She heard the baying of the hounds and saw them approaching, followed by the devil himself on a huge horse. Then she fainted.

When she revived, a young man was bending over her. She asked him if he had seen the Wild Hunt, but he said he had not. They exchanged confidences, and she learned that he too was a disappointed lover. He promised her revenge if she, for her part, would promise to be his.

After many meetings he told her that on the following evening the lovers would meet at Daddy's Hole, where she could take her revenge. She did so, stabbing them both. As soon as the crime was committed, a tremendous storm blew up and the Wild Hunt could be heard approaching. The Demon Hunter, the young man who had tempted her to murder, came galloping up, seized her and leaped into the depths of Daddy's Hole. She was never seen again.

Devon has a number of other stories about the Wild Hunt, also called the Yeth Hounds ('Yeth' being a corruption of 'Heath') or the Wish Hounds. In the 1850s an old man at St Mary Tavy, named Roger Burn, declared that he had heard them baying, with the huntsman sounding his horn and the whip cracking, while working in fields near the village. Shaugh Bridge, over the river Plym on the south-western edge of Dartmoor, is reckoned to be a favourite haunt of the devil and his Wild Hunt. He attempts to lead unsuspecting travellers to the edge of the Dewerstone Rock, and then chivvy them over the cliff to fall to the river below. Once, after a heavy fall of snow, his cloven hoof-prints were seen across the cliff face.

One of the unsolved mysteries of Britain is that of the Devil's hoof-marks, which appeared on the morning of 8 February 1855, after heavy snow over a wide area by the estuary of the Exe. There were hundreds of these marks, sprinkled liberally almost everywhere, some on the ground, some on roofs and the tops of walls, some in open fields and some in village gardens. They were said to have resembled the marks made by a donkey's hoof, about four inches long and two and a half inches wide, and they occurred in single file, never in pairs. Naturally they disappeared with the thawing of the snow, but in the meantime the story had been taken up by the Press and given wide publicity. The search for the solution to the problem of finding a hoofed animal which could climb high walls, walk over roofs and hayricks and traverse the countryside from Starcross to Exmouth, crossing the estuary of the Exe en route, in a single night, caught the public imagination. The devil was only one of many ingenious suggestions. The likeliest was made a few years ago by a naturalist, who pointed out that the marks were very like those that would be made by a short-tailed field vole squatting in the snow!

The Guinness Book of Records states that the worst recorded storm in the United Kingdom occurred at Widecombe on 21 October 1638, the casualty total being 60. The actual figures were four killed and 62 injured. The storm struck on a Sunday afternoon, when a service was in progress in the church, where most of the casualties occurred. Predictably, the devil was blamed. Several 'explanatory' tales, in which he features, circulated and are still remembered.

The victim in one of the most widely known is Widecombe Jan, a young man who made a pact with the devil, to the effect that if ever the fiend found him sleeping in church he was welcome to his soul. That afternoon the devil spotted the feckless youth, sound asleep during service, and all the fuss and commotion were caused when he claimed his trophy. Another version says that some of the damage was caused by the devil dealing with a party of boys whom he found playing marbles on a tombstone in the churchyard. Yet another portrays the devil in a foul temper after losing his way on the moors while going to collect a soul: 'Dressed in black and mounted on a black horse, he enquired his way to the church, of a woman who kept a little public-house on the moor. He offered her money to become his guide, but she mistrusted him on remarking that the liquor went hissing down his throat; and finally had her suspicions confirmed by the glimpse of a cloven hoof, which he could not conceal by his boot.'

In *Devon Villages* S. H. Burton identifies the pub as The Tavistock Inn at Poundsgate; the money which he gave to pay for his drink changed to dead leaves.

Much of the damage was done, apparently, by a pinnacle which was struck by lightning and came crashing down into the church. An early account of the disaster mentions that 'another man had his head cloven, his skull went into three pieces, and his brains thrown on the ground whole; but the hair of his head, through the violence of the blow, stuck fast to a pillar near him, where it remained a woeful spectacle a long while after.' As for Widecombe Jan, the sleepy originator of this calamity, he was killed by being dashed against a pillar, where the bloody evidence of his guilt and punishment, as it was believed, remained for a considerable period.

The devil is no stranger to Widecombe. Evidently encouraged by his success in taking toll of the local inhabitants, he once even attempted to trap the soul of an ecclesiastic. This was Bishop Bronescombe, Bishop of Exeter from 1258 to 1280, who with a party of attendants lost his way on the moors while travelling from Widecombe to Sourton. Sabine Baring-Gould describes the details of his subsequent encounter with the devil:

> The Bishop was overcome with fatigue and was starving. He turned to his chaplain and said,
>
> Our Master in the wilderness was offered by Satan bread made of stones. If he were now to make the same offer to me, I doubt if I should have the Christian fortitude to refuse.'
>
> 'Ah!' sighed the chaplain, 'and a hunk of cheese as well!'
>
> 'Bread and cheese I could not hold out against!' said the Bishop.
>
> Hardly had he spoken before a moorman rose up from a peat dyke and drew nigh; he had a wallet on his back . . . .

Needless to say, there was bread and cheese in the wallet. The moorman was willing to share it but only if the Bishop would get off his horse, doff his cap and address him as 'Master'. This the Bishop was quite prepared to do 'when the chaplain perceived that the man had one foot like that of a goat. He instantly cried out to God, and signified what he saw to the prelate, who, in holy horror, made the sign of the cross, and lo! the moorman vanished, and the bread and cheese remained transformed to stone.'

The place where this occurred is still known as Brandescombe's Loaf, or, alternatively, Bread and Cheese. It is on the slopes of Amicombe Hill. And there is an additional memorial to the event in Exeter Cathedral itself, for the Bishop was so ashamed of nearly yielding to temptation that, by way of atonement, he set about rebuilding the edifice. On the same hill, not far from Brandescombe'

Loaf, are the Slipper Stones, so-called because here the Bishop lost his slippers.

St Dunstan was a figure who emerged from an encounter with the devil with much less credit. On one occasion the saint had bought up a large stock of barley, for brewing beer, which he hoped to sell in competition with the local beverage, Devonshire cider. The devil offered to blight all the apple trees, so that there would be no cider, in return for Dunstan's soul. The saint, ever one to drive a hard bargain, argued with him, and eventually a compromise was reached whereby the devil had Dunstan's soul for certain days each year, while, for his part, he would blight the apple trees on three days: 17, 18, and 19 May. These, at least in the nineteenth century, were still known as St Dunstan's Days, and country folk awaited them anxiously, to see whether the old pact held and their apple trees would be blasted by frost. One gathers that, for some reason, Devon people had no great opinion of St Dunstan.

Another version substitutes a brewer named Frankan for St Dunstan. He is sometimes referred to as St Frankan, and his feast as 'Francimass'.

The devil also once collected a clerical soul at Dawlish – or rather, between Dawlish and Teignmouth, where the event is still commemorated by two spectacular rocks, the Parson and the Clerk. The victim was an elderly priest, consumed by ambition to become the next Bishop of Exeter. Having eventually been promised the See when it fell vacant, he was delighted when the incumbent Bishop became ill. The invalid went to stay at Dawlish, to try to restore his failing health, and there his would-be successor took to visiting him, hoping to find him growing steadily worse.

Crossing Haldon Hill on one of the journeys to Dawlish, the priest and his clerk lost their way during a thunderstorm. The priest lost his temper, too, and scolded the clerk, who was supposed to be the guide.

'I'd rather have the devil himself as a guide!' he shouted.

Immediately a countryman appeared and guided them to the coast, where their horses plunged over a cliff and all perished.

An embellishment of the story makes the countryman a horseman, who invites them to his mansion, to shelter there till the storm is past. They are invited to share a meal, at which the priest seems to recognise among the guests the faces of old colleagues whom he had supposed were dead. While they are eating and drinking, news is brought that the Bishop is dead, and the priest says he must return to Exeter at once. His host escorts him to the door, sees him mounted and bids him farewell. As he and the clerk ride away they look back and are terrified to see that the brightly-lighted mansion has become a heap of jagged rocks, now surrounded by the swirling, incoming tide. They struggle frantically to escape, but the waves crash around them. The bodies of the horses are found on the beach next morning, but those of the men are never seen.

Another version gives the further detail that, on leaving the mansion, the horses refused to budge.

'Devil take them!' shouted the priest, whipping and spurring them.

'Thank you, sir,' said the host. 'I will.'

And with that he slapped their rumps and they galloped madly into the sea. Some versions also contain word-play between 'sea' and the 'see' coveted by the parson.

Farther along the coast, on the Dorset border, the village of Uplyme has a story about a seventeenth-century mayor of Lyme Regis, whose soul was carried off by the devil. The mayor, whose name was Jones, was notorious for his persecution of Nonconformists in the days after the Restoration. Local dissenters, driven out of the town, used to hold their services at White Chapel Rocks, on Pinhay Cliffs. To get there they had to walk along a cliff path; above was a recess still known as 'Jones' Chair'. There Mayor Jones used to sit every Sunday, to note the names of the congregation walking along to the service, with a view to taking further action against them. When he died, the devil sent a ship for him. Outward bound from Lyme, this ship was hailed by a passing vessel and gave the following answers to enquiries:

> Sailed from Lyme.
> Skipper's name, Satan.
> Cargo, Old Jones.
> Destination, Mount Etna.

Whereupon, says the story, the ship 'disappeared in flames and smoke, leaving an extremely sulphurous atmosphere'.

In his endeavours to capture human souls, the devil adopts many ruses. To Mary, a servant girl on a farm in the village of Marwood, he appeared as a lover. Mary, having had no luck with boys and being afraid of being left on the shelf, declared that she would get a lover, even if it were the devil himself. One day she visited Barnstaple Fair, said to be one of his notorious haunts, and there she was accosted by a handsome young man with a fine tenor voice. He followed her home and thereafter visited her frequently. The farmer and his family liked him and often invited him in to join in convivial evenings, though they were rather puzzled by the fact that, when they started to light the lamps, he disappeared.

One night, during a heavy storm, a loud thumping sound was heard. Tracing it to its source in Mary's room, the farmer found her wedged almost inextricably between the bed and the wall. As he found he couldn't move her, he fetched the farm men, ten in number, and they couldn't help her, either. So then (and here the tale becomes even more far-fetched) he sent for twelve parsons, who also failed to move the bewitched girl. Finally, the rector of Ashford, who was said to have considerable experience in dealing with such situations, arrived. He addressed the devil, asking him whether he would wait till a freshly-lighted candle had burned out before he claimed Mary's soul. The devil agreed, whereupon the parson blew out the candle and placed it in a box, which he had built into a wall of Marwood church. There it stayed, while Mary lived out her life.

A very similar story is told of a nameless girl who lived in Bridgerule, near Holsworthy. Here the girl is the daughter of a cottager and lives with her mother. The demon lover arrives as a handsome gentleman, who drives up in a carriage and four. After a period of courtship, the girl promises to go away with him. But the mother is suspicious and consults the local priest, who tells her what to do. When the lover arrives to claim the girl, she asks for time to change into some better clothes, and the man agrees to giver her 'until that candle is burnt out'. At the first opportunity, the mother blows out the candle and runs to the priest, who puts it in a box and walls it up in Bridgerule church. The devil, realising that his secret is discovered, drives off in a rage. He and his carriage plunge into a bog on Affaland Moor and disappear in an explosion of blue flame.

The distance between Bridgerule and Marwood, the two villages associated with these stories, is thirty miles direct – much more by road.

The squire of a certain Devonshire village – we do not know his name – sold his soul, and his skin, to the devil and called a neighbour as a witness to the transaction. On his death, the neighbour went in distress to the parson and asked what should be done about fulfilling the terms of the contract. The parson told him to go to the church on the night after the funeral, but be sure to take a live cock with him.

At midnight the devil appeared, opened the grave and proceeded to flay the corpse. When he had finished, he held the skin up against the light filtering in through a window and commented,

'It wasn't worth coming for, after all. It's full of holes.'

At that moment, the cock crew. The devil wheeled round and exclaimed,

'And if it hadn't been for that bird under your arm, I would have had your skin, too.'

As it was, the man got home safely.

The devil and another disinterred corpse feature in a North Devon story for which a logical explanation is preserved.

The corpse belonged to Joseph Gould, a prosperous farmer of the hamlet of Mockham, near Charles on the edge of Exmoor, who died in 1817. Although a lifelong Baptist, he was buried in the Charles parish churchyard, there being no Baptist burial-ground then available, and the funeral service was conducted by a Baptist minister. In an age of strong religious prejudice, the burial there of a Nonconformist, who had never been baptized according to Anglican rites, outraged many of the more bigoted parishioners. They were sure that the devil would come and carry him away.

Joseph Gould died in August. On Christmas Eve the choir, returning from carol-singing around the parish, paused by the churchyard wall and noticed, poised on top of it, a huge packing case. When one of them touched it, it started to rock. Peeping over the wall, they saw that Joseph Gould's grave had been opened. There was a deep, black hole, and from the depths the sound of shovels could be heard. The choristers, who were mostly boys, naturally panicked and went shrieking to their homes, crying:

'The devil's in the churchyard, digging up old Joseph Gould!'

· Sure enough, when a few of the bolder villagers summoned up sufficient courage to go and investigate, all they found was the empty grave. The coffin and the packing-case had both vanished.

However no secret was made of the explanation. A week or two earlier a tombstone erected over Joseph Gould's grave had been found in the road outside the graveyard, split in half. The more ignorant of the villagers said that the devil had dropped it as he carried it away. One of Farmer Gould's employees, however, knew better. He remembered his master as a kindly, God-fearing man. Human prejudice and not the devil was the agency at work.

'If they won't have his stone, be damned if they shall have his body, neither,' he resolved.

So, with another man to help, he went to the churchyard on Christmas Eve, dug up the coffin and placed it in the packing-case they had brought with them. They put it in a cart and took it to the Baptist chapel, at some distance from the village, where Joseph Gould had worshipped. Then they dug a deep grave in the floor of the chapel, interred the coffin there, and left the broken tombstone propped up against a wall.

Much later, the coffin was moved to a new Baptist burial-ground, together with the broken tombstone.

The fact that Joseph Gould was unbaptized would certainly have troubled the prejudiced for it was a widespread notion in Devon that at baptism the devil, driven out of the child, escapes by way of the north door of the church. For this reason that door is often known as 'the Devil's Door'.

Tavistock had a celebrated singer who used to take solo parts in the church choir. One night, returning decidedly the worse for a convivial evening at Horrabridge, he was carried by his donkey to a place where he saw demons dancing in a ring. On being invited by their leader to join in the dance, he exclaimed in terror:

'Stop, Mr Devil, I say! I am a righteous man and a psalm-singer to boot, in Tavistock church; stop, or I'll give you such a stave as shall startle all the devils in hell!'

Whereupon he threw back his head and uttered such a note that the startled donkey, bucking, threw him off its back and into a ditch. There he was found next morning by a neighbour. Ever afterwards he bore the honorary title, 'Psalm-singer to Old Nick'.

Another Tavistock story is of an old woman who, mistaking the time, got up at midnight and set out for market. Somewhere on the moors, in the small hours, she heard the cries of the Wild Hunt and saw a frightened hare, which was evidently the quarry. Being kind-hearted, she gathered up the creature and hid it in one of her panniers. Presently the devil himself appeared, in the form of a black-clothed horseman, cloven-hoofed, horns sprouting from his head, and riding a headless horse. He asked her if she had seen the hare, but she replied 'No.'

After he had passed, she released the hare from the pannier. It turned into a beautiful young lady in white, who told the startled old woman that she was not an inhabitant of this world, but was suffering punishment for a crime committed during her earthly life. She said that she was doomed to be constantly pursued either above or below ground by evil spirits, 'until I could get behind their tails, whilst they passed on in search of me'. In return for the old woman's help in fulfilling this condition, she promised her, as a reward, 'that your hens shall lay two eggs instead of one, that your cows shall yield the most plentiful store of milk all the year round, and that you shall talk twice as much as before, and your husband stand no chance at all in any matter between you to be settled by the tongue!'

It is said that from then on the affairs of the old woman prospered.

Other appearances of the devil in Devon include one, early in the nineteenth century, at Moreston Farm, Bratton Clovelly. On this occasion the devil came for Mr James Rice, the farmer, but clumsily stumbled against a granite pillar in the kitchen. The post split from top to bottom with a loud explosion. Mr Rice jumped out of bed, seized a loaded shotgun which he always kept there, and shot the devil . . . who evidently survived, even if wounded.

At Topsham Railway Inn the devil visited four men playing cards on a Sunday evening. When one stooped to pick up a card from the floor, the devil seized his hand and refused to let go. The others eventually managed to pull their mate free, and the corner of the pub fell in.

The devil arrives in Devon every autumn on 20 September, when he spits on blackberries, making them unfit to eat after that date. This is a week or two earlier than times usually quoted for other West Country shires, but presumably even the devil cannot be everywhere at once. It is true that blackberries later in the season tend to be tasteless and infested with maggots.

2　Pixies and Fairies

PIXIES RATHER THAN FAIRIES are 'the little people' of Devon. Stories about them abound. Pixies, far from being idealised miniature human beings, are often rather ugly little men, almost invariably dressed in rags. They are timid and shy, live in remote places, often in caves or holes in rocks, venturing out only at night. They are, in general, well disposed towards the human race and have been known to lend a friendly hand with farm and domestic work. Householders, faced with some thankless task, have woken in the morning to find that pixies had performed it during the night. Nevertheless, the little creatures are not to be trifled with, for they understand magic and can make life unpleasant for anyone who offends them.

Mrs Bray, writing to Robert Southey in April 1832, mentions some of the beliefs about pixies prevalent in Devon at that time:

Some are sent, . . . to work the will of his master in the mines; to show by sure signs where lies the richest lode; or sometimes to delude the unfortunate miner, who may not be in favour, with false fires, and to mock his toils by startling him with sounds within the bed of the rocks, that seem to repeat, stroke for stroke, the fall of the hammer which he wields, whilst his labours are repaid by the worst ore in the vein.

Then the pixy flies away, laughing.

'Other pixies, nice in their persons, are the avowed enemies of all sluts or idlers . . . they sally forth to see if the maidens do their duty with mop and broom.'

If they find duties neglected, they pinch the culprit 'blue as a bilberry'.

The good dames in this part of the world are very particular in sweeping their houses before they go to bed, and they will frequently place a basin of water by the chimney nook, to accomodate the pixies, who are great lovers of water; and sometimes they requite the good deed by dropping a piece of money into the basin.

She mentions that one young woman, who thus received a sixpence, offended the pixies; she chattered about it all over the town and was never rewarded again.

Many a pixy is sent out on works of mischief, to deceive the old nurses and steal away young children, or to do them harm . . . Many also, bent solely on mischief, are sent forth to lead poor travellers astray, to deceive them with those false lights called Will-o'-the-Wisp, or to guide them a fine dance in trudging home through woods and waters, through bogs and quagmires, and every peril.

Others, says Mrs Bray, have fun with flighty girls, blowing out the candle and then kissing them 'with a smack', so that they shriek 'Who's this?'.

An old woman in Tavistock told Mrs Bray that, years before, when spinning flax, she suspected the pixies were helping her. Sure enough, one evening, as she entered her spinning room suddenly, she saw a little ragged figure disappearing through the doorway. To reward the pixy, and in the hope of gaining more help in the future, she bought some new clothes, doll-size, and left them by the spinning-wheel. In due course, the pixy returned, tried on the new clothes, and left dancing with delight and singing,

> Pixy fine, pixy gay,
> Pixy now will run away.

And that was the last the spinster saw of her.

J. R. W. Coxhead relates a very similar story about a Dartmoor farmer, who was delighted to find his corn threshed by pixies. Every morning, when he went into his barn to start work with the flail, he found a heap of corn that had been threshed overnight. So, one night, overcome by curiosity, he hid himself in a mound of straw and watched the pixy (it was only one, in spite of the prodigious amount of work performed). He was impressed, not only by the speed with which the little creature worked, but also by the ragged clothes it wore. So, being a kindly man, he suggested to his wife that the pixy needed some new clothes. She set to work with needle and thread, and by supper-time had a new suit ready for the little man.

The farmer laid the clothes on the barn floor and hid in the straw, to see how the present would be received. The pixy spotted the clothes as soon as it arrived and seized them with cries of delight.

'New toat! New waist-toat! New breeches!' it exclaimed. 'You proud! I proud! I shan't work any more!'

With that it vanished, wearing the new suit, and never came back. The farmer had to finish the threshing himself.

A story with a different ending, also by J. R. W. Coxhead, tells how a farmer discovered that his barn was haunted by pixies, who were threshing his corn by night. To reward them, he placed a large hunk of bread and a slice of cheese on the barn floor, forbidding any of his men to go near the building after dark. Every morning he found more threshing had been done and a fresh heap of corn on the floor. Came the time when all the harvest had been threshed, but, to his amazement, there was again a heap of corn on the barn floor in the morning. So he went on putting out the bread and cheese, and the pixies continued to provide corn, though no-one knew where it came from. The farmer became a very rich man and continued to feed the pixies till his dying day.

Pixies also spirit away human children. Mrs Bray relates a story, told by a Tavistock woman, who said that her mother had had a child stolen by the pixies while she was in the garden, hanging out washing. A pixy child was left in its place. The broken-hearted mother cared for the pixy child as though it had been her own. This so pleased the pixy mother that she returned the human child, which was very lucky for the rest of its life.

There are several versions of the story of the midwife who found herself attending a pixy birth, and who anointed her eyes with fairy ointment, with dire consequences. Both Mrs Bray and the Rev. S. Baring-Gould recount it with considerable detail, and Ruth Tongue heard it over the border, in Somerset. Mrs Bray locates the midwife's home at Tavistock; Baring-Gould places it at Holne. Mrs Bray does not know the woman's name, but Baring-Gould gives it as Morada, and describes her as a foreigner.

One night, Baring-Gould says it was just before harvest and a thunderstorm was brewing, the midwife was awakened by banging at the door. She opened it and saw (in Mrs Bray's version) a 'strange, squint-eyed, little, ugly, old fellow', who said his wife urgently needed her help. Mrs Bray's says the midwife felt impelled to go, despite herself, but Baring-Gould says an offer of ten golden guineas provided the incentive.

She mounted on the pillion of a 'large, coal-black horse, with eyes like balls of fire', which was standing outside the door and was soon whisked away over the moor. Baring-Gould says she was blindfolded. They arrived at a cottage, where a woman was lying in and two children were sitting by the hearth. Here the versions given by Mrs Bray and Baring-Gould diverge considerably.

In Mrs Bray's account the woman is 'decent-looking' – evidently an ordinary countrywoman, – and the cottage 'neat and homely'. The baby is born, and celebrates its arrival by boxing the midwife on the ears! The mother gives the midwife some ointment to rub on the child's eyes. She uses it, and tries some on her own, whereupon she sees things as they really are.

The mother is a lovely lady, dressed in white. The baby is wrapped in swaddling clothes of silver gauze and is very beautiful, with, however, a squint like its father. The two children are 'little, flat-nosed imps ... with long and hairy paws'.

Though naturally disconcerted, the midwife has sense enough not to show any surprise, and the pixies never suspect that she has used the ointment on herself. The ugly little man escorts her back to the horse and takes her home 'in a whipsissa'. The meaning of that word is doubtful; my guess is that it signifies something like 'in the twinkling of an eye'.

Next market-day the midwife happens to see the ugly little man again. He is going from stall to stall, pilfering articles. She goes up to him and asks casually how his wife and baby are.

'What! Can you *see* me today?' exclaims the pixy.

'To be sure I do, as plain as I see the sun in the skies,' replies the woman; 'and I see you are busy into the bargain.'

'With which eye do you see this?' asks the pixy.   'With the right eye, to be sure.'

With that, the pixy strikes her a blow on the right eye which blinds her for the rest of her life.

In Baring-Gould's version, the mother is, from the beginning, 'the prettiest little lady anybody ever did see', and the house is 'all lighted up with beautiful lamps'. After the midwife has anointed the baby's eyes, she puts the box of ointment into her pocket and forgets about it. She then stays with the lady for many days and becomes fond of her and the baby. The lady tells the midwife that she is a fairy princess (thus emphasising that she is not a pixy). As a punishment for marrying someone beneath her in rank, she and her husband have been banished to Dartmoor for a year, but soon the time will be up and they will be allowed to return.

In due course, the midwife is taken home, on horseback, as she came. After her escort has left, she finds the ointment in her pocket. She waits for several days, to see if he will come to collect it, but then, her curiosity gets the better of her, and she tries it on her own left eye.

Next morning, her cat looks the size of a dog. As she walks along the road to market, everything seems unnaturally clear, and she sees the stars, although the sun in shining.

On the way she meets the fairy prince on horseback and curtseys to him. He is surprised that she can see him. Learning that she can do so with her left eye, he strikes it, and she loses the sight immediately. To her now restricted vision the prince appears as the ugly little man she had first met. To round off the story neatly, he gives her the ten guineas he had first promised, she hands him the box of ointment, and he vanishes.

In 'The Devil in Devon' J. R. W. Coxhead quotes from The Western Daily Mercury of 6 June 1890, the following story:

A few days ago a party of men were ripping bark in a wood about four miles from Torrington. In the evening, when it was time to pick up tools, one of the men had occasion to separate himself from the party to fetch an iron which he had been using in another part of the wood. He avers that on stooping to pick up the tool a strange feeling came over him, and while totally unable to raise himself he heard peals of discordant laughter all around. It flashed across his mind that he was being pixie-led, and though he has many times heard stories of people being in a similar state, his presence of mind forsook him, and he was unable to turn his coat inside out – a sure talisman against the spells of pixies. . . .

This happened at about half-past five, and when he did not return home his wife went to look for him. She found him at about ten o'clock, crawling on hands knees in the wood and dripping wet through having fallen into a stream.

'You girt fule!' she exclaimed, when he had told her about the pixy spell. 'Why didden ee turn your pockets inside out? Then you could have come away tu wance!'

In Devon Traditions and Fairy Tales J. W. R. Coxhead quotes from The Transactions of the Devonshire Association an account, which appeared in 1928, of an encounter, by a Mrs G. Herbert, with a pixy on Dartmoor:

'I saw the pixy under an overhanging boulder close to Shaugh Bridge (on the southern edge of Dartmoor) in the afternoon. I cannot say more definitely as to the time, but I remember running in to my mother after an afternoon walk and saying I had seen a pixie – and being laughed at. This was in 1897.

It was like a little wizened man (as far as I can remember) eighteen inches or possibly two feet high, but I incline to the lesser height. It had a little pointed hat, slightly curved to the front, a doublet, and little short knicker things. My impression is of some contrasting colours, but I cannot now remember what colours, though I think they were red and blue. Its face was brown and wrinkled and wizened. I saw it for a moment, and it vanished. It was under the boulder when I looked, and then vanished.'

Mrs Herbert also claimed to have been 'pixy-led', saying,

It was about three years ago. I did not see the pixy, but, although it was a bright, fine day and I was riding on a part of the moor I know well, I was suddenly – to use a Dartmoor expression – 'mazed'. I knew the places and yet was utterly befogged. I felt I was pixie-led, and started to turn my pockets inside out. While I was doing so, I suddenly knew where I was exactly. I may add that I am psychic but do not know whether this has anything to do with any pixie experiences.

Another, and this time tragic, story of someone pixy-led on Dartmoor is attached to Rowbrook Farm, near Dartmeet. Many years ago on a winter evening, a lad employed at the farm heard a plaintive voice calling, 'Jan Coo'. He brought the other farm workers out to the yard, and they also heard it. Thereafter it called regularly every evening, and they grew used to it, – except the boy, whose name was Jan. One evening the voice was much nearer and called more insistently. Jan declared it was calling him and started to follow it. The men waited for him to return and tell them what he had discovered, but they never saw him again. Nor was the eerie voice ever heard. The pixies had claimed Jan.

A historical character, John Fitz, who lived at Fitzford, near Tavistock, in the middle of the sixteenth century, was once pixy-led on Dartmoor. He and his wife lost their way while riding over the moors.

'After wandering in the vain effort to find the right path, they felt so fatigued and thirsty that it was with extreme delight they discovered a spring of water, whose powers seemed to be miraculous; for no sooner had they satisfied their thirst than they were enabled to find their way through the moor towards home, without the least difficulty. In gratitude for this deliverance, and the benefit they had received from the water, John Fitz caused a stone memorial to be placed over the spring for the advantage of all pixy-led travellers.'

The spring, or well, is still to be seen on the moor, about a mile and a half north of Princetown, marked by stone slab bearing the inscription, 'I. F. 1568'.

Ruth Tongue records an account, given by a member of the Nettlecombe (Somerset) Women's Institute, of being pixy-led at Budleigh Salterton:

I were pixy-led once in a wood near Budleigh Salterton. I couldn't find my way out, though 'twas there, plain to see. I went all around about it three times, and then somebody coom along to find me, and I thought, How could I miss the path. They said others was pixy-led there too.'

Some so-called instances of pixy-leading have undoubtedly been caused by the will-o'-the-wisp. Baring-Gould relates that a miner crossing Dartmoor one Sunday afternoon lost his way among the bogs and was overtaken by nightfall. Greatly alarmed, he knelt down to pray, and when he opened his eyes he saw a flickering light moving before him. Although he knew it to be a will-o'-the-wisp he followed it, trusting in Providence, and presently found himself walking on dry heather.

An Exmoor legend recounts how a farm worker, returning to his cottage, became confused in a neighbouring field. He was led astray, he said, by a pixy with a lantern, but eventually managed to break the spell through hitting the light with a stick and putting it out.

Mrs Bray, in setting down her collection of pixy stories, describes the dangers of travelling over the moors in her day. Her husband, who knew the moors well, had more than once been temporarily lost there, when overtaken by a sudden mist.

'Whitchurch Down, a favourite ride with me and my pony,' she writes, 'is said to be very famous for the peril there incurred of being pixy-led; for there many an honest yeoman and stout farmer is very apt to lose his way....'?

Then she adds the shrewd comment; 'especially if he should happen to take a cup too much'!

Many remote and secluded places, especially on the moors, have particular associations with pixies. A colony is said to live on Pixie Rocks, in a combe near Challacombe. On Gidleigh Common, high on Dartmoor, a large hut circle, ninety feet across, is supposedly haunted by pixies. No horse will cross it. The villagers of Chagford claim to have heard pixies on the moors on quiet nights.

The queen of the fairies is said to have created South Down Bridge, near Tavistock, by crystallizing the drops of water in a rainbow over the stream. First becoming tiny pebbles, then great stones.

At Chudleigh Rock a cave, waterfall and creeper-hung glen are alleged to be a favourite haunt of pixies.

King Castle, an ancient earthwork near Simonsbath, is reputed to have been built by pixies, as a defence against hostile spirits from neighbouring mines.

Pixies are said to dance in a number of the stone circles on Dartmoor, including the one on Huccaby Moor. A story is told of Tom White, a young man of Postbridge, who went courting a girl at Huccaby, which involved frequent five mile walks each way over the wild moors. One summer night he saw a crowd of pixies dancing near Bellever Tor. He watched for a time and then tried to steal away but the pixies saw him. They formed a ring and danced around him till dawn, making him twirl like a top all the time. When eventually he was released, at sunrise, exhausted and frightened, he declared he would never risk such an experience again. He died a bachelor.

William Crossing, writing in 1890, gives the two chief haunts of Devon pixies as Piskies' Holt, in Huccaby Cleave, near Dartmeet, and The Pixies' Cave, a grotto below Sheepstor. Both are lonely, picturesque places, lending themselves to such fancies.

If, as some suppose, the stories of Devon pixies are based on dim and distorted memories of ancient peoples who once lived there, of small, dark, Iberian-type folk who, weak and lacking iron, were driven away to live in remote caves and glens from which they dared to venture only at night, the legacy they have left is not an unenviable one. The pixies in general, though sometimes mischievous, are simple, kindly folk, ready to do a good turn for small rewards. And some of the pixie legends are quite lovely.

We have, for example, the story of the old woman and the tulip garden. She lived in a cottage near Tavistock and took a great pride in her garden, especially her tulips. Before the cottage had been built, the site was a haunt of pixies, and they continued to come and enjoy the flowers in the garden. At night they could be heard singing to their babies and caressing them. Thanks to the pixies, the tulips not only grew unusually tall and fine but as delicately fragrant as roses.

When she died her heir destroyed the flowers and grew vegetables instead; the tulip bed was planted with parsley. The pixies were so upset that for years afterwards they saw to it that the garden grew nothing worthwhile. Instead, they transferred their attentions to the old woman's grave (which her relations had neglected), planting it with lovely little flowers and neat grass lawns.

Then there is the story of Kitty Jay. She was an eighteenth-century servant maid, and orphan, placed by the parish on a farm where she became a drudge. Seduced by her employer, she was disgraced and driven out of the parish. In despair, she hanged herself. Her body was buried at a point, below Hound Tor, where three parishes meet, – an outcast disowned by all of them. Yet it was said that for long afterwards fresh flowers were always to be found, recently placed on her grave. The pixies showed more compassion than her own folk had ever done.

A ploughman on one of the Dartmoor farms went out to plough at daybreak, before breakfast. As he grew hungrier and hungrier, hoping that his young son would shortly arrive with food in a satchel, he heard voices coming from a massive granite boulder in the middle of the field. He paused to listen and distinctly heard one say,

'The oven's hot.'

'Bake me a cake, then,' called the ploughman, who by this time was too hungry to worry about the possible consequences of accosting a pixy.

When he passed the rock again, ploughing the return furrow across the field, he found on the rock a fresh-baked cake, steaming hot. He ate it with gratitude.

K. M. Briggs recounts a story, told by the wife of a vicar who exchanged pulpits one holiday with a colleague from 'a little church in Devon, on the edge of Haldon'. This was a few years before 1962:

The house was very old indeed, long and low and thatched. It was always very dark, but I liked it, though queer things occurred. One day I was going to light the fire, and put on a stew for us, for our supper at night when we returned after a day's outing. Something disturbed our attention, and I went off, forgetting to light the fire. We came back that evening, resigned to bread and cheese. The fire was alight and the stew was hot. We had been within sight of the house all day. We had seen nobody go there, nor had we seen any smoke. Another time the same thing happened in reverse. I forgot to take off the evening meal, which was cooking, and put it aside to be heated again. I remembered it in the afternoon, by which time it should have been a crisp. We arrived to find it taken off the stove and waiting to be warmed up. I was advised, if I wanted the fire to burn up brightly, to shout up the chimney for help. It always came. The only time They disapproved was when I found a delightful nook in the heather and settled down to sew in the sun. That afternoon I lost two needles in quick succession, and then the needlebook disappeared too. I took the hint and left the nook to its owners.'

Dr Briggs comments: 'In holiday time, at least, this lady seems to have been a casual housewife. It is as well that she found a domestic spirit to help her.'

Pixies are apparently easily offended but ready to forgive. Mrs Bray relates how two servant girls, every night accustomed to placing a bucket of fresh water in the chimney corner for the pixies before going to bed, once forgot to do so. The pixies in return would drop silver coins into the bucket. On this occasion the disappointed pixies went up to the bedroom, entered through the keyhole, and began to make pointed remarks about the laziness of some folk.

One of the girls heard them and, nudging her bed-mate, suggested that they should get up and fill the bucket with water. The other, whose name was Molly, replied sleepily that she 'would not stir out of bed for all the pixies in Devonshire'. She went off to sleep again, leaving her more conscientious companion to creep downstairs and fill the bucket.

On her way back upstairs she heard the pixies discussing what punishment should be meted out to lazy Molly. One suggested treatment by pinches, another tooth-ache, another a red nose, another the spoiling of the girl's new bonnet. Eventually it was decided that she should be lame for seven years, after which she could be cured by applying a certain rare herb which grew on Dartmoor. The pixy who made the decision repeated the name of the herb which was seven syllables long. The listening girl tried desperately to remember it, she even tied a knot in her garter for each syllable.

It was useless. When she woke in the morning, all she could remember was that Molly would be lame for seven years and would then be cured by the herb, but she could not think of the name. So Molly became lame for nearly seven years. Then one day on the moor she met a squint-eyed boy who whipped her leg with a plant he was holding, and immediately she was healed. As a consolation, and to show they bore no ill-will, the pixies thereafter made her the best dancer in Tavistock.

With all this potential for mischief, the pixies were widely regarded by old Devon people as beings to be propitiated. Baring-Gould records one instance in 1879, concerning a farmer on the edge of Dartmoor:

> His cattle were afflicted with some disorder; he thereupon conveyed a sheep to the ridge above his house, sacrificed and burnt it there, as an offering to the Pysgies. The cattle at once began to recover and did well after, nor were there any fresh cases of sickness amongst them.

Since then I have been told of other and very similar instances.

A Mr Edmund Pearse, a surgeon of Tavistock, wrote to Mrs Bray in October 1835, to tell her some interesting traditions about Devon miners. He describes how, in deep mines there, crystalline formations occur which sometimes burst on exposure to air. Miners, hearing these explosions, would ascribe them to pixies, or fairies, *'whom they call small men'*. It is interesting that the pixies of Simonsbath were thought antagonistic to miners.

Pixies were often blamed for riding horses at night, the animals being lathered and fatigued in the morning. This is a smugglers' tale, well-known in many other counties; the pixies, or sometimes witches, were a useful means of disguising the activities of men commandeering horses to carry contraband.

It is in no way connected with smugglers, but I like the remark of a mother who apologised for her little boy, who was afraid to go into the Piskie House, the rocky cavern near Sheepstor. It was, she said, a *critical* place for children.

To conclude, here is a rather remarkable story, recorded in 1846, of a fox and its encounter with Dartmoor pixies. Although very like the story of the Big Bad Wolf and the three little pigs, it has interesting points of difference.

The fox, hunting as usual, found a colony of moorland pixies. He pounced on them and ate several before the rest took refuge in their houses. He then went to the first house and demanded to be let in.

'I will not let you in!' declared the pixy, in true fairy-tale style.

Whereupon the fox tore the roof open, extracted the pixy and gobbled him up. He then went to the next house, where the conversation and subsequent events were repeated.

The third house, however, was made of iron and resisted the fox's attempts to force it open. The pixy, safe inside, laughed, and the fox had to creep away to find the rest of his supper elsewhere.

Next night he came again and tried guile instead of force. He told the pixy about a field of splendid turnips not far away and offered to escort him there, with a promise of safe conduct, at four o'clock next morning. The pixy agreed but went along to the turnip field very early and was safely back in his house, with a load of turnips, when the fox arrived.

The following evening the fox reminded the pixy of Widecombe Fair the next day, and suggested that they go together. He promised to come along at three o'clock in the morning. The pixy, however, got up even earlier and was returning from the fair when his enemy appeared. The fox was very angry and tried to catch the little creature. But he crawled inside an earthenware pot he had won at the fair, and used it to roll down the hill to the safety of his home.

This time he was so tired that he forgot to fasten the door. When the fox came the following night he found the door unlatched, went in, seized the pixy and popped him into a box for future use.

Even now the pixy was not beaten. He persuaded the fox that he possessed a marvellous secret, which he would reveal if only his adversary would open the lid. Eventually the fox did so, whereupon the pixy laid him under a tremendously powerful spell and locked him in the box for ever.

> To catch a fox
> And shut him in a box
> And never let him go.

3 Witches

THE LAST WOMAN executed for witchcraft in Devon was Alice
Molland, who was hanged at Exeter in March 1684/5. In 1696
Elizabeth Horner was brought to Exeter to be tried for the same
crime before Chief Justice Holt and was acquitted. The act which
made witchcraft a capital offence was removed from the statute book
in 1736.

Considerable attention was attracted in 1682 by the trial at Exeter
of three old women, Susanne Edwards, Temperance Lloyd and Mary
Trembles, all of Bideford, who were found guilty and hanged at
Heavitree on 25 August that year. Although the victims were 'very
old, decrepit and impotent,' popular feeling was aroused against them
to such a pitch of fury that the judge dared not acquit them. They
also condemned themselves by admitting all, and more than all, of
the fantastic crimes of which they were accused, though their
incredible statements seem to us evidence of delusion and advanced
senility. The fear and hatred which they and other witches inspired
lingered in Devon, particularly in country districts, long after the law

had ceased to persecute witches. Gradually the old beliefs faded, but even today they cannot be presumed to be extinct.

A distinction is made between black and white witches. Black witches are those which use their supernatural power for evil; white witches work magic for the benefit of their neighbours. According to Sarah Hewett, writing in 1900, there were also grey witches, who possessed 'the double power of either overlooking or releasing'. I have no first-hand knowledge of either black witches or grey witches, but certainly there are still persons in Devon who are regarded by their neighbours as white witches. I say 'persons', because in Devonshire a witch can be either male or female, though a male witch would, I suppose, be more properly termed a wizard. He is also, in Devon parlance, a 'conjuror'. When a storm is brewing, a Devon villager will say, 'Ah, there be a conjuring going on somewhere'.

A 'conjuror' was responsible for detecting treasure in a barrow near Challacombe, on Exmoor. He assembled a party of helpers and began excavations. 'When the centre was neared a deadly faintness stole over his assistants.' This appears to have been a common hazard of barrow-rifling, and the conjuror kept his head better than the others, due no doubt to his professional poise. Even he, however, was overcome when a loud clap of thunder resounded and a shaft of lightning arrowed into the very heart of the barrow. When the treasure-hunters recovered, they saw an empty 'brass' pan, green and corroded, save for a shining spot in the bottom where the treasure had been. The conjuror told his terrified associates that he had seen the treasure but, as the thunder roared and the lightning flashed, 'they' – presumably the spirits guarding the barrow – 'had snatched it away'. One might suspect that conjuring of a more conventional kind was involved.

Baring-Gould recounts some stories of a parson, named Harris, of Hennock, who was 'a very locally-famous wizard, not yet forgotten'! One of them concerns some geese which had been stolen. The parson promised to discover the thief and 'put him to open shame'. Next Sunday in the pulpit he announced:

'I give you all to know that Farmer Tuckett has had three geese stolen. Now I've read my books and drawn my figures, and I have so conjured that three feathers of thickey geese shall now – this instant – stick to the nose of the thief.'

Immediately a member of the congregation instinctively lifted his hand to his nose, and the parson, who was watching for just that, thundered: 'There is the man that stole the geese.' This was good psychology.

On another occasion, a farmer who had lost a gander went to the parson's study, and asked for help in retrieving it. The parson set about 'conjuring', then opened the casement window, and the gander was thrown in, plucked, trussed and ready for roasting!

Parson Harris, who was a kindly man, brought from Exeter the lover of his servant-maid, who was pining for him. The girl was so upset and dispirited that the parson agreed to cast his spells, even although it was Sunday. Nothing happened at first, and the girl went to bed, disappointed. But at about dawn she heard a knocking at the door and found her young man standing there, breathless, perspiring and jacketless. He had just run all the way from Exeter. The reason for the delay was that all through Sunday he had worn his best jacket with his Prayer Book in the pocket, and the spell would not work until he had taken it off.

A Devonshire wizard named 'Old Baker' was evidently notorious in the 1820s. He featured in a trial at Taunton in 1823, when a woman, who had been set upon as a witch, brought an action for assault against her neighbours. One of the defendants said she had consulted Old Baker, who had advised her that blood must be drawn from the witch – hence the attack. The judge naturally wanted to know:

'Who is Old Baker?'

'Oh, my Lord, he is a great conjuror, the people say. He is a good deal looked up to by the poor people in these parts.'

Said Mr Justice Burrough, 'I wish we had the fellow here. Tell him, if he does not leave off his conjuring, he will be caught and charmed in a manner he will not like.'

Another reference to Old Baker is found in the *Report and Transactions of the Devonshire Association,* 1882, where he features as a consultant in a witchcraft case at Ashreigney. The informant, who provided the story in the 1880s, said that it occurred in his grandfather's time, which would place it in about the 1820s.

The alleged witches were a man named Durke, his wife, and a widowed sister-in-law, Deb Knight. The man did casual work from time to time for a local farmer, keeping an account on a slate and settling it, by accepting payment in kind, once a month. On one occasion Deb Knight went up to the farm with the slate and became involved in an argument with the farmer's wife, who accused her of cheating over the quantity of potatoes she had received. The dispute became so heated that the wife's little boy, aged three, tumbled off his stool in fright and, falling into the fire, was badly burned. His mother cried,

'You wicked old hussey! You've witched the child into the fire!'

Equally angry, Deb Knight replied, 'I'll let you know if I'm a witch or not, before three months are out!'

A series of disasters then struck the farm. The pigs sickened and died, at the rate of two or three a day, till none was left. Then similar trouble began to take a toll of the sheep, cattle and horses. The farmer, a deeply religious man, refused to believe that witchcraft was the cause, but when his losses exceeded £500 he was persuaded by his father-in-law (who features in the next story) to visit Old Baker. As they entered the wizard's cottage, which was near Tiverton, Old Baker looked up and greeted them with,

'Well, farmer, so you've come at last, now you've lost nearly all you had. Why not before? I would have stopped it.'

The farmer was told to take the heart of the next thing that died, stick it full of pins, salt and bury it. Old Baker added that the trouble was caused by three persons, who would appear on the farmer's homeward journey in the guise of three hares, which would come out of a gutter-hole. This happened. After the farmer had buried the heart, his stock began to recover, and there were no more losses.

The father-in-law in this story had his own experience of witches some years earlier. In those days, at the end of wheat harvest, each farm had a reaping day, when the last fields were cut. It was generally understood that anyone could come to help with the work and join in the feast that followed. Among those who apparently made a point of attending all the local reaping-days were a man named Bowden, and his wife. Both were reputed to be witches.

On this occasion, after drinking cider all day, Bowden had reached the truculent stage of drunkenness by supper-time. He wanted a second helping of meat and, instead of passing his plate along the table, he sent it spinning towards the farmer's wife at the head, breaking three more plates in the process. Whereupon she called him 'a witching old rogue'. He then became so violent that he had to be seized and thrown out.

Talking it over afterwards, the farmer and his wife were apprehensive about possible revenge by the Bowdens, and their fears were justified. Mysterious maladies began to affect their livestock, beginning with the poultry and spreading to the sheep, cows, pigs and oxen, which in those days were used for ploughing.

An unusual feature of this story is the bizarre manner in which some of the animals died. A horse, left outside the stable door for a few moments, disappeared and was found the next day in a distant quarry, dead.

'Both the fore and hind legs on the near side were passed through one stirrup-iron above the fetlock. The smith was fetched to remove the stirrup but was obliged to file it off. They then tried by every means to pass a single hoof through the other stirrup-iron, but it was impossible to do so.'

One morning an ox was found, dead, with a heavy ox-yoke stuck on the top of its horns. A few days later two of the oxen, also dead, were found in their shed, their necks jammed into a yoke intended for one. The yoke was properly fastened. The poultry fell about as if their backs were broken, and the hens laid eggs with soft shells.

After much persuasion the farmer, who did not believe in witchcraft, consulted a white witch at Barnstaple. He was told that one more animal would die. He was to cut out its heart, take it at night to the quarry where the horse had been found and burn it. While it was burning, something on the farm would start bleeding. Some of the blood must be collected and brought to the witch.

Arriving home, the farmer went out to the farmyard and looked in at a very valuable calf in one of the sheds. The animal leaped up so violently that it struck a beam six feet above and fell down dead. The farmer dealt with the heart as he had been told. While this was happening, 'two of his daughters were asleep together in the same bed. The younger awoke and found that her feet were quite wet. She struck a light and discovered that her sister's leg had burst out bleeding and that she was all but dead from exhaustion and loss of blood. A doctor was fetched, who stopped the bleeding. . . . Some of the blood was sent to the white witch, and this was the end of the troubles.'

There is another Ashreigney witch story connected with the elder of these two sisters. She married a local farmer. In the village lived an old woman alleged to be a witch. The villagers avoided her, for it was believed that a witch could exercise power only over those who did business with her. One day this farmer found the old woman in his kitchen, where his wife was selling her butter and eggs. He became violently angry and ordered the old woman out. She went, muttering that he would soon regret it.

Disasters similar to those described in the other stories soon began to trouble him. He too consulted a white witch, who stopped the series of misfortunes and told him the culprit would be punished by a mark that all could see. Shortly afterwards, the old woman was affected by an eye disorder, which gradually destroyed the sight of her right eye and was so unsightly that she was ever afterwards obliged to wear a green eye-shade.

The old woman had a beautiful daughter who was at first courted by several local men, including a young mason named Will Ford. As the old lady's reputation for witchcraft increased, the young man became frightened and jilted her daughter. Soon afterwards he fell down a well, broke both his thighs and was crippled for the rest of his life. Shunned and disheartened, the girl went into a decline and pined away. On her death-bed she accused her mother:

'Oh mother, you drew the circle for Will Ford, and I have walked into it, and now I am dying.'

Both she and her mother died soon afterwards.

From the same source comes the story of a witch at Membury, containing an extraordinary wealth of detail. The witch was a woman named Hannah Henley. She lived in a hut in a wood and, unlike the usual description of a reputed witch, was not a decrepit old woman but a 'pattern of neatness and cleanliness. She generally wore short petticoats, with a large white apron, white as the driven snow, a plaid turnover, and a satin poke bonnet. Cats she had in any number, and of all colours.' She was famous for making apple dumplings, or crowdy pies.

However, she was evidently a cadger, particularly at a certain neighbouring farm, although 'she never asked like begging; she demanded'. The farmer, his brother, and his wife gave her whatever she wanted for a long time – 'corn, bread, milk, flour, beer, sometimes money' – but at last grew tired and refused. The brother, who had been very generous, was the first to say no.

'You'll not live long to use it yourself,' Hannah told him. He died in agony within three weeks. Not long afterwards the farmer's youngest child wanted to give Hannah a walnut it was playing with. The nurse refused, so Hannah stooped down and drew the sign of a cross enclosed in a circle on the ground. That night the child turned round and round and became giddy. It fell ill and died four days later.

More trouble followed. 'The milk would not set, the butter could not be made, bread put to bake only ran about the oven. . . .'

Hannah continued to visit the farm, although she was unwelcome. One day the mistress refused to see her and hid in the pantry, telling a servant to say she was not at home. Hannah knew better.

'Tell your missus that she shall not move out of the pantry now, even if she wishes,' she said.

And, sure enough, even her husband could not pull her out. He became so angry that he went to Hannah's cottage with a loaded gun. But when she dared him to shoot her he could not do it.

Troubles continued. Horses injured themselves in the stables at night; sheep died at the rate of eight or ten a day. At last the farmer fetched a white witch from Chard, who came and lived in the house for the best part of a month. He had a bed made up in the parlour and slept there by day, working at dusk. A maid-servant crept downstairs one night and looked through the key-hole.

She saw this man on his knees before his book, and sparks of fire flashing about the room. . . . Next morning she told the mistress that she believed the parlour had been on fire, and was sharply reproved for her pains and told not to meddle again, lest something dreadful should happen to her.

The wizard ordered six bullocks' hearts to be hung in the fireplace. 'Two in the centre were stuck with pins, and the other four with new nails. These were slowly melted, and as they melted the witch's heart was to be melted too.'

'Old Hannah came to the house day after day, begging for relief and saying that since such and such a day she had had no rest'. The kind-hearted mistress would have helped, but the farmer and the wizard would not allow it. The affair came to a ghastly climax just before Easter.

The wizard:

had a large number of nails driven into a butt. . . . This was taken
to the top of the hill and set rolling till it came to the bottom.
This was Thursday, and in the afternoon old Hannah came again
to the house, saying she was dying and begging for wine or spirits.
The white witch then felt sure that he had gained; and at four
o'clock in the morning went towards the hut in the wood. This
was Good Friday morning. He found the window was broken,
and, looking about, he saw high above him, in a tree, the witch
in a sheet, with a smutty kettle hanging by her side. There she was
left for the bettermost folks to see, and also the servants.

Then the tree was cut down, as she was too high to be got at;
and, as the tree fell, the witch fell into a gulley. She was laid out
on a 'kit', with just a sheet over her; and then it was seen that her
flesh was very much torn, as if by pins or nails; and inside the hut
blood marks everywhere. This was caused, so they said, by
struggling with the devil, who pulled her through the broken
window.

After her death a box on one side of her bed was opened, and
in it money to a fair amount was found, with tea, sugar, bread and
suchlike; while on the other side, two smaller boxes, containing
toads of various sizes.

From Good Friday till the following Wednesday, the corpse
was visited by scores of people from all parts; and then was buried
at four cross-roads, between Membury and Axminster; and afterwards horses used to shy when passing the grave.

The informant adds that the white witch was paid £100 for his
work. White witch or black, what he did sounds uncommonly like
murder. An attempt was made to kill the cats, but they all escaped.
The informant said that the hut was burnt, but a letter written in
1865, refers to a hut that had been empty for 20 years and identifies
it as 'the very house that Hannah Henley, the Membury witch, used
to live in'.

J. R. W. Coxhead supplies some further details. Kind neighbours
offered to stay with her, as she lay ill in her cottage, the night before
she died, but she told them to leave her alone, for their own safety's
sake, as she knew she was going to die hard that night. The inquest

was held at Axminster on 12 April 1841, when the cause of death was recorded as 'Water on the Brain'.

J. R. W. Coxhead tells another story in which a bullock's heart featured in the breaking of a spell. The white witch in this case lived at Exeter, and was consulted by a woman who had experienced a run of bad luck. She and her husband were told to buy a large bullock's heart and put it in the fire just before midnight, taking care first to lock all doors and shutter all windows. As the bullock's heart started to burn, there came a rattling at the doors and windows; the relative suspected of bewitching them was trying to break in. The pair crouched by the fire, trembling, and eventually the bullock's heart was entirely consumed and the witch went away.

Sarah Hewett has described an old Devonshire counter-measure to be employed against witches:

Take three small-necked stone jars; place in each the liver of a frog stuck full of new pins and the heart of a toad stuck full of thorns from a holy thorn bush. Cork and seal each jar. Bury in three different churchyard paths seven inches from the surface and seven feet from the porch. While in the act of burying each, repeat the Lord's Prayer backwards. As the hearts and livers decay, so will the witch's powers vanish.

Christina Hole records an instance of witchcraft recoiling on a witch in Devonshire. In 1602 a witch of Hardness, named Alice Trevisard, cast a spell on the house of a woman who had offended her, by throwing water on the staircase. Her action was seen by a neighbour, who warned the householder. Consequently, the next person to use the stairs was Alice Trevisard herself. 'Within one hour after, the said Alice fell grievously sick, and part of the hands, fingers and toes of the said Alice rotted and consumed away.'

In 1833, Mrs Bray visited Cranmere Pool, the source of the river Tavy. Her guide told her that he himself had been bewitched by 'an evil-minded old woman' who was still alive and lived near him. For seventeen weeks, he said, he could not sleep for more than an hour at a time, and could eat nothing except a few biscuits. At midnight precisely he would begin to be tormented by pricking pains in the side, which were so bad that he had to be helped out of bed. They would afflict him all night, as he sat by the bedside, but vanished regularly at six o'clock in the morning.

Predictably, Devon, like almost every other county, has a number of stories about witches who turned themselves into hares. One, often repeated, comes from the collection of Mrs. Bray written down in 1833. In this instance, the ability of an old woman to turn into a hare was used for gain. She and her little grandson, who lived with her, took advantage of an offer from the local hunt of sixpence for every hare the boy could put up. He found a hare so regularly that the huntsmen began to be suspicious. They arranged to get the hunt started with less delay than usual. Soon the hounds were hard on the heels of the hare, and 'Run, Granny, run for your life!' shouted the boy. She managed to outdistance the hounds and escaped into the cottage through a little hole in the door. The huntsmen tried to break it down, but could not do so till the parson arrived to break the spell.

'Upstairs they all went. There they found the old hag bleeding, and covered with wounds, and still out of breath. On this occasion they let her off, though the boy was soundly beaten. The woman was later arrested, 'for bewitching a young woman and making her spit pins', and this story was told in evidence against her. She was burnt at the stake.

One of Hannah Henley's accomplishments is said to have been the ability to turn herself into a hare; she was frequently chased in this form by the Cotley Harriers. As late as 1885 a man at Rose Ash, near South Molton, shot at a hare with a bullet made from a sixpence, and that same day a local woman suspected of being a witch was found with wounds in her leg.

J. R. W. Coxhead tells the story of Moll Stancombe, of Chagford, who, in the form of a hare, was often coursed by hounds but could never be caught. One of her former lovers, whom she had rejected, loaded a gun with a silver bullet and attempted to shoot her, but the gun exploded and blew off his hand. A rival witch at length revealed that she could be caught by a spayed bitch. Hare and bitch seemed evenly matched for a long time, but at last the dog managed to bite her flank as she scrambled through a hedge. The owner of the dog then went to Moll's cottage, looked through the window, and saw her putting a plaster on a wound. It corresponded exactly to the spot which the dog had bitten. In this case, the witch learned her lesson, for she never again appeared as a hare.

Vixen Tor, by Merrivale Bridge, on Dartmoor, was once the haunt of a particularly evil witch, who used to perch on a high crag and, by her spells, caused sudden dense mists to descend on the moor, luring travellers to their death in the bogs. She was finally overcome by a moorman, who had once been befriended by pixies and had been given by them a magic ring. When the witch tried her tricks on him he put on the ring, which made him invisible. Then he crept up behind her and pushed her off the crag into the bog below.

Some Devon witch stories are relatively recent. The tale of Mother Dark, of Dalwood, dates from 1881. This old woman was suspected of causing the illness of a cow, a fact confirmed by a white witch of Exeter whom the farmer consulted. The white witch promised to make Mother Dark suffer as she had made the farm animals suffer, and soon afterwards the old woman was admitted to hospital, suffering from a mysterious illness. Her ailment coincided with the end of the epidemic on the farm.

A similar story, from about the same period, comes from neighbouring Axmouth, the witch there being an old woman named Charity Perry. In this instance, too, a neighbour went by train to Exeter to consult a white witch and was told that the witch would fall ill; then the troubles she had been causing would cease. That is what happened. Charity was ill for nine days. Some interesting details are recorded. The local boys thought that she left her bedroom on a broomstick every night at dusk, using a broken window instead of the door. Under her bed she kept a box full of toads.

In December 1924, a man named Matthews, of Clyst St Lawrence, was sentenced at Cullompton Petty Sessions to a month's imprisonment for attacking a neighbour and scratching her with a pin. Matthews alleged witchcraft, asserting that the neighbour had 'ill-wished' his pig. He said that she used a crystal and insisted that the house should be searched for it, since 'the police have to protect the public in such a matter'. When a magistrate protested, 'Such a fallacy died out years ago', Matthews retorted, 'Oh, no it didn't. It hasn't with some of us'.

In front of The Hunter's Lodge Inn, between Honiton and Ottery, is a great stone on which, according to legend, witches sacrificed their victims. At night the stone was said to roll down to the river to drink, lubricated by the blood that had been shed on it.

4 Ghosts

WILLIAM III SPENT an uneasy night at Ford House, Newton Abbot, when he first landed in England, on 5 November 1688. Although he had taken the precaution of bringing a large army with him, his heart was not in the invasion enterprise and he could hardly have avoided thinking of the fate of the Duke of Monmouth, the last invader of the West Country, only four years earlier. So perhaps it is not surprising that the house has a tradition of heavy footsteps, tramping along the corridors on the anniversary of the occasion.

On about the same date, making allowances for alterations in the calendar, a coach and horses rattle over cobbles outside (and partly inside) the Royal Castle Inn on Dartmouth quay They are heard at about two a.m., which is the time that a coach arrived, in 1688, to take Mary, consort of William III, from her lodging there to meet her husband at Torbay.

Judge Jeffreys is a more unexpected ghost, for his associations are with Somerset rather than Devon. He haunts the ruins of Lydford castle, sometimes appearing in the form of a black pig.

Fitzford House, near Tavistock, is haunted by the ghost of Lady Howard, whose seventeenth century career was tragic and eventful. At midnight she passes by, sheeted in white and riding in a coach of human bones, with skulls at the four corners. It is drawn by headless horses and is accompanied by a ghostly black dog (more than one, in some versions), with only one eye, in the middle of its forehead. This dog has been given the task of plucking one blade of grass each night from the mound of Okehampton Castle and carrying it to the gate of Fitzford. It must continue to do so until all have been plucked, which will never happen, for the grass grows faster than the hound can work.

Why Lady Howard should be the restless spirit in this story seems inexplicable, for she was more sinned against than sinning, three of her four husbands having been decidedly unsavoury characters. Devon tradition credits her with having murdered three of them, but that is almost certainly incorrect.

The spectre of Squire Boone, from Norton Dawnay, near Dartmouth, appeared with a readily defined purpose after his death in 1677. He had strongly disapproved of the young man whom his daughter proposed to marry and eventually extracted from her a promise to break off the engagement. Not long afterwards, Squire Boone died, and, after waiting six months, the daughter broke her promise and married her lover. Unwisely, they moved into the ancestral home, Mount Boone, and soon the ghost of the old man started to display his displeasure. It took to roaming the house, preceded by flickering flames and accompanied by supernatural phenomena, such as the moving of heavy furniture. When the young couple tried to escape by going to London, the ghost followed them.

At Mount Boone itself, the deceased squire became so troublesome that a group of clergy was called in to exorcise him. They met with little success until the spirit appeared in visible form and amiably agreed to return to where he now belonged, if he could take his daughter with him. Father and daughter had a long conversation, and then the whole party went to the millstream, where one of the clergymen handed the ghost a cockle-shell with a hole in the bottom. The squire's task was to empty the stream with the cockle-shell, before he appeared again on earth. The ghost expressed satisfaction with the conditions, probably because it was aware of the sequel, which was that the daughter died three months later, thus accompanying her father as he had demanded.

An ancestress of Sabine Baring-Gould, who lived at Lew Trenchard and died in 1795, was a lady of such strong character and personality that several ghost stories, some of which may have had other origins, have become attached to her memory. For some time after her death she appeared to local people, including a carpenter who peeped into her vault and was chased home by the outraged phantom. More than a hundred years later Baring-Gould's visitors occasionally saw spectral figures in the old house.

Parson Froude, who lived at Rackenford in the middle years of the nineteenth century, seems to have been a typical hard-living, fox-hunting country parson, who fell foul of his more puritanical neighbours and whose reputation was blackened in consequence. He still rides at night on his black horse.

A more modern ghost is that of the parson of Luffincott, who simply disappeared one day in 1904 and was never seen or heard of again. His spirit, however, has been observed, notably by the sexton, who has tried to speak to it, but without success.

A nineteenth-century rector of Uplyme adopted a novel method for laying the ghost of his predecessor. When he became tired of the spectre appearing and occupying a chair at table, as he ate his dinner alone in the great dining-room by candle-light, he went and sat on it! Apparently the method worked, for the ghost was not seen again.

Cranmere Pool, in one of the wildest and loneliest parts of Dartmoor, is associated with many ghost stories. As the site is more bog than open water, the will-o'-the-wisp may be responsible for some of the tales, which, however, have become very confused. One of the basic and most circumstantial concerns an Okehampton merchant of the seventeenth century named Benjamin Gayer. One of his duties as mayor of Okehampton was to administer a fund, maintained by public subscription, for ransoming Christian sailors from the Turks – a laudable charity, much needed in those days. When the Turks captured several large merchantmen laden with goods belonging to Gayer, he was faced with ruin and decided to reimburse himself from the fund. In due course he died, much troubled by a guilty conscience, and his restless spirit haunted Okehampton.

Years later, the ghost had become such a nuisance that twenty-three clergymen were asked to exorcise it. They were unsuccessful, until one of them adjured it in Arabic. At this the spirit acknowledged defeat and retired into the body of an unbroken colt. The best horseman in town received the Holy Sacrament and then slipped an unused bridle and bit over the colt's head. He mounted it and galloped away to Cranmere Pool, never allowing the animal to turn its head during the journey. When they reached the Pool, the horseman slid off its back, but the colt galloped on and vanished in the depths of the water.

An addition to the story describes how the spirit was doomed to spend its time, till the Day of Judgement, making trusses and bonds of sand. According to another version, its task was to bale out the Pool, using a thimble with a hole in it.

In yet another version, the merchant becomes an old farmer. The number of clergymen assembled for the exorcism is reduced to seven, and the best horseman in town is the farmer's servant boy. It is the boy, not the colt, who may not turn round, but he is inquisitive and disobeys at the edge of the Pool. The colt vanishes in a ball of fire. In a final flurry, the colt lashes out with its hoofs and knocks out one of the boy's eyes.

There is another legend of a 'conjuror', who keeps a spirit named 'Bingie' in the Pool. It has to try to drain the waters with a wicker oat-sieve. One day it discovers that a sheepskin, which it found on the moor, can be laid over the bottom of the sieve to make it watertight. This way it quickly empties the Pool, pours the water down the hill and drowns the town of Okehampton.

Another ghost with an apparently hopeless task is the wraith of a lady buried, for some unremembered sin, in unconsecrated ground near a holy well at Coffinswell. At midnight every New Year's morning she is permitted to leave her grave and take 'one cock's stride' towards the churchyard. She will arrive there, and find her hope of salvation, on the Day of Judgment.

Peter Tavy also has a ghost associated with a grave in unconsecrated ground. Having committed suicide following a tragic love affair, a man named Stephen was buried there with a stake through his heart. He continued to haunt the place until exorcised by a priest, but the spot is still known as Stephen's Grave.

A ghost which frequents the site of a cottage at Marlpits Hill, near Honiton, is identified, from the location and by his dress, as a man who volunteered for service with Monmouth's army in 1685 and escaped from the Battle of Sedgmoor. Just as he was arriving home at the cottage, exhausted, he was overtaken by cavalry and hacked to death, his wife and children watching. A curious feature of this apparition is that, on a sunny afternoon in 1904, it was seen by a whole party of schoolchildren, but not by their teacher who was accompanying them.

Devon has several stories of murdered pedlars and other wayfarers. One refers to a farm called Loosely, about three miles from Tiverton, where one night in 1643 a pedlar lodged with a farmer named Shapcott and was never seen or heard of again. The farmer exhibited all the symptoms of an uneasy conscience for the next two years and swore that he was haunted. Eventually, having recovered his normal spirits, he had a tombstone erected to the pedlar, inscribing on it some verses from the 103rd Psalm beginning, 'The Lord executeth righteousness and judgment for all that are oppressed . . .' Some time later the farmer's son, who regarded the stone as a reproach, smashed it with an iron bar. His hand withered, luck deserted his family, and he was reduced to poverty.

Another pedlar, identified as a Jew, was murdered on Carn Top, above Ilfracombe and his ghost used to be seen, haunting the bushes.

Sir William Tracey, one of the murderers of Thomas a'Becket, was a baron of Barnstaple, and several legends concerning his fate are remembered in north-west Devon. For a time he is supposed to have hidden himself in Crookham Cavern, between Mortehoe and Ilfracombe, his daughter bringing him food; and now he is condemned to remain there for ever, making 'bundles of sand and wisps of the same'. His ghost can be heard lamenting on stormy nights.

Another knight, Sir Robert Chichester of Martinhoe, is also doomed to wander along this same wild shore, engaged in a similar hopeless task. He has to 'form traces from the sand, to fasten them to his carriage, and then to drive up the face of the crag, and through a narrow fissure at the summit, which is known as Sir Robert's Road'.

Another group of stories introduces buried treasure, to which the ghost leads the observer. One of Mrs Bray's neighbours, a Mary Colling, told her the following story in 1833.

A certain house near Tavistock, called Down House, was reputedly haunted by a ghost which walked at the same hour every night. The residents took care to be in bed and asleep at that time. One night a small boy, who was sick and being nursed by his mother, cried for a drink of cool water from the pump in the yard. Although the time of the ghost's appearance was near at hand, the mother bravely went downstairs with her pitcher and was accosted by a tall man who placed a hand on her shoulder.

'In the name of God why troublest thou me?' she demanded.

'It is well for thee that thou hast spoken to me in the name of God,' was the reply, 'this being the last time allotted to me to trouble this world, or else I should have injured thee. Now do as I tell thee, and be not afraid. Come with me and I will direct thee to a something which shall remove this pump; underneath it is buried treasure.'

The treasure was uncovered, and the ghost told her to use it well for the benefit of the farm, promising that anyone trying to steal it or to molest her would suffer for it; her child would now recover. Then a cock crew, and the ghost faded away.

On Trow Hill, above Salcombe Regis, is a field where in about 1811 a farmer was led to a buried treasure by the apparition of a lady in grey. One of his plough oxen sank into the ground just where the ghost had been seen, and on investigation the farmer found a very large and valuable treasure. It was a happy event, for the man had a big family which he was finding difficult to keep on his small acreage. But after his discovery he prospered, and was able to give each of the children £1500 when they married.

Chettiscombe, near Tiverton, possessed a haunted chapel in which a vast treasure was reputed to be hidden. There was a legend that anyone courageous enough to spend the night there, braving the numerous ghosts, would be directed by one of them to the treasure. Two farmers agreed to undertake the ordeal, and sure enough, found the treasure, in a field not far away. They said one of the spirits appeared in the form of a white owl and revealed the secret.

As in other counties, the stories that have been collected are probably only a fraction of those still in circulation.

The road between Postbridge and Two Bridges on Dartmoor is haunted by a mysterious phantom whose chief characteristic seems to be a pair of large hairy hands. They grasp at the handlebars of motor-cycles, causing the riders to finish up in the ditch, or rap at the windows of parked cars and caravans.

The Old Inn at Widecombe is haunted by the ghost, not of Tom

Pearse's grey mare, but of a friendly character named Harry, who has frequently been seen walking through solid walls, especially in the direction of the kitchen. Not far away, on the moors, is a place marked on the map as Jay's Grave, said to be that of a pregnant girl, Mary Jay, who committed suicide. Her ghost is sometimes seen, apparently laying flowers on the grave. The Old Inn, too, has a ghost of a child, who can sometimes be heard crying, but is never seen.

Another inn with two ghosts is the Who'd Have Thought It at Milton Coombe, near Yelverton (a pub frequented by Sir Francis Drake). They are a former landlord, Abe Beer, and an earlier phantom who seems to be a cavalier. One of them occasionally rings the bell for service.

The Church House Inn at Torbryan, near Newton Abbot, has a ghost which is heard more often than seen. Of the few people who have observed it, one described the apparition as a monk; another as an old man, sitting in the bar. A different monk has a chair left vacant for him in The Pig and Whistle at Littlehempston, near Totnes, and is familiarly known as Freddie. The more erudite local residents believe him to be Brother Joseph, a monk of nearby Buckfast Abbey, some four hundred years ago.

Bishop Lacy Inn in Chudleigh, the oldest building in the little town, has a clerical ghost said by some to be Bishop Lacy himself, a fourteenth century bishop of Exeter. The inn was once his summer residence.

A barmaid at the Old Smugglers' Inn near Teignmouth was badly frightened night after night by a ghost which she said she felt was present. No-one would believe her until the landlord found, in a batch of old prints he had purchased, one showing the murder of a woman in the very room occupied by the barmaid.

Dean Combe, near Mary Tavy, had a ghost which apparently arrived by mistake. He was a master weaver who was so enthusiastic about his work and so assiduous that, on the day after his death, he took his accustomed place at his loom as though nothing had happened. The weaver's son was frightened and called in the parson to exorcise the ghost. This was done by conjuring it to come downstairs and flinging a handful of earth from the churchyard in its face. The spirit then became a black hound. The parson gave it a nutshell containing a hole and set the phantom the task of emptying the pool below the waterfall.

Devon seems to have fewer poltergeists than certain other counties, but Sabine Baring-Gould records an instance which created
much attention at Sampford Peverell in 1810. The events followed
the usual pattern of rappings, bumps and throwing of articles, but
much of the evidence is apparently suspect, having been provided by
a clergyman of dubious character, who was later unfrocked.

Ottery St Mary parish church has an effigy, of John Coke, which
was said in times past to step out of its niche and prowl around the
church at dead of night. Its behaviour was attributed to the uneasy
conscience of John Coke, who was alleged to have murdered his
brother for an inheritance or, according to another version, to have
shot him accidentally. There seems to be no sound basis for either
tale.

In *Haunted England,* Christina Hole, tells a strange story of what
appears to be spirit guidance. About the middle of the nineteenth
century, a young man staying at Exmouth awoke at midnight with
the feeling that he had to get up immediately and go down to the
ferry. Although he argued that the ferry-boat would not be there,
because the ferryman was sleeping on the other side of the estuary
at Starcross, he could not resist the impulse. To his surprise, the
ferryboat was waiting. The ferryman said that some person unknown
had told him a passenger was waiting on the Exmouth side. Still
wondering whether he was dreaming, the young man got into the
boat and crossed to Starcross, where he felt impelled to take the next
train to Exeter.

There his impulses ceased, and he spent the rest of the night
wandering about the streets, grateful at last to find a hotel open
where he could have breakfast. Over the meal his waiter chatted
about the Assizes, which were then being held in the city, so he
decided to drop in there for an hour or two. The case in progress
when he entered was a murder trial, of a carpenter. The accused
maintained that at the time he was working at a big house some
miles away, but could bring no evidence to support his alibi, as the
family of the house were absent.

There was, said the carpenter, one man who could exonerate him.
A young man, who was a friend of the householder, had called
during the day and, finding the family away, had stayed taking for
a time. The young man had borrowed the carpenter's pencil to make
an entry in his notebook. Unfortunately the carpenter did not know

the young man's name and had no idea where to find him.

On hearing this, the young man asked to be allowed to give evidence. He testified to being the young man in question and produced the pocket-book in which he had made a note with the carpenter's pencil. The case against the prisoner naturally collapsed. But we are left wondering about the nature of the guidance which brought the young man to Exeter.

By way of contrast, two stories collected by Mrs Bray introduce ghosts with natural explanations. One concerns the period of the Civil War, when a party of Parliamentarian soldiers set about despoiling Fitzford House and other royalist enclaves in and around Tavistock. The information that the landlord of the King's Arms Inn was a royalist delighted them. But, as they gleefully made their way to the cellars, they were stopped by a pale figure of a woman in a white robe. It was the inn-keeper's daughter, wrapped in a white sheet and aided in her role by the fact that she had got up from a sick-bed where she was dying of consumption. She played her part so well that the troopers fled in panic, leaving the cellars intact.

The other describes the terror of a small boy, He was studying a nightmarish painting in his candle-lit room at Sydenham House, near Tavistock, just before going to sleep, when he heard alarming sounds approaching along the corridor. They consisted of regular-spaced stumpings, alternating with the muffled tread of a slipper-clad foot. It was, in fact, a one-legged footman on his way to bed.

Like many other counties, Devon has a number of stories of animal ghosts. Black dogs are especially renowned, and Theo Brown, a resident of Chudleigh, has collected many examples of the apparition. A nineteenth-century visitor to Devon set out one December afternoon to walk from Princetown to Plymouth – a sixteen-mile tramp over the moors in sparkling winter weather. For the latter part of his journey he was accompanied by a black dog, of Newfoundland type, but much larger. Being fond of dogs, he tried to pat the head of the animal by his side, but was alarmed to find that his hand passed right through it. As they were nearing Plymouth, there was a loud explosion, accompanied by a flash as of lightning, and the man fell senseless into a ditch where he was found next morning, still unconscious. Local tradition says that, at the spot where the explosion occurred, a traveller was murdered many years ago. His dog now trots along the road, looking for the murderer, whom he will kill when he finds him. Meantime he can make mistakes.

Yealmbridge, a village on the Attery, used to be haunted by a black dog apparition, which appeared at midnight when the moon was full. It walked in silence, from the direction of Boyton, near the bridge, went up the opposite hill, and disappeared along the Egloskerry road. In 1870 a correspondent to *Notes and Queries* wrote 'Ask him the hour and he will tell you. But no one has ever yet seen this midnight visitant, no one knows of his return, yet no one presumes to doubt his advent'.

Uplyme has a Black Dog Lane, and a black dog is said to walk along it at night. The creature is believed to grow larger as it approaches, until it becomes monstrous. Anyone who sees it will die within a year.

There is also a black dog who used to haunt either a farmhouse at Uplyme, or, according to another version, the Black Dog Inn. It used to sit by the fireside with the householder, who took little notice. Once, however, he tried to chase it away with a poker, and it vanished through the ceiling, doing considerable damage. During the subsequent repairs, a large hoard of coins from the time of Charles I was found in the roof. After that the dog no longer appeared indoors, but transferred itself to Black Dog Lane.

The moors above Plymouth are not the only part of Dartmoor infested by black dogs. In *Devon Villages,* S. H. Burton refers to 'the famous Black dog which haunts lanes all over the moor'. Perhaps he should speak of them in the plural. He tells the story of a Ponsworthy character named Joey Brown, who, well fortified after an evening in the Forest Inn at Hexworthy, fell in with a black dog on his way home. Courageously he tied his scarf around the animal's neck, led it home and locked it in a stable for the night. When he brought his neighbours and friends to admire his captive in the morning, they found the stable occupied by a large black sow, wearing Joey Brown's scarf!

Black Hounds, of course, run with the Wild Hunt – a common legend, which also occurs in Devon. Sabine Baring-Gould says that in old times the Wild Hunt was known locally as the 'Wish Hounds'. J. R. W. Coxhead has heard them called the 'Yeth Hounds' or 'Heath Hounds'. He writes:

The sound of the Dark Huntsman's horn and the fierce cries of the Yeth Hounds are supposed to have been heard many times in lonely parts of the moor by belated travellers, and by resident inhabitants of the Dartmoor area. It is said that two of the favourite haunts of the spectral huntsman and his pack of demon hounds are Wistman's Wood and the Dewerstone Rock.

He adds that when, on a stormy night in 1677, Sir Richard Cabell, lord of the manor of Brook in Buckfastleigh parish, died, the Demon Hunt raged around the house all night, waiting for the soul of the wicked knight.

Devon tradition regards unbaptised infants as the special prey of the Demon Huntsman.

Another story relates how a man, returning from Widecombe fair to Chagford one dark and stormy night, encountered the Wild Hunt on Hamel Down. He saw the 'jet-black hounds with glowing eyes' bounding past, followed by the Demon Hunter, to whom he called:

'Hey, Huntsman! What sport have you had? Give us some of your game.'

'Take that', said the Huntsman and tossed him a parcel.

The man could not see what he was carrying until he reached home. On unwrapping the parcel in the courtyard, by the light streaming from the doorway, he found himself looking in horror at the dead body of his own small child.

A different type of animal spectre, the Black Hen and her chicks, has appeared from time to time in a toadstool circle in a meadow. It seems they can be conjured up by a spell. Some years ago, a vicar, who was a keen student of magic, left a book on the subject open on his study table while he went to conduct a service in the village church. As he was preaching, one of his servants back at home started to read the book aloud; it happened to be open at the page describing the spell for producing the Black Hen. Sure enough, the hen and her chicks walked into the study, but, as the servant continued reading, they grew larger and larger until they were as big as bullocks. Meantime a violent storm had blown up, and the vicar, sensing what was wrong, brought the service to a hurried conclusion and hastened home. There he was just in time to reverse the spell, keeping the hen and chicks busy during the process by throwing them grains of rice.

5   Other Supernatural Beings

THE RIVERS Tamar and Torridge are each said to have a resident nymph or genius, who once argued about the quickest route to the sea. They quarrelled so vigorously and so long that they fell asleep. Torridge awoke first and crept silently away, hoping to steal a march on his brother. Tamar, awaking suddenly and finding what had happened, stormed away southwards, dislodging great stones in his course, and soon reached the sea. Whereupon Torridge, discouraged, turned sadly northwards.

Coxhead gives a different version. There is only one nymph, Tamara, the lovely daughter of an earth-gnome. Her two suitors are young giants, the spirits of the Torridge and Tavy. They are put to sleep, enchanted by Tamara's father, who also turns Tamara into a river. In this version, Tavy wakes first and hurries to his own father, a giant living on Dartmoor. The old giant changes him into a stream, so that he may bound happily down the hill to join Tamara.

Later, Torridge also awakes and goes to a local wizard to ask if he too may be allowed to join Tamara. But he is in so much of a hurry, that he confuses the wizard, who sends him in the wrong direction. So Torridge never links up with Tamar.

The earth-gnomes also feature in an ancient story about the founding of Fernworthy, an old farmstead, now submerged by Fernworthy Reservoir, Dartmoor. When, long ago, the first house was built at Fernworthy, the earth-gnomes who lived there in a fairy hill were enraged and determined on revenge. So one winter night they crept in and stole the baby of the farmer of Fernworthy, the first child born in the new house.

The power of the earth spirits of Dartmoor was still remembered as late as the nineteenth century. A Lancashire man acquired several thousands of acres on the moor and began reclaiming the land with the aid of every modern invention, which in those days included steam ploughs and steam threshing-engines. One day he was accosted by a moorman who warned him to be careful. Said he,

'I valled asleep, and then I saw the gurt old sperit of the moors, Old Crockern hisself, grey as granite, and his eyebrows hanging down over his glimmering eyes like sedge, and his eyes deep as peat-water pools . . . Sez he to me, Bear Muster Vowler a message from me. Tell Muster Vowler, if he scratches my back, I'll tear out his pocket.'

The warning was justified. The money was drained from Mr Fowler's pocket before he succeeded in draining Dartmoor's peat bogs.

At one time there were so many giants in Devon that some of them fled to Somerset. One was the giant of Grabbist, who went first to Exmoor and then established himself at Dunster, where a number of tales are told about him. He occasionally ventured back to Devon, wading out to sea as far as Lundy, where he used to catch great shoals of fish. He was a kindly giant.

The two giants of Plymouth are even known by name. They were Corineus and Gogmagog, who engaged in a wrestling match where Plymouth now stands. Corineus was a Trojan hero who, according to Geoffrey of Monmouth, sailed to Albion (Britain) with Brutus when expelled from Italy. Landing in Devon, they found the country occupied by a tribe of giants, with whom they engaged in battle. Eventually the quarrel was decided by single combat between

Corineus and Gogmagog. Gogmagog broke three of the Trojan's ribs but Corineus, maddened with pain, seized his adversary and tossed him into the sea off Plymouth Hoe. Two huge figures commemorating the giants were carved in white limestone overlooking the harbour, but were destroyed, after existing for many centuries, in 1671. Brutus himself, according to local tradition, founded Totnes.

A giant is said to be buried at Kenford, beneath Haldon Hill, the grave being marked by two stones, one at the head, the other at the feet. The stones were some distance apart, but how far is unknown, for it was said that, no matter how often the space is measured, the result is always different.

Mrs Bray, writing in 1832, says she heard a tradition that the bones of a giant were discovered when the foundations were dug for the Abbey-house at Tavistock. Some of the bones and their sarcophagus were still extant and in her husband's possession. One thigh-bone was 21 inches long and 5½ inches in circumference; the other was 19½ by 4½. They were said by local people to be the bones of Ordulf and his wife.

Ordulf was the son of an earl of Devon, who lived in the reign of Edward the Confessor. He is said to have been about nine feet tall, and stories are told of his prodigious strength. He once tore down the gates of Exeter, and destroyed part of the city wall with his bare hands in order to gain admittance. He could stride across a river ten feet wide.

There are a few stories of dragons in Devonshire. One lived by the river Exe, between Dolbury Hill and Cadbury Castle, a few miles north of Exeter. Each hill is crowned by a prehistoric fortress. The dragon was said to pass between the two of them, guarding a great treasure that was concealed in one or both. It was a fiery creature, so may possibly owe its origin to the will-o'-the-wisps in the marshy meadows by the river. An old rhyme asserts:

If Cadbury Castle and Dolbury Hill dolven were
All England might plough with a golden share.

In the 1950s an old lady at Cullompton mentioned to me that both hills held buried treasure.

Other fiery dragons have been seen by local residents, around Challacombe, on Exmoor.

6 Churches, Saints and More Treasure

DEVON HAS A DUAL ecclesiastical tradition. By the time of the Saxon invasion in the seventh century AD, Christianity had become well established, and many of the churches, and the villages around them, are of Celtic foundation. Some of the Saxons were Christians, too, by this time, so they also established churches as they settled the land.

One of the Celtic townships is undoubtedly Braunton, which was, in the earliest extant records, Brannoc-minster. St Brannoc, its founder, came from Wales in the fifth century, having been told in a vision that he should found a church on the other side of the sea, in a place where he would meet a sow and her litter. This instruction he obeyed, and there is a boss in the church nave, carved with a sow and litter, to commemorate his obedience.

Other Celtic saints perpetuated in the names of Devon villages include St Kea, whose village is Landkey (*Llan Kea*), St Fili at Filleigh, and St Budoc at Budshead (Budocs-hide). Celtic saints with church dedications in the county include St Kerrian (in Exeter), St

Rumon, St Petrock, St Indract, St Winwalloe (now called Onolaus, with a church at Portleham), and St Nectan. A Celtic saint, Endelienta, had a chapel on Lundy and may possess other dedications in Devon, under the guise of St Helen (Elen).

No sooner had the Saxons settled in Devon than they started to acquire their own local saints. One of the best known is St Urith, or Hieritha, who lived on a farm at Swimbridge. When she became a Christian, her angry heathen stepmother incited the farm labourers to kill her with their scythes. The church dedicated to her at Chittlehampton is said to be on the site of her martyrdom, and was a place of pilgrimage till the Reformation. Urith was a popular mediaeval saint in Devon, and many children were named after her.

Another Christian girl allegedly murdered by a heathen step-mother was St Sidwell, of Exeter. She was martyred while at her devotions at a well outside the city walls, and again a church was erected on the site.

The best-known Saxon saint of Devonshire is St Boniface. Originally known as Winfrith, he was born at or near Crediton. Although some writers have considered him the greatest of all Devon men, he seems to have been both arrogant and bigoted, his desire to convert the heathen Friesians in the forests of Germany surpassed only by his hatred of the Celtic Christians, who lived all around his home in Devon. Much of his energy in Germany was directed to the undoing of the work already accomplished by Celtic (Irish) missionaries.

Religious intolerance frequently manifested its ugly head in Devon. One occasion was the Prayer Book Rebellion in 1549. The new Prayer Book was introduced on Whitsunday of that year and was used in all English churches, including Sampford Courtenay, where the congregation disliked it so much that on the following Sunday they compelled their priest to go back to the old style of service. The new one was just 'a Christmas game', they said.

Authority was brought in to ensure that the new edict was obeyed. Justices of the Peace addressed the parishioners in a field near the church, and one of them, William Hellyons, was so eloquent and domineering that the villagers lost their tempers. A farmer named Lethbridge hit at him with a billhook, felling him to the ground, and within minutes the crowd had hacked him to pieces.

Now they were committed to rebellion, and for a time things

went reasonably well. A party of gentry, who came out from Exeter
to deal with them, returned without achieving much. The peasant
army occupied Crediton, where they linked up with a force sharing
similar ideals, who had marched up from Cornwall. Together they all
proceeded down the road to Exeter, flying banners bearing the Five
Wounds of Christ and carrying the pyx under a lavishly decorated
canopy. Most of them were farmers and labourers, led by priests, but
they were joined by a few minor gentry. They besieged Exeter for
weeks during the summer but were eventually defeated by a
Government force sent down from London; pitched battles, in which
they displayed incredible valour, were fought at Fenny Bridges and
Clyst Heath. They made a last stand at Sampford Courtenay itself on
17 August, and then retribution descended on the survivors in a
fashion reminiscent of the infamous Judge Jeffreys after Sedgmoor.
The Rev. Robert Welsh, vicar of St Thomas, Exeter, and one of the
rebel leaders, was hanged from the tower of his own church, dressed
in his Mass vestments.

Local tradition credits many mediaeval churches with subterranean
passages, linking them, as a rule, with neighbouring castles. Often
these tunnels are reputed to be the hiding-places of treasure. In her
Traditions, etc., of Devonshire, Mrs Bray who is always sensible when
discussing such matters, records local traditions about Tavistock at
the beginning of the nineteenth century.

There is much talk about this place about a mysterious and
subterranean passage (I should like to find it out) that leads all the
way from the Abbey to the gateway of Fitzford. A great deal of
wealth in coin and plate, including, as I was told, 'a crucifix as
large as life', being there deposited. Mary heard an old woman say
that she was told by her great-grandmother that during the civil
wars a waggonload of plate was carried in there and never
afterwards brought out. An inhabitant of this town, I am likewise
informed, once discovered, while rooting up an apple-tree at
Fitzford, some steps; and, digging still deeper, found an entrance
which led underground. Several persons went down, but none
presumed to follow up the discovery, as it ought to have been
followed. I hear also (but pray observe I do not vouch for the
truth of any of these tales) that a man named Bickley, whilst
employed in raising sand in a place called Jessop's Hay, dug up,

as he imagined, a bag of fine sand, which proved to be a bag of gold dust. He also discovered a pavement supposed to be that of the passage. Everybody, I observe, has a tale about this old passage; but, question them closely, and you are sure to find they heard it from somebody, who heard it from somebody else, and so on - a sort of evidence to be cautiously admitted in a statement of facts.

Local tradition here seemed to have its sights fixed on the period of the Civil War, which, in Mrs Bray's time, was less than two hundred years distant. An older legend of treasure at Tavistock relates to the days when the Abbey still possessed an Abbot. One avaricious incumbent dreamed of a waterfall; behind it was a cave filled with immense treasure. When he awoke and went to look for the place, he eventually found it at what is now Abbot's Weir, on the river Tavy. Like Moses, he struck a wall of rock with his staff, and the cave opened to display its secret. He stayed there all day, partly to gloat and partly to avoid being seen by anyone who would want to share the booty. When darkness fell, he piled as much as he could on his mule and, mounting it himself, set out for home. The mule rebelled at the extra weight and, bucking, tossed the abbot into the weir, where he was drowned, together with his treasure.

During the Civil War the Harris family, of the estate of Radford, Plymstock, lost treasure which was not recovered for nearly two hundred years. It consisted of 23 pieces of silver plate, though as tradition refers to 'gold and silver in blocks', there may be a further instalment waiting to be found. It is all said to have been part of the booty brought back from the Spanish Main by Sir Francis Drake, for Sir Christopher Harris who had been a personal friend of his. When Radford was besieged by Parliamentarian forces during the Civil War, the treasure disappeared. Some thought it had been concealed by the steward to prevent its falling into the hands of the Roundheads; others supposed that the Roundheads actually seized it. At all events, it was lost sight of until December 1827, when it was discovered by farm workers enlarging a potato-cave at Brixton, about two miles from Radford. It found its way eventually to a London auction.

In 1935 an old woman living at Kingskerswell told a member of the Devonshire Association of a treasure she had heard of in 'a big country house in Devon somewhere'. It belonged to an old man who died suddenly, before he had time to tell anyone where it was. Later he began haunting the house, to the terror of the three resident maid-servants (one of whom was the mother of the informant).

The coachman, hearing of their experience, arranged to change bedrooms, so that he would see the apparition. In due course, the old gentleman appeared and beckoned him to follow. They went downstairs,

> into an underground cellar place what he'd never seed afore and never yerd tell of. And though 'twas all pitch dark, more like a dungeon 'twas, the coachman could see where he was to because of the light what went wi' the ole gen'lman. And th' ole gen'leman led the coachman right up to a blue stone there was in the floor of this yer underground cellar, and he said, 'Lift up that stone'. And the coachman didn't know however anybody could lift up that there stone, but he tried and was surprised that he could lift 'n to once. And under that stone was like a tin box, and he was full o' money. And when th' ole gen'leman seen that his money was found, he went and nobody never seed 'n no more.

The coachman managed to get the tin box out of the cellar and had enough to keep him in comfort for the rest of his life.

Treasure still undiscovered belongs to John Cann, a Royalist, who, fleeing from the Roundheads, lived for a time by the Bottor Rocks, near Hennock. Eventually bloodhounds tracked him down, and he was taken out and hanged. Meantime he had secreted his treasure somewhere in the vicinity, and a blue flame is said sometimes to hover over the place where it is hidden.

Near Challacombe, on Exmoor, some 350 years ago an old man went looking for treasure in a moorland tumulus, then called Brokenbarrow.

> Having pierced into the bowels of the hillock, he found therein a little place, as it had been a large oven, fairly, strongly, and closely walled up; which comforted him much, hoping that some good would befall him, that there might be some treasure there hidden to maintain him more liberally, and with less labour in his old years; wherewith encouraged he plies his work earnestly until

he had broken a hole through this wall, in the cavity whereof he espied an earthen pot, which caused him to multiply his strokes, until he might make the orifice thereof large enough to take out the pot, which his earnest desire made him no long a-doing; but as he thrust in his arm and fastened his hand thereon, suddenly he heard, or seemed to hear, the noise of the treading or trampling of horses, coming, as he thought, towards, him; which caused him to forbear, and arise from the place, fearing the comers would take his purchase from him; but looking about every way to see what company this was, he saw neither horse nor man in view. To the pot again he goes, and had the like success a second time; and yet, looking all about, could ken nothing. At the third time he brings it away, and finds therein only a few ashes and bones, as if they had been of children, or the like. But the man, whether by the fear, which yet he denied, or other causes, which I cannot comprehend, in a very short time after lost senses both of sight and hearing, and in less than three months consuming died. He was in all his lifetime accounted an honest man.

This account, from S. H. Burton's book *Exmoor,* is quoted from Thomas Westcote's *A View of Devonshire in MDCXXX.*

7 Local Heroes and Rogues

DEVON'S GREATEST HERO is, of course, Sir Francis Drake. Belief in witchcraft persisted in the county long after his time, so it is not surprising that many of his fellow countrymen shared the conviction, widespread in Spain, France and other continental nations, that Drake was a magician.

The story of him playing bowls on Plymouth Hoe and refusing to let the appearance of the Armada interrupt his game is a favourite in English history books, but the Devonshire version goes on to say that, when he had finished, Drake commanded a large baulk of timber and a hatchet to be brought. He then chopped the timber into short lengths, tossing each log into Plymouth Sound, where it became a fireship; by this means he defeated the Spanish. Incidentally, old records refer to the game as 'kales', a form of skittles, rather than bowls.

A related legend tells how Drake was one day whittling a stick on Devil's Point, overlooking Plymouth Sound, and, as the shavings fell into the sea, they became fully rigged ships.

In Plymouth, a town which idolised him, he was also credited with bringing a water supply from Dartmoor. When the local washerwomen complained of shortage of water Drake searched on the moors till he found a clear spring. Then he galloped back to town, and the stream followed him. In fact, he did cut a canal, which may still be traced, for the purpose.

Another well-known story is his reputed interference with the marriage of his second wife, Elizabeth, who thought she was a widow. Drake had been away for seven years, and Elizabeth, yielding to pressure from her family, who persistently tried to persuade her that he had perished at sea, agreed to marry another suitor. The wedding party was already at church when one of Drake's cannon-balls, fired from the antipodes through the centre of the earth, landed with a loud explosion between the bride and groom. This the bride took as a sign that her husband was still alive and displeased with what she proposed to do, so she called off the wedding. Next day Drake himself arrived and claimed her.

Other accounts say that the cannon-ball fell from the sky on to the bride's train as she went to church. One version describes Drake, disguised as a beggar, calling at Elizabeth's house for alms. But, as he tells his story, he cannot resist smiling and immediately Elizabeth recognises him. The wedding, incidentally, was about to take place at Elizabeth's home at Combe Sydenham, in Somerset, not in Devon.

There was a tradition that in times of great national need the cannon-ball would start to roll. It closely resembles the better-known legend of Drake's drum which was hung in Buckland Abbey, his old home, at his urgent request, as he lay dying off Porto Bello. It is said to beat of its own accord when England is threatened by enemy attack. Many Devon people, in a more credulous age, firmly believed that other English naval heroes, including Nelson, were Sir Francis reincarnated, as he had promised, when England needed him.

There are many records of Drake's popularity in Plymouth, where he became mayor in 1582. As Professor W. G. Hoskins says, 'Crowds followed him in the streets, and ballads were written and sung about him.' When, after a voyage to the Spanish Main, he anchored in Plymouth Sound on a Sunday morning in 1573, the whispered news caused St Andrew's Church to empty as though it were on fire, and the preacher was soon left preaching to himself.

Legends of Sir Francis have even become confused, through the passing of the years, with tales of the Wild Hunt. It is said that he leads his pack of black hounds over Dartmoor at certain seasons and that whoever hears their baying may take it as a sign of his own rapidly approaching death.

Drake's reputed promise to return is reminiscent of Arthur, who, according to legend, is also sleeping until his country needs him again. Arthur's associations are with Somerset and Cornwall rather than with Devon, but Shoulsbarrow Castle on Exmoor (just within the Devon border) is said to have been one of his fortresses. That other early hero, King Alfred, is believed to have defended Shoulsbarrow against the Danes.

From Exmoor, too, comes the story of Joseph of Arimathea. On a voyage to Glastonbury, with the young Christ on board, he ran his ship on the beach at Glenthorne (by County Gate) in stormy weather. Joseph and Jesus went searching for fresh water in the combe, but they were unsuccessful, so Christ caused a spring to rise. It has never since failed.

Another storm at sea is held to have been responsible for the building of the little church of St Michael on the summit of Brentor, four miles north of Tavistock – a landmark visible for many miles in every direction. Robert Giffard, a merchant of Tavistock, is credited with its erection about the year 1140. Storm-tossed in the English Channel, he made a vow to St Michael that, if ever he were permitted to reach Plymouth Sound, he would build a church on Brentor to help other mariners in danger of shipwreck.

A story popular with Devon folk in past centuries concerned Sir Peter Carew, who lived, in the reign of Henry VIII, in a mansion called Mohun's Ottery, on a hill above the Otter valley. He was the youngest son of Sir William Carew, who, finding the boy intelligent, sent him, at the age of twelve, to school in Exeter. Peter, however, had other ideas about education. He wanted adventure and sport and spent much of his time playing truant and being flogged for it. When eventually reports of his unruliness reached his father, Sir William was furious. Hurrying down to Exeter he fastened a dog collar round Peter's neck and had a servant lead him back to Mohun's Ottery.

'If you behave like a mischievous puppy, you shall be treated as one,' he exclaimed.

Despairing at achieving any improvement in his son at Exeter, Sir William packed him off to London, as a pupil at the newly-founded St Paul's School. The results were no different. Peter had had enough of school. As the result of a chance meeting, he was then taken under the wing of a Frenchman, whom he accompanied to the French court. After many difficulties he was at last given the chance to acquire a military training, including managing horses and weapons, at which he soon excelled.

With the French army he went campaigning in Italy. When it disbanded, he transferred to the service of the Prince and Princess of Orange and was soon in high favour. After a time he insisted he must return home to see his parents and was sent off in high style, with a purse of gold, retainers, a gold chain round his neck, and a letter of introduction to Henry VIII. The king also took an immediate liking to him and guaranteed him a position at Court as soon as he returned from visiting his parents.

So, back to Mohun's Ottery rode Peter, tall, broad, and mounted on a splendid horse. He was still only eighteen years old. His parents, 'sitting together in the parlour' failed to recognise him and when, without any explanation, he knelt down and asked their blessing they were astonished, 'much musing what it should mean that a young gentleman so well apparelled, and so well accompanied, should thus prostrate himself before them'

We hear that, when they realised who he was, they were over-joyed, but one feels that Sir William, seeing the gold chain around his son's neck, must have been uneasily reminded of the dog collar.

Another story of the Carews, this time concerning the branch of the family living at Haccombe, near Newton Abbot, involves a dispute over land between them and the Champernownes of Dartington. After much argument, the head of each family agreed to an unusual duel. They would ride together, each on his best horse, to Tor Bay, and the one who rode farthest into the sea would win the estate.

Both had ventured far out when Champernowne's horse collapsed under him, and its owner, in danger of drowning, cried out for help. Carew immediately went to his assistance and brought him safely to land on his own gallantly struggling, but nearly exhausted horse. Appropriately, the sequel to the story deals with the reward to the horse rather than the future of the manor, which, of course, went to

Carew. The animal was turned out to grass, became a family pet and never did another stroke of work for the rest of its long life. Its shoes were taken off and nailed to the door of the little church of St Blaise, on the Haccombe estate, where, I believe, one of them is still to be seen. Needless to say, some writers tend to discount the story and maintain that the horseshoes were nailed there as a defence against witchcraft.

Clearly men of the Devon gentry in Tudor and Elizabethan times were autocratic and impulsive. Sir William Coffin of Alwington is another example. Riding one day through nearby Bideford he paused to enquire about a commotion outside the church. He found he had chanced upon the funeral of a poor peasant. The family and friends had gathered for the ceremony, but the priest refused to perform it until he was paid. Knowing that the widow was unable to produce the cash, he was demanding the dead man's only cow.

Sir William angrily commanded the priest to perform the ceremony at once. But the cleric was stubborn, and refused. Whereupon Sir William told the crowd to throw him into the grave instead and bury him, – which they were delighted to do. Only a last-minute repentance, when he was almost buried, and a promise to do what was required, saved him.

After the incident the priest sent a vigorous complaint about the treatment he had received to the Bishop of Exeter, and the matter was raised in Parliament. Sir William, however, was adamant and made such a good case that an Act was passed, regulating and limiting the amount of burial fees chargeable to poor people.

One of the local heroes of the Civil War was Squire Henry Bidlake, of Bridestowe, not because of great deeds he performed, but because of his ingenuity in eluding the enemy when fleeing for his life. Having fought with the Royalists in a losing battle, he found himself pursued by Parliamentarian soldiers, who surrounded Bidlake House. The Squire, however, dressed himself in ragged clothes and walked calmly out of the back door. Accosted by a soldier in the courtyard, who asked if he had seen Squire Bidlake, he replied,

'Aye, sure. He was a-standin' on is awn doorstep a foo minutes agoo.'

He reached the house of one of his tenants, a Mr Veale, but the troopers searched there, too, so again he had to hide, this time in the case of a grandfather clock that stood in the hall. He had a bad moment when one of the soldiers, looking at the clock and seeing that the hands pointed to the hour, remarked,

'What, doan't he strike, missus?'

'Aye, aye, mister, there be a hand here as can strike, I tell ee,' said Mrs Veale.

Just then Henry Bidlake was seized by a bad cough which often troubled him. He had the presence of mind to adjust himself in the cramped space, so that the weights could fall behind his back and allow the clock to strike. It made such a noise, striking the hour, that the noise of his cough was drowned.

It seems that the troopers were also looking for Mr Veale, since there is a record that they hanged a boy of ten or twelve in the garden, for not revealing where his father was. They cut him down before he was dead, but whether he ever recovered is not known.

During the late seventeenth and eighteenth centuries literate travellers began to visit Devon and note their impressions. Prominent among them are Celia Fiennes, Daniel Defoe, William Marshall and John Wesley. Their journals mainly record their valuable observations of life in Devon, but Wesley, predictably, had some adventures of his own. At North Tawton he was harassed by a mob led by a clergyman and some local gentry, who brought a huntsman and hounds to drown the preacher's words. At Southernhay Green, Exeter, another mob tried to overturn the table from which he was speaking. At Tiverton the mayor announced:

'There is the old church and the new church, that's one religion. Then there is the Pitt Meeting, the Meeting in Peter Street, and the Meeting in New Street – four ways of going to heaven, enough in all conscience – and if people won't go to heaven by one or other of these ways, by God, they shan't go to heaven at all while I am mayor of Tiverton.'

A celebrated Devonshire cleric of the nineteenth century was Parson Jack Russell, who bred the spirited little dogs which still bear his name. He was passionately fond of hunting and no doubt, had he lived earlier, he and Wesley might well have crossed swords. Having been educated at Blundells School, Tiverton, he became perpetual curate of Swimbridge, Barnstaple, a post which he held until 1880. One of the stories told about him describes how a curate, whom he had invited to preach, was very slow over breakfast one Sunday morning. So they mounted their horses and took a short cut

over the fields to avoid a long detour by road. 'Coming to a stiff
gate, Russell, with his hand in his pocket, cleared it like a bird, but
looking round, saw the curate on the other side crawling over the
gate and crying out in piteous tones, 'It won't open'.

'Not it,' was the reply, 'and if you can't jump a gate like that I'm
sure you can't preach a sermon. Good-bye.'

Nevertheless, for all his prowess in the field, Russell was said to
be a good preacher and conscientious priest.

A nineteenth-century character, unfairly described as an eccentric,
was Peter Orlando Hutchinson, of Sidmouth. One wishes there had
been more like him. When, in true Victorian style, a scheme was
proposed to 'restore' the parish church, Hutchinson objected to the
part of the plan that involved destroying some fine fifteenth-century
glass and the medieval chancel. He even presented a petition to the
Queen. When all else failed, he himself purchased the chancel and
the glass, had it all dismantled and re-erected in his garden, two
hundred yards away. And there it still is, in good repair, though it
is private property and not normally open to the public.

The churchyard at Heanton Punchardon contains the grave of
Edward Capern, Devon's 'Postman-Poet'. In his tombstone is set the
bell he used to ring on his daily rounds. He was born at Tiverton
but moved with his family to Barnstaple while still young, where he
was grossly overworked in a lace factory. Later he became postman
on an extensive rural round in the Bideford area, and he used to
write poems during his mid-day halt at Buckland Brewer. Good
friends helped to sell his books of poems to local gentry and others,
and for the latter part of his life he received a pension from the Civil
List. His portrait, in Bideford Library, reveals an erect, forceful,
bold-faced man, and we are not surprised to learn that he had a good
opinion of his own ability as a poet. It is, however, not shared by
modern readers, who find his verse insipid and pedestrian. He had a
well-developed sense of rhythm, which swings his songs along. A
verse from one of the best of them runs:

> O, the postman's life is as happy a life
>   As anyone's, I trow;
> Wandering away where dragon-flies play,
>   And brooks sing soft and low;
> And watching the lark as he soars on high,

> To carol in yonder cloud,
> He sings in his labours, and why not I?
> The postman sings aloud.

Edward Capern died in 1894.

Mrs Bray, writing in 1833, gives an account of another lowly Devon character, 'Old Nanny, the watercress-woman'. Her correct name was Anne Burnaford James, and her grandfather was a distinguished clergyman. When Mrs Bray heard of her, she was about eighty years old and living with her widowed daughter, who tried to maintain her three children by keeping a small shop. But, says Mrs Bray,

> 'the mainstay of the family is Nanny.
> Poor old soul! she is up with the lark, and oftentimes during summer she goes up to Dartmoor to gather hurtleberries, called by the country people, hurts. And sometimes she's away to the woods for nuts or blackberries; or else to the hedges and fields for herbs and elderberries. She frequently rises on a frosty morning, long before day, and walks four or five miles to pull watercresses, when the stream where they grow has been half-frozen. She told me that one morning, after coming out of the water into which she had been obliged to go, to gather the cresses, her clothes were frozen about her. These vegetables and herbs she sells, and supplies persons who make elderberry-wine or blackberry-syrup. The poorer class have a great opinion of old Nanny as a doctress, and she is the most kind and useful person in the world to them; and does cures, and is very clever in dressing a wound. No one better understands the medical qualities of different herbs, which she says are too much despised and neglected by the real doctors. She finds many rare ones on Dartmoor; and always turns her apron before she goes there in search of them, because she was once pixy-led on the moor.'

The extreme isolation and insularity of peasant life in Devon to within living memory is something we may find difficult to appreciate. Baring-Gould mentions a woman of Widecombe, who said she would like to move elsewhere, but there was no getting her husband away 'from atop o' Widdecombe chimney' – meaning the adjacent moors on the level of Widecombe church tower. He records also that: 'In a cottage near Sherrill lived an old woman absolutely alone, who for sixty years never once allowed her fire to go out.'

The Doones of Badgworthy feature as the villains in R. D. Blackmore's classic, *Lorna Doone*. They are not the product of his imagination but were real people, and many traditions and memories connected with them have been collected. (Badgworthy Water is an Exmoor stream which forms the boundary between Devon and Somerset.)

In his *Devon Traditions and Fairy Tales* J. R. W. Coxhead quotes the Rev. J. R. Chanter's article 'Lorna Doone', which appeared in *The Western Antiquary*, Vol. III, in 1884. This, he thinks, is the earliest known version of the Doone story:

> The ruins of a sort of rude village, long forsake and deserted, may be traced in an adjoining valley, which, before the destruction of the timber, must have been a spot exactly suited to the wants of its wild inhabitants. Tradition states that it consisted of eleven cottages and was, about the time of the Commonwealth, the dwelling-place of the Doones, a daring and successful gang of robbers who were the terror of the country around and who, for a long time, escaped undetected among the wild, bleak hills of Exmoor, where few thought it safe, or even practicable to follow them. They were not natives of this part of the country but, having been disturbed by the Revolutions, suddenly entered Devon and erected the village alluded to. . . . The idea was prevalent that, before leaving their previous home, they had been men of distinction and not common peasants.

After giving several instances of the Doone's activities the writer describes the incident which led to the end of the Doones.

> They broke into and robbed a house at Exford, in the evening, just before dark – there was only a woman servant in the house and a child – the woman concealed herself in the oven, but the Doones murdered the child, and the woman from her concealment heard them make to the infant the barbarous remark, which has ever since been kept alive as a couplet in the district:
>
> > If anyone asks who killed thee,
> > Tell 'em 'twas the Doones of Badgery.

It was for this murder that the whole countryside rose in arms against them and, going to their village in great haste, succeeded in capturing or destroying the whole gang.

In a later version of the story, the Doones not only kill the child but cook and eat it, washing it down with some of its father's ale.

The Doones were not the only wild moorland family supposed to practise cannibalism. Similar allegations were made against the Greggs who, at some unspecified date in the past, lived in a cave near Clovelly and terrorised their neighbours, until they were rooted out and executed.

The Gubbinses, a gang at Lydford in the sixteenth century were, according to S. H. Burton, eliminated by inbreeding and intemperance. Baring-Gould quotes the following passage from a seventeenth-century writer, Fuller:

I have read of an England beyond Wales, but the Gubbings land is a Scythia within England, and they be pure heathens therein. It lyeth near Brentor, in the egde of Dartmore. . . . They live in cotts (rather holes than houses) like swine, having all in common, multiplied, without marriage, into many hundreds. Their language is the drosse of the dregs of the vulgar Devonian; and the more learned a man is the worse he can understand them. Their wealth consists in other men's goods, and they live by stealing sheep on the More, and vain it is for any to search their Houses, being a work beneath the pains of a Sherriff and beyond the powers of any constable. Such their fleetness, they will outrun many horses; vivaciousness, they outlive most men; living in the ignorance of luxury, the Extinguisher of Life, they hold together like burrs; offend one, and all will revenge his quarrel.

Baring-Gould, writing in 1900, adds:

It cannot be said that the race is altogether extinct. The magistrates have had much trouble with certain persons living in hovels on the outskirts of the moor, who subsist in the same manner. They carry off lambs and young horses before they are marked, and when it is difficult, not to say impossible, for the owners to identify them. Their own ewes always have doubles.

Sarah Hewett, writing in the same year, describes another savage family who lived fifty years earlier in Nymet Rowland, in central Devon, and are strangely similar. Their name was Cheriton, and Mrs Hewett emphasises that they had no connection with either the Gubbineses or the Doones. She says in her *Nummits & Crummits* that the family was orginally one of respectable small farmers, who owned their own land and hence could not be evicted. 'Then a son married badly, and the children of this union grew up idle and dissolute; consequently the farm was neglected and in a short time it fell into a low state of cultivation. Each successive generation sank lower in the social scale till a condition insensible to shame was reached.'

Like the Gubbinses, they had all things in common, including wives and children. They chased away visitors with sticks, stones, pitchforks and filthy language. The farmstead became completely derelict.

The thatch was stripped from the rafters, and the rooms below received all the rain which fell, . . . The windows had long been denuded of glass and in winter were stuffed with bundles of hay or straw to protect the inmates from the severity of the weather; the air had free passage from basement to roof. A person standing in what was at one time the kitchen could see the clouds passing and the birds flying above the roof. The doors were nowhere. The living room was almost destitute of furniture, and in place of seats a hole had been dug in the lime-ash floor in front of the fireplace, which was on the hearth. Into this hole the legs of the members of the family rested as they sat on the bare floor around the fire.

In this hovel resided as many Cheritons – men, women and children – as could find resting-places; the surplus members of the family found shelter and repose in holes cut into hayricks and woodstacks.

The patriarch of the tribe, Christopher Cheriton, slept at night, and reclined during the greater part of the day, in solitary state, within the friendly shelter of a cider cask well bedded with hay and dried ferns.

In spite of the primitive conditions, the Cheritons fed well 'on game and every portable kind of dairy produce . . . brought thither by the sons, who were noted poachers and purloiners of other men's belongings.'

Their eventual fate was obscure, though Mrs Hewett mentions that by her day they had left the district, some of the younger members having emigrated.

Bampfylde Carew of Bickleigh, near Tiverton, was a rogue of a different type. His father was the scholarly vicar of Bickleigh who sent his son, born in 1693, to Blundell's School at Tiverton. The boy was intelligent almost to the point of precocity, with a lively, inquiring mind that tended to question convention.

One day he and his school-mates went hunting with the school pack of hounds. Carried away by excitement, they careered through standing corn-fields and eventually killed a deer in a private park. Carew and two companions, who had been ringleaders in the escapade, quickly made off. By chance they met a party of beggars, with whom they threw in their lot till the storm should have blown over.

Beggars and vagrants were common in those days. Henry VIII's suppression of monasteries left hordes of poor and infirm persons, who had depended on the religious houses for charity, without means of livelihood. Large numbers of them wandered about the countryside in bands and were joined by many able-bodied rogues and vagabonds and unfrocked priests. To the reign of Elizabeth I, when the problem began to be alarming, belongs the jingle,

> Hark, hark, the dogs do bark,
> The beggars are coming to town;
> Some in rags, and some in jags,
> And some in a velvet gown.

By Carew's time the beggars had long been well organised and even had their own elected 'King', chosen for life at a conclave somewhere in the vicinity of London.

Carew enjoyed the careless, improvident, open-air life of the beggars and stayed with them for some time. Then, hearing that his parents were grieving, he dutifully returned home. But, having tasted freedom, he could not settle down to civilized life and soon returned to join the beggars – an early example of a 'drop-out'.

A beggar had to have a speciality, in order to coax alms from the people, so Carew became a Tom o' Bedlam, shamming madness. With his background and intelligence, he soon stood out above all his companions. He seems to have been an accomplished actor and was forever thinking up new tricks. In a fit of aberration he married the daughter of a distinguished Newcastle surgeon but soon left her and resumed his vagrant life. While he was in London for a gathering of the beggars, the King, an old man named Clause Patch, died, and Carew was elected King.

After a lively career, he was arrested, tried at Exeter and sentenced to seven years' transportation to Maryland. An iron collar was fastened around his neck, but he managed to escape and persuaded a tribe of Indians, who befriended him, to file it off. Eventually he managed to return to England and apparently rejoined his gipsy and beggar friends at Crediton. His end is uncertain, but one version of his story says that he was so moved by an eloquent sermon that he repented his misdeeds and settled down to an obscure, uneventful life with his wife and family. He seems to have died at Bickleigh in 1758.

In 1833 Mrs Bray of Tavistock was quite familiar with professional beggars and some of their tricks. She and her husband encountered an Irish vagrant who asked for her baby, alleged to be in danger of dying from fits, to be baptised immediately. Mr Bray obliged and also gave the woman a shilling, but Mrs Bray was more suspicious and did not respond to a request for clothes for the baby. She said the infant looked remarkably healthy, 'a fine, bouncing child, as rosy as a rose, that could not have been very far from two years old at least, with stout limbs and firm flesh; and the little fellow looked the very picture of health, smiling and well pleased to undergo the rite of baptism, a ceremony to which, no doubt, he was pretty well accustomed'. She adds that a few days later the Brays met a neighbouring clergyman who had also had the privilege of baptising the same baby.

She mentions a neighbour, a retired naval officer, who was naturally charitably disposed towards old sailors. He gave a shilling and a glass of grog to any old sailor coming to his door, and, says Mrs Bray, 'it was marvellous to see what a number of veteran blue jackets paid him a visit in the course of a year'. Eventually a servant, suspecting that his master was being exploited, arranged for the next visiting sailor to be followed. Sure enough, he went to the den of a certain old woman in the town, took off his bluejacket and handed it in for use by the next beggar, who could hire it for a few pence.

Two Devon rogues were villains, who employed criminal methods to dispose of unwanted heirs. One of the stories bears a resemblance to the well-known fairy-tale of the children who were delivered to a woodcutter to kill, but were saved by his compassion. A little boy, heir to the estates of the Bampfyldes of Poltimore (near Exeter), whose parents died, became the ward of a powerful, grasping and unscrupulous baron. This man ordered one of his servants to take the boy into a forest and there deliver him to a forester, to be brought up as a foundling.

The boy was reared by the forester's wife and grew up to become a handsome, intelligent youth. Meantime, the baron evaded enquiries about the missing heir with stories of his Continental education and travels. An old retainer of the Bampfyldes became suspicious and eventually undertook the long journey to the distant estate where the baron lived. There, by diligent enquiries, he managed to find the forester and see the boy, in whom he immediately recognised the Bampfylde family likeness. When he revealed to the boy his true identity, the youngster soon escaped and returned to Devon, where he took over the family estates.

The second story is even more scandalous, for the deceit was practised by Squire Northmore, of Sheepstor, on his own son. The father was determined that his second son should inherit the estate in preference to the oldest boy, who had a slight mental handicap. So he arranged for the press-gang to kidnap his lawful heir and carry him off to sea.

After enduring for a long time the hardships of sailors in the Navy in those days, the boy was told by one of his ship-mates the true facts of his abduction. Naturally he was enraged and vowed vengeance. Next time the ship put in at Plymouth for refitting, he collected a party of shipmates and marched to his father's home at Sheepstor. The Squire hid in the roof, but the sailors ransacked the house and burnt all the papers they could find, including the deeds of the estate.

There is no happy ending to the story. It is said that the boy went back to sea and was not heard of in Devon again. The father tried to drown his shame and remorse in drink and became a notorious alcoholic, while the estate went downhill fast.

Another Devon squire overtaken by his own evil deeds was Sir John Fitz, of Fitzford, Tavistock, who was the only son, born late in life, of John Fitz. His father casting his son's horoscope just before his birth, asked the midwife if the birth could not be delayed for an hour, as he foresaw calamity if it took place at that moment. Young John, left an orphan at the age of fourteen, was married to the daughter of another Devon landowner, Sir William Courtenay, while still in his teens. Once he became of age and acquired control of his estate he surrounded himself with dissolute companions. In a drunken quarrel he murdered a neighbouring landowner, Nicholas Slanning, and fled to France.

After a time his wife obtained a pardon for him; he returned and led a quiet life for a few years. Then the old wild streak became dominant again. When his wife objected to his habits and companions he turned her out, together with their young daughter to the indignation of his powerful father-in-law. The case of Nicholas Slanning was now reopened, and a claim was made for compensation to be paid to the heirs. Sir John Fitz was summoned to London to appear in the courts. Setting out in fear and apprehension, he became mentally deranged before he reached the city. At Reading he attacked the innkeeper and his wife, declaring that they were in league with his enemies. Having killed the innkeeper, he turned his sword on himself, and so perished.

Yet another wicked squire was Shilston Upcott, who lived on Upcott estate at Broadwoodwidger in Tudor times. An effigy supposed to be of him is to be seen in Broadwoodwidger church. Lawless and undisciplined, he preyed on his neighbours and tenants, stealing their cattle and helping himself to anything else he fancied.

One evening he shot a valuable cow belonging to a neighbour. The villagers heard an explosion and, on searching, found Shilston Upcott lying in a pool of blood, cut almost in half by chain-shot. As his servants carried him indoors he died, so they laid the body on a bed upstairs and sent messengers to fetch his relations. When they arrived, not many hours later, to everyone's astonishment the bedroom was empty. After a prolonged search the body was found in a well in the courtyard.

Naturally ghost stories developed around these gruesome events. There were tales of screams and shouts, explosions and the trampling of horses' hooves. Several intriguing questions remain unanswered, however. The chain-shot must have been fired from a light cannon. Assuming this had been done by the aggrieved neighbour, how did he get the cannon to Upcott and contrive to get Shilston in the sights? Who took the body from the bedroom and dumped it in the well? How did they get it into the courtyard without being seen? And why did they do it?

During the eighteenth century the coast of North Devon, like the coasts of Cornwall, became notorious for its smugglers and wreckers. Many of the stories about their blood-thirsty deeds seem to have gathered around a man named Coppinger, known in Devon as 'Cruel' Coppinger. They were set down by the Rev. R. S. Hawker, vicar of Morwenstow at the end of the eighteenth century, but whether they all really belong to Coppinger is doubtful.

Coppinger was the Danish captain of a ship that foundered in a storm off Hartland Point in December 1792. He was the only survivor of the wreck. When he struggled to land, and saw a crowd of local people assembled, he thought that he was about to be knocked on the head, as was the pleasant custom of those times, so, dashing through the throng, he jumped on a horse and galloped away, stark naked. The horse naturally went back to its stable, where the farmer took pity on the shipwrecked mariner. Coppinger settled down there, helping on the farm and later marrying the farmer's daughter.

When his father-in-law died, Coppinger inherited the farm and quickly changed his ways. He set himself up as leader of all the wreckers, smugglers and other bad characters in the district, to the horror of his wife and mother-in-law. He even robbed the older woman of her life savings, tying his wife to the bedpost and threatening to flog her unless the money was handed over. Many tales are told of Coppinger's ingenuity in arranging for ships to be wrecked and his ruthlessness in dealing with any survivors. Also of his skill in outwitting excisemen and preventive officers.

At last, realising that all good things must come to an end, he collected his booty and prepared to depart. Local people saw him one evening hailing a large ship that lay offshore, by the Gull Rock. A boat came to fetch him, and the ship sailed away. No-one in Devonshire saw or heard of him again, and local tradition suggests that the ship went down that very night, in a terrible storm. A study of the local registers corroborates some of the details of the story, but not others.

Just as smuggling stories have clustered around the personality of Coppinger, so highwaymen tales have attached themselves to Tom Faggus. Tom was an Exmoor highwayman, born at North Molton, who appears as a minor character in *Lorna Doone*. Research suggests that he actually existed and lived in the seventeenth century. The stories associated with him are in the Dick Turpin class. He outwitted the law by a mixture of ingenuity and audacity; he robbed the rich to help the poor; he had a faithful mare named Winnie, who carried him on many a marathon ride, and who came to his assistance whenever he was in a tight corner.

Tradition says he was an honest blacksmith, who was ruined by a lawsuit with Sir Robert Bampfylde and lost all his possessions. This is why he became a highwayman. Once during his career he held up his old enemy, Sir Robert, but handed back his loot, remarking that it was against the accepted code for one robber to steal from another.

On another occasion he accosted a party of troopers sent out to arrest him, claiming that he too was on the same errand. As he was dressed and spoke like a gentleman, and had an impressive document which appeared to be his commission, they allowed him to take charge. He ordered them to attend to the priming of their guns, instructing them to discharge and re-load. As soon as the guns were empty, he whipped out his own pistols, held up the entire troop, took their money and galloped off.

At Swimbridge he was once surrounded in a cottage, so he put his hat on a fire-fork and pushed it up the chimney.

'He be trying to get out of the chimbley,' shouted the crowd. Somebody shot at the hat, which fell.

'Got en!' someone cried. 'He be daid.'

They all ran to get in at the front door, while Faggus slipped out through the back.

The same fire-fork, it is said, is the one exhibited in St Anne's chapel museum, Barnstaple.

There is even the legend, common to other highwaymen, that Faggus once had his horse shod backward, to deceive his pursuers. This is said to have happened at Alcombe smithy.

Nicholas Mason, who lived in the late eighteenth century in a cave by the Tamar, obtained a living by robbing farmhouses in the neighbourhood. He used to enter by climbing down the chimneys, which so puzzled his victims that they thought the burglaries were the work of the devil. Eventually his lair was discovered by a pack of hounds, Mason was overpowered, taken to court and hanged.

Not all these local rogues were men. One of the notorious women of history was Elfrida, daughter of Ordgar, Earl of Devon in Saxon times. King Edgar, having lost his first wife and hoping to remarry, heard rumours of Elfrida's beauty and sent a trusted courtier, Ethelwold, down to Devon to report. On seeing the beautiful girl, Ethelwold himself fell in love with her. So he informed Edgar that she had been much over-rated – she was just an ordinary country girl who had been brought up with Devon rustics and was lacking in grace and refinement. On the other hand, he said, she was an heiress, for her only brother was childless, and he himself would rather like to marry her for her money.

The king consented. Back to Devonshire rode Ethelwold, to settle matters with the Earl and to marry Elfrida with all reasonable speed. In due course, she presented him with a son; Edgar consented to be god-father. And that, thought Ethelwold, makes me safe, for, whatever happens, the king cannot now get rid of me and marry Elfrida without breaking the laws of the church.

Presently rumours began to reach Edgar, who determined to go down to Devon to see for himself. Ethelwold heard of this with alarm, but could do nothing to prevent the visit. So he agitatedly confessed to his wife, who apparently heard for the first time of his deceit and what she had missed by it. He begged her to disguise her beauty when the king came. Of course, this was asking the impossible of a beautiful woman, let along one smarting with resentment at having been cheated out of a crown. When Edgar arrived she was magnificently dressed and looking her most ravishing. Edgar fell in love with her as promptly as Ethelwold had and, contrary to Ethelwold's pious hope, was not deterred by the possible censure of the church. Out hunting with Ethelwold, he killed him with a javelin thrust. Then, as soon as was decently possible, he married Elfrida.

Subsequent events reveal her as a thoroughly bad character. After the death of Edgar, she had her step-son Edward murdered in order to clear the way for her own son, Ethelred, to ascend the throne. And Ethelred was the ill-advised monarch in whose reign the Danes spread havoc over England.

A lady with whom one feels considerable sympathy, though her trial and conviction would seem to be fair, was Eulalia Page, executed for murdering her husband in 1591. She was born Eulalia Glanville, a member of a respectable and wealthy family resident at

Barnstaple. Her relatives disapproved of her lover, George Stanwich, variously described as a naval lieutenant, and an assistant in her father's shop. Instead, they married her to an old Plymouth miser, whose purpose in marrying was to beget an heir and disinherit his relatives.

Eulalia's consent to the wedding had been obtained by deceit on the part of her family, who intercepted letters from George and convinced her that he had grown tired of her. When Eulalia discovered the truth she was very angry, especially as her new husband was an avaricious old man, who had economised since the wedding by dismissing the maidservants and making her do all the household work. She and George met, and it is assumed that they decided to get rid of the old man. When he was found strangled in his bed one morning his wife was tried for murder, found guilty and executed, together with her lover. Popular tradition says that her own father was the judge who pronounced the sentence.

There is some doubt about the details of the case. The judge, if indeed he presided on that occasion, would have been her brother, not her father. If she was hanged, it was contrary to the law, which at that time laid down the penalty for the murder of a husband by a wife as burning. However, the story became popular in Devon. Ballads were written about it, and it is said that it became the subject of a play by Ben Jonson.

Mary Baker, alias Princess Caraboo, was a relatively innocuous rogue. She was born at Witheridge in 1792, the daughter of a shoemaker, and, as she grew up, gained a reputation as a wild young tomboy, playing cricket and bowls with the boys and indulging in swimming and fishing. She followed the usual pattern of going into service at the age of sixteen. Mary was visiting her parents five years later when she fell out with her father, who beat her for wearing too fancy a dress. This led to a break with her family and she travelled to London, where she married (or so she said) a man named Bickerstein, who not long afterwards deserted her.

A year or so later she appeared in Bristol. One evening in April 1817, she arrived at a cottage in nearby Almondsbury and made signs that she wanted to sleep there. She appeared to know no English, nor any other language that was tried. A magistrate, Mr Samuel Warrall, was sent for; intrigued by the situation and impressed by her behaviour, he invited her to his home. There she remained for some months, a source of interest to the intelligentsia of Bristol. She let it be known, by signs and sketches, that she came from a country in the East called Javasu, her father being Chinese and her mother Batavian. She herself was a princess, named Caraboo. She volunteered a mass of information about her country, none of which could be proved incorrect, and even gave many words of the alleged language, as well as the letters of its alphabet.

Eventually someone enquired into her past and traced her back to the shoemaker's family at Witheridge. After an attempt to brazen it out, she confessed to the imposture. Even so, there was considerable admiration in Bristol and Bath for her skill, and verses were written in her honour. Here is one:

> Plague on that meddling tell-tale Neale,
> Eager thy history to reveal,
> And mar the pleasing fable;
> Too sudden came the *denouement*
> Which proved thou art from down-along,
> Where dumplings grace each table. . . .
> But heed him not – for on my soul
>   Whether at Bristol, Bath or Knole,
> I admired thy Caraboo.
> Such self-possession at command,
> The by-play great, the illusion grand;
> In truth, 'twas everything but *true*.

Her Bristol friends packed her off to Philadelphia, where she lived for many years, afterwards returning to Bristol where she died in 1864.

We now cross the threshold between the rascally and the eccentric, though some doubt exists as to the nature of our next character, Joanna Southcott. Was she a conscious impostor or simply a victim of delusions and mental derangement? Probably the latter, though she seems to have had lucid moments, and there is no denying that she did very well, financially, from her prophecies.

Joanna Southcott, born in 1750, was the daughter of a peasant farmer of Gittisham. She went in service at Exeter, following the usual pattern of her class, and was still there, unmarried, in 1790, when she attended a revivalist meeting held by an itinerant Methodist preacher. Baring-Gould, describing the evangelist's methods, writes: 'He shrieked and threatened till sometimes the whole congregation fell flat and rigid on the floor, when he would walk in and out among them and revive them by assuring them they had received pardon for all their sins, were elect vessels, and that their election was sealed in heaven.'

To the emotional and semi-literate Joanna, probably approaching the menopause, this was heady stuff. Before long she was being visited by spirits and seeing visions. It was revealed to her that she was the Woman of the Book of Revelation, Chapter 12. By 1792 she had already collected a group of followers, and the Exeter Methodists, whom she had now joined, held a meeting to enquire into her spiritual state. In their presence she signed a statement declaring that her calling was from God, to which she appended a note that the 58 persons present, including Methodist preachers, assented to the truth of the statement.

To one minister she gave some sealed packets, containing, she said, her prophecies, for safe-keeping until the time came for them to be opened. When, however, she went about claiming this minister, who was called Pomeroy, as her disciple, he became alarmed and, in a misguided moment, burnt the prophecies. From that moment he became the arch-enemy of Joanna and her adherents, who continually denounced him, while at the same time maintaining that the prophecies he had destroyed were all being fulfilled.

After that, Joanna prospered. She sold books of prophecies and warnings; she sold copies of her letters of denunciation of Pomeroy and other backsliders and opponents; she also sold sealed passports to heaven. The passports cost twelve shillings or a guinea, according to circumstances. Her books were mainly ungrammatical, wandering nonsense. In one of them she described her struggles with the Devil, who naturally came off worse.

Eventually she announced herself pregnant, with a child, to be named Shiloh, who would be the second Messiah. Her followers were agog with excitement and showered her with expensive presents. She now had, it is said, well over a hundred thousand adherents, in all parts of the kingdom, two of her most loyal strongholds being Leeds and Bristol, where she went to live in 1798.

In 1792 she had prophesied that, previous to the birth of the

Messiah, she would be as dead for four days but would then be revived and delivered. So when, in 1814, she did actually die, the expectation that she would be resurrected after four days ran high. It was disappointed. She was not only dead but not even pregnant, a fact which some doctors had suspected for months. Her death was caused by dropsy.

Nevertheless, her influence remained. For years afterwards her disciples looked for her return on earth. Many of the men had vowed never to shave or cut their beards till she reappeared, and presumably went to their graves unshorn. As late as 1860 small groups in Devonshire were still confidently awaiting her resurrection.

Even now belief in her lingers on. She bequeathed to the world the famous Joanna Southcott's Box, which is supposed to contain a panacea to all the ills of the world. At present it is kept at Bedford and must not be opened till 24 bishops have assembled to watch the procedure, which so far they have declined to do. The Box has, however, been X-rayed, and has been shown to contain a pistol, and other unidentified articles.

Mrs Bray tells of a farmer who, shortly before her time (she wrote in 1833), tried to translate Scripture in terms of his own life, though not exactly on the lines of Joanna Southcott. He lived about a mile from Tavistock and was held to be a scrupulously honest and respected citizen.

He was also an excellent master to his labourers; and such a lover was he of all the country customs that, whilst he lived, he might be considered as the representative of old manners and past times. Every festival throughout the year was duly observed by him and his household and his men working on the farm had their full share of all the sports. No house displayed such an abundance of shrove cakes; May-day had its honours, and, as Christmas was crowned with evergreens, the yule-logs were noble and roast beef and plum-puddings feasted the poor; whilst all the games and frolics of that season were celebrated with the honours their antiquity required.

This magnificent old man had, however, one notable eccentricity; 'He considered himself a profound theologian, controverted the doctrines of the Established Church and, in his advanced years, chose to give an example of patriarchal living that scandalized all the neighbourhood.'

What he did was, after study of the *Book of Genesis*, to follow the pattern of Abraham. In his later years the patriarch took his wife's handmaid as a kind of concubine, to raise more children for him, and this old farmer decided to do the same. He was not lacking in respect for his wife, to whom he had been married for forty years, he assured his neighbours who came to remonstrate with him. She would always have first place of honour. No, he was simply living according to the old Biblical law. There was nothing sinful in it.

It was, however, more than his wife could stomach. She took herself off to another part of the parish, to live with a married daughter. The old man regretted this, but continued to do his duty by sending round to her, about every other day, a basket of 'the best things his table or farm could afford'. Carrying the basket to her mistress was a part of the duty of the complaisant hand-maid.

The old farmer then foretold that he would father five children by his hand-maid. And so he did. Their names were Abraham, Isaac, Jacob, Sarah and Mary. The last one should have been called Rebecca, but the hand-maid, showing a little initiative at last, insisted that it should be Mary, after herself. The farmer agreed that it was a good name, and said he hoped the child would be worthy of it.

We could wish to know more of the story, especially what happened to the hand-maid and the five children when the old man died. But there it ends abruptly.

He certainly got away with his eccentricity, which came close to bigamy, unlike the unfortunate Duchess of Kingston, who was tried and condemned for the offence in 1776. This seems to have been a miscarriage of justice. When aged eighteen she had spent a holiday with an aunt in Hampshire, where she met a young naval lieutenant with whom she had a brief love affair. The pair persuaded a local clergyman to marry them at eleven o'clock one night in a ruined church. Two days later the lieutenant, who was a grandson of the Earl of Bristol, had to rejoin his ship, and they never afterwards lived as man and wife.

That was in 1744. Later, the lieutenant, presumably with her agreement, instituted a plea for the annulment of the marriage. It was heard by the Consistory Court of the Bishop of London, which had no difficulty in granting the plea, especially as no register had been signed. In 1769 the lady married the Duke of Kingston and lived happily with him for seven years. No-one raised the least objection.

But when the Duke died in 1776 and left his enormous fortune to his wife, his disappointed nephews brought a charge of bigamy against the Duchess. The finding of the Consistory Court, they claimed, was invalid. The Duchess naturally contested the charge indignantly and must have been surprised and appalled when her peers found her guilty. She fled to the Continent, thus escaping the death penalty, and lived there until her death in 1788.

The Duchess was a member of the Devon family of Chudleigh. Another county character, who was unlucky according to which traditions you accept, was a Mr Varwell, of Brixham. It is said that when William III landed there in 1688 the tide was out, and Varwell volunteered to carry him ashore. This little man was so elated with the honour that he then mounted a pony and rode bare-headed in front of the Prince's escort all the way to Newton Abbot. William, impressed and probably amused by such enthusiasm, gave Varwell a short document which would admit him to the royal presence in London, to receive a reward.

In due course, Varwell set off for London, assuring his fellow citizens that he would certainly come back a lord. He boasted so much, however, both at home and in London that he became an easy prey for the unscrupulous. At his London inn a party of rogues made him thoroughly drunk, kept him in that condition for a week or two, stole his precious document and used it. One of them went to the palace and, armed with the passport and circumstantial details of the story gleaned from the boasting Varwell, collected His Majesty's gratitude in the form of £100. After his recovery, the chastened Varwell also went to the palace and tried to explain what had happened, only to be rejected as an impostor. Varwell's friends and relations, however, maintained that the second part of the tale was a fabrication. He had presented his paper to the king and been duly rewarded.

Thomas Westcote, the seventeenth-century writer on Devonshire, records the story of the improvident Lord of Dyrwood, whose estate was on the outskirts of Exeter. Like so many other Devon aristocrats, he played havoc with his inheritance and was finally reduced to selling it. His great weakness was gluttony: he bargained his last property for a year's food, on condition that it consisted of what he considered a choice and exotic dish, the skins of roasted geese, known locally as goose-vells. When the year was up he contested the agreement, on the grounds that some of the skins had belonged to ganders, not geese, and got away with it. The ruse did him little good, for, within a few years, the remainder of the estate had gone and he was in great need.

'Oh Dyrwood, Dyrwood!', he is reported to have mourned, as he begged a drink at the well of his old home, 'had I known thy water to be so sweet I would never have sold thee.'

One of the loveliest girls ever bred in this county was Dolly Trebble, an orphan, who lived with her brother at Princetown at the turn of the eighteenth and nineteenth centuries. Trebble was her married name; her maiden name is unknown. As Dolly blossomed into womanhood she naturally attracted the attention of the men of the neighbourhood, including Sir Thomas Tyrwhitt, a local estate-owner. Recognising the danger-signs, her brother kept a close watch over Dolly until, to get him out of the way, Sir Thomas secured him a post in London. He was appointed candle-snuffer in the House of Lords, with the ends of the wax tapers as a perquisite – apparently quite a valuable source of income.

Meanwhile another suitor appeared on the scene. He was none other than the amorous Prince Regent, who, during a visit to Dartmoor, caught sight of Dolly and immediately began to lay siege. Tom Trebble now enters the story. He was a handsome young moorman who took it upon himself to look after Dolly when her brother left home, and he had no opinion of Sir Thomas or the Prince Regent. He did the right thing. He came on horseback, set Dolly on the pillion and trotted over to Lydford, where he married her in the church. Then the pair set up house; for years afterwards their cottage was known as Dolly's Cot. It stood in a pathless wilderness by the river Dart. Their married life there was happy, though, after Tom's death, Dolly's last years were spent in some poverty, and she was obliged to work in a tin-mine. It is said that she kept her good looks well into old age.

Presumably the Prince Regent had better luck with another Devonshire girl (or maybe Devon was not her home county), for a little later in the same century the vicar of Widecombe was said to be his natural son, sent there to keep him out of the way. He lived for many years with his widowed sister, also said to have George IV as her father. At any rate, brother and sister lived, according to local gossip, better than his stipend would warrant, and the sister's only daughter was sent to be educated at one of the most exclusive schools in London.

This girl, Caroline, was a handsome, wayward lass who grew into a thoroughly autocratic, self-centred and undisciplined woman. She married a Mr Darke, who visited her uncle one day on business, and led him a dog's life. Soon after her marriage her uncle died, leaving his estate to her, and she bought the local manor. Thereafter she insisted on being called Lady Darke, and as such she is remembered.

Baring-Gould records some memories of this eccentric and forceful lady:

'She kept nine or ten horses in her stables – some had never been broken in; some she rode on, others were driven in pairs. . . . If a visitor of distinction was expected, she sent for him her carriage and pair with silver-mounted harness. For ordinary use she employed her brass-mounted harness; but Bill, her husband, was despatched to market in the little trap in which she fetched coals. . . . She was an implacable hater; and, living in the wilds, half-educated, she was superstitious and believed in witchcraft, and in her own power to ill-wish such individuals as offended her. She was caught on one occasion with a doll into which she was sticking pins and needles, in the hope of thereby producing aches and cramps in a neighbour.'

Yet she was also kind-hearted and generous, and she loved entertaining:

At one time she played on the piano after the meal to get her guests to dance, but the cats tore the instrument open and made their nests and kittened among the strings, and the damp air rusted the wires. Then she bought a barrel-organ and forced her husband to turn the handle in the corner and grind out music for the dancers. However, on one occasion, having tasted too often a bottle within reach though out of sight, he fell forward in the middle of a dance and brought the instrument down with him. . . . He died at last in one of the fits to which he was liable,

having retired to rest by mistake *under* in place of *on* the bed.
Lady Darke had him buried in a pig-cloth.

In her later years her eccentricity became more pronounced. She
ruled the household with an iron rod and yet did nothing:

The house was infested with cats and dogs, and her servants did
not dare to get rid of any of them or to drive them out of the
rooms. The large room over the kitchen she alone entered. The
door was padlocked, and the key of the padlock she kept attached
to her garter. . . . It [the room] was found, after her death, to
contain a confused mass of sundry articles to the depth of three
feet above the floor, the accumulation of many years. Bureaus were
there with guineas and banknotes in the drawers, and quantities
of old silver plate, bearing the arms and crests of men of title who
had been about the Court of the Prince Regent; and the whole
was veiled in cobwebs that hung from the ceiling. . . .'

Among the accumulation were large collections of letters, all of
which were destroyed, so that no clue remained as to the real identity
of Lady Darke.

With mention of two other ladies we conclude this chapter. One
was Lady Mount Edgcumbe, of Mount Edgcumbe, near Plymouth,
who, in the eighteenth century, was buried in a trance. After the
funeral a sexton crept down to the vault to rob the corpse of its rings
and, being unable to pull one of them off, cut off the finger.
Whereupon Lady Mount Edgcumbe sat up, climbed out of her coffin
and walked home, her finger-stump dripping blood.

Finally, Devon has a claim to be the home of Old Mother
Hubbard. She is identified by some with the housekeeper at Kitley
House, Brixton, around the year 1805. As at least some of the
rhymes about her are, however, much older than that, it may be that
she simply passed on verses that she had learned when young.

8   Legends and Memories

THE FRONTIER between legends and memories is a diffuse zone
rather than a fine demarcation line. We remember incidents that
made an impression on us in our early life. We remember stories our
grandfather told us. Some of those stories were told to him by his
grandfather. But our memories are notoriously faulty; and the longer
the chain, the greater the chance of error. By the time a memory has
become a legend, the details tend to be suspect. The fact that the
legend exists is proof that something happened, but exactly what and
when and where is uncertain.

There is a story, which frequently occurs in books on Devonshire,
concerning septuplets. As far as I can ascertain, it was first committed
to writing by Thomas Westcote in 1630. As he tells it, a poor
labouring man of Chulmleigh, already blessed by many children,
decided to absent himself for seven years, to avoid any further
additions to his family. Within a year of his return is wife presented
him with seven sons at a birth, giving rise to the obvious comment
that he might just as well have stayed at home.

Appalled by this overwhelming responsibility, the poor man put all the babies in a basket and took them down to the river. On his way he met the Countess of Devon who, hearing whimpers from the basket, asked him what was inside.

'Only puppies, not worth the rearing,' said he.

'Let me see,' demanded the Countess, 'I want a dog.'

The father, trembling, made every excuse he could think of, but, of course, the more reluctant he was to open the basket the greater was the Countess's determination to see its contents. At last he gave in and, falling on his knees, confessed what he was about to do. The Countess's reaction was prompt and commendable. 'She hasteth home with them, provides nurses and all things else necessary. They all live, are bred in learning, and being come to man's estate gives each a prebend in this parish.' He adds that seven crosses were set up near Tiverton to commemorate the event, though all had disappeared by his time.

Baring-Gould gives a different location to the story. He puts it at Hensleigh, near Tiverton, some fifteen miles from Chulmleigh. The poor man is a tailor. The babies are reared by the mother, the Countess paying the expenses. They are educated at Buckfast Abbey and, having been ordained to the priesthood, are found seats in Tiverton, four becoming rectors and three their curates. He adds a comment that sheds some light on the general state of affairs in Tiverton: 'As they were all of one birth, they loved each other, and never disagreed; and that was – so it is averred – the only instance within a historic period that the rectors of the four portions of Tiverton have agreed and have got on smoothly with each other and with their curates!' He concludes by saying that all seven died on one day and were buried on the spot where the Countess saved their lives.

It is such a good story that it seems a pity that doubt has to be cast on at least some of the details, for the reason that an almost exactly similar one is told of a mediaeval knight, Sir Thomas Bonham, of the village of Wishford in Wiltshire. There is the same absence of seven years, in order to avoid increasing a family, the same multiple birth, and in this instance there seems to be supporting evidence in a Bonham monument in the parish church, and a tradition that, until almost within living memory, the sieve in which the babies were carried to church for baptism was preserved there.

Who can say where the truth lies? In fact the story is an international legend type, known not only in England, but in such countries as India, Germany and Denmark, as well as in the medieval legends of the saints.

Another legend involving small children – in this case only one baby – is told of a young wife who lived in a cottage by Blackingstone Rock, overlooking the river Teign on the eastern edge of Dartmoor. Hearing the merry sounds of Moretonhampstead Fair one fine July day, she left the child asleep in its cradle and ran down to the fair for an hour or two. While she was gone, three ravens swooped down, plucked the baby out of the cradle and carried it off to the top of Blackingstone Rock. Next day its remains were found there in the raven's nest.

Ravens will attack sickly lambs and might well peck at a helpless baby, but to carry a child to the top of Blackingstone Rock would seem to be a most unlikely feat. And how could it be known that three ravens were involved unless someone saw them? How could three ravens cooperate to carry anything through the air? One can imagine, however, that this moral tale would be popular with puritanical preachers, eager to dissuade young people from going to fairs. Another legend with moral overtones is the story of the sheep which hanged a man, once popular in Devon. The man was a sheepstealer, who, having purloined the sheep, hoisted it on his back to carry it home. It was fastened with a rope, which the thief had twisted around his own neck. On the way, growing tired, he sat on a stone to rest, and the sheep slipped off, strangling him by its weight. The occurrence was, naturally, regarded as an act of God.

Another often-repeated legend is that of Childe, the hunter, who is said to have been a rich Saxon landowner of Plymstock. Lost on the moors when out hunting one winter day, he was at last driven to the extremity of killing his horse, disembowelling it, and creeping inside its carcase to keep warm. Even this did not save him, and next day he and the horse were found, frozen stiff. Before he died he managed to make a will (for he had no direct heir) using his blood to sign his name to the following couplet:

> He that finds and brings me to my tomb
> My Land at Plymstock shall be his doom.

The monks of Tavistock were first on the scene, and they were bearing the corpse to their Abbey for burial, when they encountered the men of Plymstock determined to thwart them. The Tavistock party got the better of the meeting, however, by throwing a temporary bridge over the river Tavy and so crossing over to the safety of their own land.

This seems to be the accepted version of the story, though Mrs H. P. Whitcombe, writing in 1874, gives a different couplet, a different period (she says Childe lived in the reign of Edward III) and adds that the will was written with the blood of the horse. Childe is, in fact, a Saxon title, not even a proper name. It seems that the legend may have originated in a squabble between Tavistock and Plymstock over certain lands. Childe's desperate attempt to keep warm may be true – but similar stories are told of other characters in other places – for instance, the Saxon bishop Elsinus who was caught in a blizzard when crossing the Alps. It would seem fairly certain that the will was made beforehand and that the contents were known in both Tavistock and Plymstock.

Disputes over an inheritance are frequent in every age and county; we have already noted some in these pages. One of the most notorious cases in Devon was that of North Wyke, which began in about 1658 and dragged on into the next century. In 1658 the estate was in the hands of young John Weekes, who was seriously ill with tuberculosis. His mother and umarried sister, Katherine, lived with him, but the next male heir was his uncle, also named John.

Whether he was a relation or not is unknown, but about this time a rascal named Richard Weekes appeared on the scene. He seems to have hatched a plot with John's mother and sister, who were doubtless worried about what would happen to them in the likely event of John's death, to induce him to make a will favourable to them. They so worked upon the invalid that he eventually did so, making the unusual provision that the will could be revoked by word of mouth. The will settled the estate on Richard, though the mother and sister understood that it was to be shared out between the three of them.

Just before John died, however, the mother and sister learned that Richard had outwitted him, so they persuaded John to revoke the will verbally. This was on a Saturday in 1661, and on the same day

John Weekes died. Next morning Richard arrived with a gang of retainers and ransacked the house, turning the mother and sister out of doors, with blows and abuse, and completely neglecting John's body, lying upstairs. To make matters doubly sure, Richard then approached the uncle John and persuaded him, when drunk, to make over to him, for the sum of £50, any rights he might have in the estate.

Richard was now firmly in possession and remained so until his death in 1670. The case, however, offering as it did ideal material for endless litigation, occupied the lawyers for all parties concerned, for a further thirty years, until the estate was drained dry. When all the money was gone, the lawsuit was abandoned, with nothing settled, in 1701.

An unsavoury story at a lower social level refers to a cholera outbreak at Sheepstor in 1832, when the village shopkeeper and his wife died. This isolated outbreak, in a village which had few dealings with the outside world, was so surprising that an enquiry was instituted, which brought to light the following events.

Not long before, a man, his wife and two children, living in Plymouth, had died within a few hours of one another. The man, apparently very poor, was a congenital cadger and was constantly begging from his relations and friends. It was therefore with small expectations that his two brothers, on hearing of the deaths, went round to see whether he had left anything worth having. They were astonished to find a hoard of £50 or £60 and a bank book showing a balance of a further £70. Whereupon they first quarreled and then started to fight over the corpses. The affray became so noisy that the neighbours called the police, on which the brothers, grabbing what they could, fled.

One, the greedier and more violent of the two, took some of the clothes the dead man had worn. Fearing arrest, he went up to Sheepstor and begged lodging with the shopkeeper and his wife, who were in some way related to the fugitive. From the infected clothes this innocent couple caught the disease and died, whereas the villain of the story escaped scot-free.

The legend of Berry Pomeroy Castle is another example of a disputed inheritance – in this instance a treasure. A young man of Totnes, the nearest town to Berry Pomeroy, had a dream in which he saw himself wandering around the ruins of the castle (which, in fact, he did frequently) and stopping in front of a splendid old fireplace. He stepped inside it and, looking up the chimney, spotted an irregularity in the masonry. Chipping away the mortar, he uncovered a secret hiding-place, which contained an iron pot filled with gold. In the morning he told his dream to his wife, and they laughed about it.

But on two successive nights he dreamt the same dream so, awaking just after midnight, he determined to test the truth of it. Dressing without disturbing his wife, he set out, in pouring rain and a gale, to visit Berry Pomeroy Castle.

On the bridge over the river at Totnes, struggling against the storm, he met a doctor returning from a late call. Surprised to see anyone out so late and in such weather, the doctor reined in his horse and asked if anything was wrong. The young man, John Nokes, recognising the doctor, felt foolish and tried to think of an excuse, but the doctor soon extracted from him the real reason, laughed, and told him to go back to bed.

'Dreams', he said, 'are just imagination; but, anyhow, you can go and look if you want to just as easily in the morning.'

So John went home to bed.

In the morning he made his postponed visit to Berry Pomeroy, found the fireplace and the chimney, but saw that the hiding-place had been recently tampered with and that the pot of gold was missing. He went home resentful and disappointed and thereafter always insisted that the doctor had tricked him that night and taken the treasure. Perhaps it was a coincidence that the doctor, who had hitherto been short of money, soon afterwards showed signs of being wealthy.

Naturally, the Civil War was a time when many fortunes changed hands. One farmer, whose name is not recorded, certainly did well out of the troubles of the time. A Dr Thomas Clifford, ancestor of the noble family of Clifford, fleeing from the Roundheads and closely pursued, tossed a bag of gold coins over the hedge of a field in the parish of Trusham, in the Teign valley. It fell into a lime kiln and was found next morning by the farmer who rented the field. He had sufficient common sense not to tell anyone and later spent the money in careful instalments, using it to build up a prosperous business.

Dr Clifford was, on this occasion, flying from a surprise attack on a house in Bovey Tracey, where he had been playing cards with other

Royalists. It is said that the cavaliers owed their escape to the greed of the Roundhead soldiers. As they fled, one of the officers gathered up handfuls of gold coins and threw them out of the window at the feet of the soldiers, who could not resist stopping to pick them up. This allowed the Royalists time to get away.

King Charles ii himself, when he was still Prince Charles, featured in a Devon escape story during his flight from the Battle of Worcester. He had managed to reach Lyme Regis, but found a force of Roundheads already assembled and was obliged to retreat inland again, the enemy close behind him. In his flight he came to the mansion of Coaxden, in Chardstock parish, then occupied by a loyal Royalist family named Cogan. When he arrived, urgently needing to be concealed, he found Mrs Cogan sitting in the parlour, sewing. There was no time to lose, for the Roundheads were near the front door, so she made him creep underneath her voluminous hooped skirt, a style then fashionable. Her husband, seeing the soldiers arrive, came in and saved her the necessity of rising from her chair. He showed the Roundheads over the house and introduced them to Mrs Cogan, who played the part of a haughty lady indignant at the intrusion and remained seated in her chair, sewing. When the Roundheads left, disappointed, Charles remained for a meal before travelling to safer refuge at Trent, in north Dorset.

A much older story of a subterfuge of war belongs to Saxon days and depends on the identification of Membury Castle, at Brinnacombe near Axminster, as the site of the Battle of Brunanburgh, which many authorities place in Northumberland. The two antagonists were the Saxon King Athelstan and the Dane Anlaf. On the night before the battle Anlaf, entered the English camp disguised as a minstrel to obtain information about the disposition of Athelstan's forces. He collected a pouchful of money, which was his undoing, for, thinking it indignified to accept, he hid it in a hole in the ground, and was seen by an English sentry.

Athelstan was informed and moved his quarters and the disposition of his forces. When Anlaf attacked next morning he committed his best troops to a fierce onslaught on what he supposed were the king's quarters. This Varangian guard massacred an unfortunate contingent under the Bishop of Sherborne, which had arrived during the night and camped on the spot just vacated by the royal bodyguard. They were then attacked on the flank by Athelstan, with his fresh troops, and eventually defeated with great slaughter.

Leaving aside the controversial question of whether Brunanburgh could have been in east Devon, the story bears a close resemblance to the legend of King Alfred entering the Danish camp disguised as a minstrel, which also belongs to the West Country, though just over the county border, in Somerset. Oddly enough, the story of the surprise attack at Bovey Tracey, adds that, on the previous evening, Cromwell himself spied out the situation, disguised as a Puritan preacher.

Several traditions about historical events have survived over the centuries from distant times. The earliest concerns the Roman invasion of Britain, when the subjugation of the West Country was undertaken by the Second Legion under Vespasian in AD 49. The legend is that Vespasian besieged the oppidum, which then represented Exeter, for eight days but was caught in the rear by a British army, which had come to relieve the fort. The result was a draw, with such severe losses on either side that both leaders were well content to make peace.

Something similar happened during the Norman Conquest. Towards the end of 1067, William the Conqueror himself marched into the West Country, to quell an incipient rebellion centred around the person of Gytha, mother of the dead king Harold, who had taken refuge in Exeter. When he reached a point four miles from the newly re-fortified city, leading members of the council rode out and sued for peace, offering allegiance and hostages. Evidently there was a conflict of opinion within the city, for when the delegation returned, the terms it had negotiated were quickly repudiated, and Exeter prepared to withstand a siege. William was naturally indignant at this change of front and, a ruthless man, he had the eyes of one of the hostages put out in full view of the citizens lining the city walls. He then laid violent siege to the city for eighteen days. At the end of that period, both sides began to realise that time was running out. The citizens of Exeter knew that they could not hold out much longer, especially as, in the midwinter season, supplies of food were becoming exhausted. William, for his part, was uneasily aware that, while he was engaged in this far corner of his new kingdom, troubles of a more serious nature might be hatching elsewhere. So again delegates of the opposing forces met, and agreement was reached. The people of Exeter were to open the gates, admit a garrison and acknowledge the king. William was to refrain from plundering and sacking the city and from punishing it in any way. And while negotiations were being concluded, Gytha and her followers, who represented the hard core of resistance, slipped out to board a ship and sail to safety around Land's End.

There is an old belief that Exeter is not really in Devon. Cecil Torr, writing in 1921, says,

I have not been out of Devon since 1914, or rather, I have not been out of Devon 'ceptin' Axeter town, as people used to say. Henry VIII took Exeter out of Devon and made it a county by itself. In old conveyances of land in Devon ... the covenant of Further Assurance often has the words 'so as for the doing thereof the persons comprehended within this covenant be not compelled or compellable to travel out of the county of Devon unless it be to the citie of Exon'.

Professor W. G. Hoskins estimates that, at the time of Domesday book, the total population of Devon was no more than between 60,000 and 80,000, with Exeter, the largest town, having perhaps 1,500 inhabitants. There were three other 'towns' of some 300 to 400 people, namely, Barnstaple, Totnes and Lydford, and Okehampton 'a new town, was just struggling into existence'. He further informs us that in the twelfth, thirteenth and early fourteenth centuries there was a movement on the part of rural landowners to establish 'boroughs' – 'places where tenements were held in free burgage, by payment of a money rent', with weekly markets and, in many instances, an annual fair. The idea was to increase the manorial income by rents, market tolls and other levies. Over seventy such boroughs were created by optimistic landowners, far more than in any other English county, but more than half of them never developed, owing to unsuitable siting and lack of interest. He mentions Ashburton, Tavistock, Plymouth, Torrington and South Molton as examples of successful colonisation of this sort and Rackenford and Noss Mayo as instances of failures.

Rivalry used to exist between Exeter and the village, or small town as it then was, of Bradninch, a few miles away. Bradninch claimed to have been founded earlier and therefore to have priority over Exeter. This claim was substantiated by the alleged fact that when they met, the mayor of Exeter was obliged to hold the mayor of Bradninch's stirrup when he mounted and dismounted. Thomas Westcote, writing in 1630, states 'there be gentlemen yet, I thank God, living that have seen the recorder of Exeter hold the recorder of Bradninch's stirrup'. Though he adds, 'you will think, purchance, it was in merriment, and to say the truth, so do I also'.

Apparently many jokes were formulated at the expense of Bradninch. Exeter chroniclers describe how their mayor sent a dinner invitation to the mayor of Bradninch. The messenger found the Bradninch mayor working on a ladder, for he was a thatcher. When given the document he held it upside down, for he could not read. When the messenger pointed this out, he lost his temper and indignantly demanded a 'more discreet and civil messenger', before he would give an answer.

West of Lydford, Devon has a tongue of territory extending for several miles west of the Tamar and including the village of North Petherwin. The traditional reason for this, advanced by resentful Cornishmen and having no basis in fact, is that the commissioners who fixed the boundary were made drunk by interested Devonians, and wandered far out of their way when they resumed their survey after lunch.

In East Devon a well-known legend describes how a prolonged quarrel was settled between the parishes of Honiton, Farway, Gittisham, and (in some versions) Sidbury, over boundary marks. Isabella, a thirteenth-century Countess of Devon, went with the officials of these villages to the territory in dispute and threw her ring in the air. Where it fell was henceforth to be the point where the parish boundaries met. Ever since, the field has been known as 'Ring-in-the-Mere'. It seems an extravagant method of deciding a squabble, especially if one assumes that the ring was probably lost.

Traditions and legends have survived concerning the beginnings of some of the Devon towns. Barnstaple, for instance, owes its origins, it is said, to St Brannock, tutor to the children of an Irish king, Brychan, who was involved in invasions of the north Devon and Cornish coasts in the early fifth century. One of the earliest antiquaries who has left us an account of Devonshire, Leland, visited the county in the reign of Henry VIII, and says that 'it was full of fables about Branock's cow, his staff, his well and his serving-man, Abell'. Mrs Whitcombe, writing in 1874, had heard a story of his wonderful cow which was killed, chopped in pieces and set to boil in a cauldron; miraculously the saint caused it to emerge whole and sound.

Another Irish saint of this period, St Nectan, was considered by some to be the grandson of King Brychan. He was martyred at Clovelly by having his head cut off. Straight away he picked it up, set it in place, and walked away whole. This is said to have happened on the site of the church of St Nectan, Hartland.

Tavistock grew up around its abbey. The site was selected in Saxon times after Ordulf, Earl of Devon, had seen it in a vision. When saying his prayers one night, Ordulf looked up and saw a pillar of fire, 'brighter than the sun at noonday'. During the night he was told by an angel, in a dream, to build an oratory to the four evangelists in the place where the fire had been burning. On investigation, he found the site already marked out by four stakes. Baring-Gould, who tells the story, offers a logical explanation. At certain seasons, he points out, 'a good many pillars of fire may be seen around Tavistock, when either the furze is being burnt or the farmers are consuming the "stroil" – the weeds from their fields'. It is, in fact, the good old Devon custom of 'swaling'. As for the four stakes, Baring-Gould says these were ordinary field-boundary stakes, known locally as 'termons'.

Later, during the fourteenth century, there was a legend that Bideford Bridge was built on woolpacks. After many lives had been lost on the turbulent ferry crossing, the lord of the manor, Sir Theobald Grenville, determined to build a bridge if at all possible, but for a long time his plans were thwarted through failure to find a firm foundation beneath the tidal mud. Then the parish priest, Richard Gurney, dreamt on two consecutive nights of a spot where a rock (which according to some versions had rolled down the hill into the river) offered a chance of success. Even so, the rock was buried too deep beneath the ooze and water, so woolpacks were piled upon it to raise the level sufficiently for work to begin. The story is not impossible, but it could also bear the interpretation that the bridge was built with money raised from the trade in woolpacks. Earlier in this chapter Lydford is listed as one of the only five existing towns at the time of the Domesday Book. Doubtless because of its early importance, virtually the whole of Dartmoor was included in the parish of Lydford, which was thus the largest parish in all England. Corpses had to be carried from all over the Moor to Lydford church for burial.

Several places in the county have traditions of the plague, both the medieval Black Death and the epidemic of 1666. There were also several outbreaks in 1571, 1591, and 1604-5. Professor W. G. Hoskins suggests that the Black Death may have affected Devon more severely than the rest of England, to judge from the mortality figures. Certainly the deanery of Kenn was 'the worst-hit deanery in the whole of England. It lost 86 parsons from its 17 churches in two years'.

Templeton, near Witheridge, has no village centre but consists of well-spaced farms; even so it was not immune from the Black Death. An old man, John Palfriman, of Witheridge, testified to the Bishop of Exeter in 1440 that

> during the great pestilence the servants of the rector of Witheridge were compelled to go to Templeton with a cart to collect the bodies of the dead for burial. There was no-one else to bring them in. The old man goes on to say that one corpse fell off it on the way, and the next day a man was sent to look for it and brought it into Witheridge, for which he was paid one penny.

The story was told to John Palfriman by his father, who had been in the service of the rector of Witheridge at that time.

Mrs Bray records a tradition, current in 1833, that certain prehistoric stone circles on Dartmoor, at Merrivale Bridge, above Tavistock, were used as a plague market during one epidemic, which she thinks occurred in the seventeenth century. When the plague was raging in Tavistock (which lost 522 of its citizens in 1625), people from the surrounding villages used to leave their goods in these circles; the Tavistock people then collected them and left payment. In this way the villagers hoped to avoid contamination. For many years afterwards these stone circles were known as 'The Potato Market'. According to one tradition, the money was left in bowls of water.

Tavistock was one of the four stannary courts of Devon, the other three being Chagford, Ashburton and Plympton. Under the Stannary institutions the tin-miners of Devon and Cornwall were exempt from villeinage and most other feudal laws and were regulated by their own courts – a concession based on their great importance to the Crown, as producers of a semi-precious metal used in coinage. The existence of these independent courts was a frequent source of friction with the civil authorities for centuries. One understandable cause for exasperation was that a tin-miner could 'pitch bounds', or start digging a tin mine, on a man's land without notifying him of his intention. Special enactments had to be passed to prevent the miners starting work in or around 'churches, mills, houses and gardens', and there was no prohibition against mining the highways. From very early times tin-mining had been carried on by small independent miners, but from the sixteenth century onwards it tended to fall into the hands of corporations and companies.

The twin scourge of the towns of Devon, as of London, until very recent times, was fire. Once a fire started the wooden, thatched houses, packed closely together, gave it every chance to spread, and many towns and villages were burnt out time and again. Tiverton has recollections of two particularly disastrous fires, one in 1731 destroying about 300 houses and an earlier one, in 1598, consuming the whole town – 600 houses in all. In the 1598 conflagration some fifty persons are said to have perished. The fire swept through the entire town in less than two hours. Another, though less disastrous, fire occurred there in 1612. By 1731 some of the more important merchants' houses were built of stone, 'and covered with Slatt', and these escaped destruction. The fire on this occasion was able to take a firm hold on its prey because

the Fire-Engines being usually kept in the Church, at a considerable Distance of the Place where the Fire began, it was some time before they could be brought thither and put in order to do any service, and through the Hurry and Confusion which the People were in upon this Occasion, one of the largest of them was brought without the Arms necessary for working it. . . .

By the time the arms had been fetched, the fire was so well established that the fire-engine had to be quickly abandoned and was burnt with the rest of the town. Some 2,000 people were made homeless.

Calamitous fires swept Honiton in 1672, 1699, 1747 and 1765. On the last occasion, the heat was so intense that the church bells melted. At South Molton 70 houses were destroyed in a great fire in 1641, and another conflagration occurred during a violent storm in the night of 26 November 1703 – a storm remembered long afterwards all over the West Country. Crediton lost 460 houses in a fire in 1743, and Ottery St Mary 111 in 1866.

It was in the hurricane of 1703 that the first Eddystone Lighthouse was swept away, with its occupants. The second lighthouse, finished in 1709, stood for nearly 50 years, but was then destroyed by fire. Of the three keepers on that occasion, one went mad from his experience and another swore that, as he stood looking up at the blaze, some of the molten lead had run down his throat. Although it seemed impossible that he was not killed instantly if this had happened, when he died 12 days later nearly half-a-pound of lead was found in his stomach.

The phenomenal tempest that struck Widecombe on Sunday, 21 October 1638, has already been mentioned (see page 20). Mrs Bray supplies a graphic description of the terror of the villagers, most of whom were in church for evensong, conducted by Rev. George Lyde. The sky became so dark that the congregation could hardly see each other, and the parson, breaking off his discourse, got his choristers to sing the psalm that refers to 'Him who maketh the clouds His chariot, who walketh upon the wings of the wind, who hath His way in the whirlwind and in the storm'.

> At length the whole face of the heavens became covered by dense and black clouds, and all was dark as midnight. In a moment this was fearfully dispersed, and the church appeared to be suddenly illumined by flames of forked fire. . . . A ball of fire also burst through one of the windows and passed down the nave of the church, spreading consternation in its passage. Many of the congregation thought it was the final judgment of the world; some fell on their faces, and lay extended like dead men upon the ground; others beat their breasts, or cried aloud with terror; many wept and prayed.

She lists the casualties. The parson's wife was scorched

> but her child, seated by her in the same pew, received no injury. A woman who attempted to rush out was so miserably burnt that

she expired that night. Many other persons, likewise, in a few days after, died from the same cause. One unhappy man had his skull so horribly fractured that the brains were found cast upon the pavement in an entire state.... Several seats were turned upside down, yet those who were on them received no injury.

Beams came crashing down. Stones were shaken from the tower. A pinnacle collapsed and, falling, killed a woman. A man saw his dog picked up by the whirlwind, thrown out of the door and killed. And through it all the minister remained in his pulpit and, as the storm passed, concluded the service with prayer. The total casualty figures were four killed and sixty-two badly burnt or injured by falling masonry. No wonder that the memory of the visitation lived on for centuries.

A whirlwind of remarkable intensity visited Tavistock on the morning of 22 August 1768. Having laid flat an orchard at Bere Ferris, it progressed up the valley till oposite Tavistock and then veered towards the Moor. Through Rowdon Wood, which lay directly in its path, it carved a swathe about forty yards wide. 'It tore up vast oaks and flourishing ashes by the roots, lopped the largest limbs of some, twisted and shivered the bodies of others, carried their tops to a considerable distance, and, in short, made such a devastation as a battery of cannon could scarce have effected'. Eye-witnesses who lived in a house overlooking the wood and valley said that they were fetched out-of-doors by a noise like 'half-a-dozen coaches rolling over the pavement'. They ran out and 'saw a large cloud, like a woolpack, come tumbling up the vale (with a most frightful noise) and shaking all the hedges and trees over which it passed, as if it would have shivered them to atoms'.

Severe blizzards swept Devon in 1861, 1881 and 1891, and, in the present century, in 1947 and 1962/63. In the 1947 storm 120 Devon villagers were completely cut off by drifts for three days and some for much longer. Trains were stuck in snow-drifts, ponds and canals were frozen sufficiently to allow skating, and Postbridge, Ponsworthy and Blackaton ran out of bread and had to be supplied by a mail-van which eventually managed to get through by a circuitous route.

As a maritime county, Devon naturally has many stories of smugglers and wreckers, of whom an example has already been noted in 'Cruel Coppinger' (see page 87). The old dishonest trade flourished almost into modern times, for Baring-Gould, writing in 1899, refers to an old woman, 'only lately deceased', who had engaged in it as a young woman. She used to walk along the beach at Cawsand, carrying her baby, and was often teased by the customs officers.

'That's a quiet baby you have there', joked one of them on one occasion.

'Quiet her may be,' retorted Mrs Grylls, 'but I reckon her's got a good deal of spirit in her.'

Which was true enough, the 'baby' being a jar of brandy. Smugglers used to bury them in the sand and dig them up when the way was clear.

Bob Elliott, a celebrated smuggler of Brixham, was so successful that on one occasion he had every cave and other hiding-place he used so stocked with liquor that there was no room for another barrel. It was then that a further load of brandy kegs arrived. There was no alternative but to hide them for a day or so in Bob's cottage, where he happened to be lying incapacitated with gout. He accepted the kegs with great reluctance, as he knew that the customs officers had been watching him for some time.

Sure enough, the excise-men came round and demanded to search the house. The family met them, weeping, with the news that Bob had died during the night, so the excise-men decently left them to their grief. During the day a very large coffin was delivered to the cottage, for Bob had been a massive man. That night three customs officers met a party of men carrying the coffin along the road to Totnes. Behind it walked the ghost of the dead man!

The customs men fled.

Their superior was less gullible. After hearing this report, he went round to Bob's cottage the same evening and, standing outside the window, he could hear Bob himself describing what had happened. The smugglers received the shock of their lives when he walked in, but, in fact, the officer was powerless to act against them for he had not caught them in the act, and it was only his word against theirs.

It is not only coastal areas which have smuggling associations. Smugglers and preventive officers operated inland as well. Halsbeare Farm, near Blackborough, in east Devon, has a smuggling story reminiscent of the Wiltshire Moonrakers. As in Wiltshire, the smugglers, surprised by the excise-men, hastily dumped their brandy kegs in the nearest pond. But, on this occasion, it was the excise-men who raked the pond and retrieved the brandy.

Although they had not caught the smugglers, they strongly suspected John Frost, the farmer of Halsbeare, of being involved. A summons was issued against him and required him to go to London for his trial. Frost rightly objected that he would be ruined, for whether he won or lost the case, the farm could not continue satisfactorily during his absence. So his young daughter took his place. Mounted on a farm horse, she is said to have ridden to London and back on two occasions, and to have cleared her father's name. She is regarded as a local heroine.

Smuggler's Leap, a cliff on the coast between Lynmouth and Martinhoe, takes its name from a desperate encounter between a smuggler and an excise-man. Trying to avoid the officer, who was overtaking him, the smuggler urged his horse to swerve and plunged over the precipice. In a wild effort to save himself, he clutched at his pursuer, and they fell together on the rocks below.

Shaldon, by the Teign estuary, has a 'Wreckers' Window' – a circular window high in the lime-washed wall of a house. A light shining there masqueraded as a lighthouse. More than one ship out at sea was wrecked on the Ness Rocks. The window was also used for signalling to smugglers.

Not far away, about three miles from Teignmouth, is Sithwell Chapel, the haunt of an evil priest in the sixteenth century. A highwayman, rather than a smuggler or wrecker, he murdered travellers, whom he waylaid on the neighbouring heath, hiding his spoils under the altar in the chapel. The bodies he threw down the well.

An appropriate punishment for this villain would have been the Iron Cage, which used to stand at Iron Cage Gate on Black Down, above Mary Tavy. Convicted robbers were locked in the cage, exposed to all weathers, and left to die.

Most smuggling and wrecking stories belong to the seventeenth, eighteenth and early nineteenth centuries, and especially to the period of the Napoleonic Wars, but the coasts of Devon were subject to alarms and attacks at almost every period of history.

During the reign of Henry IV a raiding party of barons and knights, who should have known better, attacked and burnt Plymouth and then made their way to Dartmouth, intending to give it the same treatment. They met with such robust opposition, however, from the woman as well as the men, that they were thoroughly routed, many were slain, and a number were taken captive. It being the practice in those days for high-ranking prisoners of war to be held to ransom, the citizens of Dartmouth saw no reason why they should not make a profit, even though they did not belong to nobility. So, 'a boisterous troop of plain western men', they hauled their prisoners before King Henry and suggested he take some action. The king, 'who took great pleasure to talk with these lusty Devonshiremen, himself caused their purses to be stuffed with golden coin'. The Dartmouth men went home in continuing high spirits, leaving their captives with the king, who proposed to collect a ransom for them for himself.

Less fortunate were the inhabitants of Lundy Island in the reign of William III. A ship, claiming to be off course, dropped anchor off the island and sent a boat ashore to pick up some milk for the captain, who was sick. They said the ship was a Dutchman. When they had obtained provisions for several days, the sailors reported that their captain had died and asked if they could bring the corpse ashore for burial in consecrated ground. The islanders agreed, and the coffin was brought ashore and laid in the chapel. Within a few minutes, the sailor, accompanied by the captain, rushed out and rounded up the islanders. The coffin had held arms, not a corpse, and the sailors were French; England was then at war with France. While the islanders were held prisoner, the enemy ransacked the island and then sailed away, leaving the people of Lundy destitute.

Frenchmen came to north Devon more peaceably a little earlier in the seventeenth century, when England and France were not at war, but France was energetically ridding herself of her Protestants. Numbers of Huguenots came as refugees to Barnstaple, where they were cordially received and many of them settled. Samuel Pepys married one, a girl of 15. Baring-Gould notes the metamorphoses of some Huguenot names into forms that Devon men could under-stand. L'Oiseau is translated into Bird; Roches becomes Roach; Blanchepied becomes Blampy; Fontaine is Fountain. The neatest of all, in my opinion, is Boursaquotte, which became the purely Devon 'Buzzacott'.

Another influx of Frenchmen occured during the Napoleonic Wars, this time as prisoners of war. At first they were housed in prisons at Plymouth and on old ships anchored in the Hamoaze, but these soon became so overcrowded that a new prison (the one that is still in use!) was built for them at Princetown, on Dartmoor. Later they were joined by numbers of Americans, when America entered the war on the French side. Pronounced class and race distinction evidently existed among the prisoners, the French and Americans despising one other, the white Americans cold-shouldering the blacks, the wealthy French living in comparative luxury and going on parole down to the towns, while their poorer fellow citizens fought each other for the meagre supplies of food and were clad only in blankets. The mortality rate among the 12,000 or so prisoners housed at Princetown between 1809 and 1814 was rather more than ten per cent.

9   Devonshire Life and Tradition

BOTH DARTMOOR AND EXMOOR were ancient 'forests' or areas
devoted to the chase. As in other English counties, the local residents
retained a mass of rights and customs, which in general they clung
to tenaciously . . . though not tenaciously enough. The rights of
chase on Dartmoor came into the hands of the Princes of Wales in
the time of Edward III. They applied, however, only to 'venison and
vert', 'vert' being the right to cut living trees. All other rights were
retained by the inhabitants of the village adjoining the moor, which
are known as 'Venville parishes.'

Although much of the moor has now been enclosed and large
tracts of it are used for quarrying, there are still extensive areas over
which cattle, sheep and ponies roam freely. Baring-Gould records
that in his time farmers from other parishes, who were not entitled
to free grazing, often used to turn their livestock on to the moor and
take a chance:

In order to detect these and exact a fine from them certain

drivings are ordered, locally called 'drifts'. The day when a drift is to take place is kept a profound secret till it is proclaimed early in the morning. Then a messenger on a fleet horse is sent round very early to announce it. On certain tors are holed stones, and through these horns were formerly passed and blown on such occasions. There are drifts for ponies, and drifts for bullocks. A drift is an animated and striking scene. Horsemen and dogs are out, the farmers identifying their cattle, the drivers and dogs sending the frightened beasts plunging, galloping in one direction towards the place of gathering. When all the beasts have been gathered together, an officer of the Duchy mounts a stone and reads a formal document which is supposed to authorise the moormen to make their claim for fees. Then the Venville tenants carry off their cattle without objection. All the others are pounded, or else their owners pay fines before being allowed to reclaim them.

Baring-Gould says that from time to time the moormen tried to extend their territory by organising 'drifts' over moorland outside the traditional limits. Usually they were resisted, often by force, and battles occurred in which clubs and whips were used.

During the centuries following the acquisition of the forest rights on Dartmoor by the Black Prince, a tradition arose whereby the adjacent farms steadily encroached on the moor. Whenever a tenant died, his heir had the right to enclose ten more acres of land. In periods when controls were relaxed, many farmers and estate-owners took larger slices of the moor, without waiting for a death. These new fields were known as 'new-takes'.

In addition to large-scale filching of land, Dartmoor was the scene of much 'squatting'. It was popularly believed that, if a man could erect a cottage between sunrise and sunset and have a fire burning on the hearth, he had a legal right to live there. One such hut, thought to be the last squatter's home on Dartmoor, is Jolly Lane Cot at Hexworthy. It is said that Tom Satterly, an ostler at Two Bridges Inn, built the place (with the help of friends, of course), for his 18-year-old bride, Sally. They chose Old Midsummer Day for the enterprise, because all the local farmers, some of whom might have interfered, were away at Holne Ram Fair. Sally was still living there, as a widow, in 1900, according to some versions of the story; other accounts say that the old woman was the daughter of the house-builder.

This cottage is of stone, with walls in places five feet thick, but, in parts of Devon where stone is not readily available, Devon cob is widely used. Cob is puddled clay, mixed with straw and trodden into a kind of putty, for building walls; a frame of boards was sometimes erected, but the consistency of properly worked cob is such that it will hold together without the frame, if the wall is wide enough. Devon cob, like the chalk cob of counties farther east, is durable and warm. It will last for generations, provided it 'has a hat on'. Once the roof is removed, allowing water to percolate and then freeze, the cob soon disintegrates. This is why cob garden walls are always provided with a capping of their own, generally of thatch. Writing in 1669, Count Magalotti noted that the town of Axminster was 'a collection of two hundred houses, many of which are made of mud and thatched with straw'. The same comment would probably have applied to most Devon towns of that day.

When Cecil Torr cut through the cob wall of an old house at Wreyland in 1919 he found embedded in it, in such a position that it could only have got there when the cob was wet, a silver coin that could be dated between 1216 and 1249.

Mrs Bray of Tavistock, writing in 1833, gives a description of a typical Devon cottage of her time. Some of the sort, fortunately, still survive:

> the walls, generally of stone, are grey and, if not whitewashed (which they too often are) abound with lichen, stonecrop and moss. Many of these dwellings are ancient, principally of the Tudor age, with the square-headed mullioned and labelled windows. The roof is always of thatch, and no cottage but has its ivy, its jessamine or its rose mantling its sides and creeping on its top. A bird-cage at the door is often the delight of the children; and the little garden, besides its complement of hollyhocks, etc., has a bed or two of flowers before the house of the most brilliant colours. A bee-hive, and the elder, that most useful of all domestic trees, are seen near the entrance. . . .'

Walter Raymond lived in one such cottage on Exmoor for a time, from 1905, and although it was just over the border in Somerset it must have been typical of an Exmoor cottage of that date. He says it had oak beams, a half-door, chimney seats and a bread-oven. He paid a shilling a week rent.

Elizabeth Bidder, of Sheepstor, has left some memories of life in a Dartmoor parish in the reign of William IV. She was the eldest daughter of a peasant family from what is known as the 'bettermore' class, and so she was sent to school . . . at Walkhampton, four miles away. She walked the eight miles each day.

> After school hours, and often before them, the children were sent on the moor to gather the wool left by the sheep on the furze bushes and brambles. When gathered, the wool was cleaned, carded and spun into yarn for those of their neighbours who had no spinning wheel. In addition to woollen garments, all the straw bonnets and hats for the household were made at home, the raw material being had for the gathering, after the harvest was over.

> The family produced a surplus of hats, which they sold. They also made their own straw mats and beehives and their tallow candles. Tea was made from local herbs, packet tea from the shops being reserved for special occasions. Metheglin, an intoxicating liquor, was made from honey flavoured with herbs. Other Devon moorland families used to collect long brambles which, peeled, were used for hoops in crinolines.

S. H. Burton recalls life in Moretonhampstead, an old wool town:

> There was spinning and weaving in the cottages; a mill at the bottom of Lime Street and – later – another on the Bovey Tracey road. . . . The shops had little half-doors, with fleeces hung above them. . . . Drinking, wrestling and wool gave Moreton plenty to do. There was tanning, tallow chandling and rope-making, too. And on the upper floor of every inn was one long 'dormitory', where the guests and drunks slept hugger-mugger.

'New-take' land, appropriated by farmers and estate-owners living near Dartmoor (see page 119) was usually enclosed with 'new-take walls', a form of drystone walling. Many of the older walls were simply heaps of stones that happened to be found lying nearby, unshaped and unselected. Such walls tend to be unstable, stones of too small a size having been used; others are networks of stones with holes which one can see through. Some time in the second half of the nineteenth century a moorman, John Bishop of Swincombe, developed a more durable type of wall, 'ordained to stand', as he put it. He employed much larger blocks of granite, often brought from distances by sledge and levered into place by means of a crowbar. ''Tis surprisin' what you can do with a laiver or two,' he used to say.

Almost the whole of Dartmoor was reckoned to be in the parish of Lydford, an arrangement which created problems, especially in bad weather. Mrs Bray tells the story of a gentleman caught in the snow on Dartmoor, who was profoundly thankful to see smoke rising from the chimney of an isolated farm. The two occupants of the house were a farmer and his old mother. They agreed to provide him with food and shelter for the night and a stable for his horse. Indeed, the son gave up his own bed to the traveller and went to sleep on the settle in the chimney corner – where, the traveller reflected when he woke in the middle of the night, it must certainly be warmer than in his bedroom.

As he lay there, shivering, he kept thinking about a large chest in a corner of the room, the old woman had given an evasive answer when he had asked what was in it. After a time, curiosity compelled him to get out of bed and lift the lid. To his horror, he found himself looking down at a corpse.

He crept back to bed and spent the rest of the night wakeful and apprehensive. He felt sure he had stumbled across a den of murderers, who made a practice of doing away with travellers who chanced to stay there for a night. Every minute he expected to hear a stealthy footstep outside his door, and he prepared to fight for his life.

However, nothing happened, and he eventually went down to a good hot breakfast, feeling rather ashamed of his suspicions. Having eaten, he summoned up enough courage to admit that he had peeped into the chest, and asked about the corpse.

'Bless your heart, your honour, 'tis nothing at all,' said the farmer. ''Tis only fayther!'

He explained that his father had died a fortnight ago but that, as all the roads and tracks were blocked by snow, there was no alternative to keeping the body in the house until they were able to get down to Tavistock to bury it. 'So mother put un in the old box and salted un in. Mother's a fine hand at salting un in.'

The traveller was quite put off his breakfast, which happened to be home-cured bacon. That, too, must have been 'salted in' by the old lady, and he couldn't help wondering whether he might have got a slice of 'fayther' by mistake! He could never afterwards bring himself to eat bacon. S. H. Burton identifies the place where this occurred as Warren House Inn, near Postbridge.

Several interesting funeral customs survived until well into the nineteenth century on and around Dartmoor. Mrs Bray writing of Tavistock in 1833, records that, until a short time before, the sexton used to carry his spade 'not shouldered but, to use the military phrase, reversed, before the clergyman at every funeral.' At Manaton it was the practice to carry a coffin three times round an old granite cross in the churchyard before burial. The procession had to make the circle sunwise. A rector of Manaton, Rev. C. Carwithen, having preached in vain against this allegedly pagan practice, eventually smashed the cross and buried the fragments.

The custom of tolling the church bell at the passing of a parishioner has not long been discontinued. Hearing it, men working in the fields would bare their heads and speculate about who had died. The tolling of the bell was thought to help the soul on its way to heaven. When in the early nineteenth century the Duke of Bedford offered the parishioners of Tavistock the choice of a church organ or bells, they chose the bells. At a later date, a lady living in Tavistock gave the town another bell, for the specific purpose of tolling it when a poor person died. This bell was alway known as the 'poor bell'.

Baring-Gould comments on 'the extraordinary fascination' which funerals had for Devonshire people. He notes: 'That which concerns the moribund person at the last is not how to prepare the soul for the great change but how to contrive to have "a proper grand buryin".'

He says, too, that weddings attracted little interest and that often the parents of the bride and bridgroom did not attend.

The bell-ringers' rules for St Petrock's church, South Brent, are still extant and are said to be observed by the present-day bell-ringers:

If any ringer shall curse, swear or profane the name of the ord Almighty, or promote gaming, or debauch in the Society room, at any meeting of the ringers, he shall pay twopence for any such offence or be excluded.

If any person, at time of meeting, abuse either the Lord Chief or any other ringer, he shall pay twopence; and if any ringer strike another he shall pay 6d for the first offence, one shilling for the second, and be excluded for the third.

That when any ringer is chosen Lord Chief or Crier, every ringer shall behave in a sober and decent manner, penalty for breaking this rule 6d.

If any ringer talks in the Society in a ridiculous manner, penalty 6d.

Mrs H. P. Whitcombe, writing in 1874, notes:

At Hatherleigh it was usual in days gone by for the church bell to announce by distinct strokes the day of the month after the church clock had struck five and nine, morning and evening .... The curfew still tolls at eight o'clock, closing with the tolling of the day of the month. Some writers assert that a peal is always rung on the church bells after a funeral, the *same* as after a wedding; but this is incorrect. This is done only occasionally, and then the bells are muffled.

If all this is correct, the church bell-ringers must have had virtually a full-time job, for they would have needed to be available at certain hours every day.

At Ottery St Mary, during the same period, the curfew bell was still rung at eight p.m. every day, except Sundays and the extended Christmas period, between Michaelmas and Lady Day. On Sundays, throughout the year, it was tolled for a quarter of an hour at 8 a.m.

A function associated with many Devon churches, as also churches in other counties, was the Church Ale. It was in effect a forerunner of the modern village fête, its purpose being to raise funds for the church. At least, that was the intention in most Devonshire villages, though in other parts of England there are instances of its being regarded as a festivity for which the parson paid the bill.

The custom in Devon seems to have been for everyone in the parish to be assessed for a share of the expenses. For this he was entitled to attend the ale and drink as much as he liked. Traditionally the Church Ale was held in the church house, where also the ale was brewed for the occasion. It is interesting that in Devon the drink normally consumed was ale, not cider.

Kingsbridge, or rather, the neighbouring village of Dodbrooke, had its own special brew of ale, known as 'White Ale'. It was said to contain a secret ingredient, 'grout', introduced long ago by a German surgeon attached to a regiment stationed nearby. Traditionally it was drunk with a lacing of Jamaica rum, which made it extraordinarily potent.

Church Ales died out with the rise of Puritanism. A church session presided over by the Bishop of Exeter in 1595, when Puritanism was in the ascendant, prohibited all 'Church or parish ales, revels, May games, plays and such other unlawful assemblies of the people of sundry parishes unto one parish on Sabbath day and other times'. It took more than a bishop's decree, however, to stop many of the cheerful old customs, as we shall see.

It was important to make sure that the ale was of proper strength and not adulterated. This was the function of the ale-taster. S. H. Burton describes the procedure. 'He would enter the premises without warning, command a mug of ale and pour some of it on the wooden bench. Then he sat in the puddle, motionless, for about half an hour. If the ale had been adulterated with sugar his leather breeches would stick to the bench.'

Ashburton still appoints an ale-taster, with other officials, at its annual Court Leet and Court Baron in November. These two courts were traditionally called to deal with local rights and duties and to enquire into felonies. All freeholders are called upon to attend, on penalty of a fine. Twenty are appointed to form a grand jury, to look into all matters concerning tenancies, transfers of properties, public nuisances and other matters of public interest to the town. They also appoint the portreeve, the bailiff, two ale-tasters and the bread-weighers for the coming year. The ale-tasters make their rounds in July, and any innkeeper whose ale passes the test is entitled to hang a sprig of evergreen over his door.

Other officials formerly appointed by the Ashburton Court-Baron included two pig-drivers, a scavenger, two viewers of watercourses and two viewers of the market. Tavistock used to have an official dog-whipper, for a sixteenth century entry in the churchwardens' accounts contains an item 'for whyppyng dogs owt of the churche'.

Lydford, a borough notorious for its Stannary courts, used to have the privilege of choosing its own coroner, who, says Mrs Whitcombe, was invariably the most aged man in the place. Its annual fair was held on a Sunday in autumn and used to be centred around and in the church. Puritan influence notwithstanding, Mrs Whitcombe was able to report that, even in her time (1874), fairs in some villages were still held on the Sabbath.

Lydford's reputation for legal severity prompted some verses, composed in 1644, which achieved wide publicity, through being uncomfortably near the mark. The first verse is:

> I oft have heard of Lydford law,
> How in the morn they hang and draw,
>   And sit in judgment after;
> At first I wondered at it much,
> But soon I found the matter such
>   As it deserves no laughter.

Another misdemeanour subject to severe penalties in medieval times in the diocese of Exeter was grazing cows in the churchyard. A thirteenth-century Exeter synod directs the prohibition against 'the rectors of churches or parish priests, to whom the custody of burial-grounds chiefly belongs'. Sheep were excluded from this ruling.

Uplyme also had memories of a Court Leet which was held until about 1913, and met in the local inn, the Talbot Arms. Its functions were to receive the rent of tenants on the estate and to elect certain officials, including a constable and a hayward, the latter being in charge of the village pound. The proceedings always ended with a dinner.

The chief official in Honiton until 1846 was the portreeve, who was then superseded by a mayor. The annual fair, now held on the first Tuesday after 19 July, used to be a Whit-Monday event. Honiton has an official town crier, who announces the opening of the fair with the proclamation:

> Oyez! Oyez! Oyez!
> The Glove is up and the Fair has begun.
> No man shall be arrested until the Glove is taken down.
> God Save the Queen!

Each phrase is repeated by the assembled school-children, who then scramble for heated pennies, thrown from a hotel window.

The glove refers to a gilded glove, carried on a staff by the town crier at the opening ceremony. In the Middle Ages it was a recognised sign that traders from outside could now enter the town and trade without restriction. Exeter had a huge glove that was carried in procession and placed on the roof of the Guildhall at the opening of its Lammas Fair. Brent Fair, too, had its glove.

At Paignton Fair a giant plum pudding was hauled through the streets and later distributed to the crowd. The tradition is now reserved for special occasions, such as the institution of the new borough of Torbay in 1968.

Holne, on the margin of Dartmoor, has a Ram Feast. At one time the ram was chased wildly over the moors and then slaughtered. Later the event became more decorous. In 1896 a writer in the *Transactions of the Devonshire Association* says that it had been discontinued for more than a hundred years, but that there had been revivals in more recent times. Enquiring from some of the oldest residents in Holne, he learned that 'a lamb was decorated with flowers, roses being specially used, and led to the "Plat Park". Here it was killed, dressed and prepared for roasting.'

After roasting it was carved into portions which were sold, and an afternoon and evening of games and sports followed. There was some controversy about the correct date for the revel, but majority opinion favoured 6 July.

According to another version, after the ram lamb had been run down on the moor, it was fastened to a granite post for slaughter, and roasted whole, unskinned. At midday it was sliced up for disposal to the crowd, and young men would struggle for a slice to present to their girls. The granite stone, the traditional place of sacrifice, stood, six or seven feet high, in the middle of a field.

Kingsteignton also had a ram-roasting, which was held at Whitsun. The custom was revived, for the first time within memory of anyone then living, in 1885. On Whit Tuesday:

at 2.30 p.m. a procession started on its way to a large field; in front, the lamb, adorned with flowers and ribbons, was carried by the two sacrificing priests; then came the Bovey Brass Band and next the four-year-old Queen of the May, accompanied by maids of honour and pages. Maypole dancing, donkey racing, athletic sports and dancing were thoroughly enjoyed and, meanwhile the ram lamb had been roasted, cut up and sold.

A legend attached to the ceremony attributed its origin to an occasion when Kingsteignton was short of water and asked its priests to intercede with the gods. In answer to their prayer, a torrent of water came rushing down from Rydon estate. A ram lamb was sacrificed in gratitude. Traditionally, it was said, the stream had to be diverted a few days before the revel and the bed cleaned, so that the lamb could be roasted there.

On page 73 is a description of how Sir Francis Drake brought water to drought-stricken Plymouth, by finding a suitable spring on Dartmoor and conjuring it to follow him down to the port. To commemorate this benefaction Plymouth now has a Fyshynge Feaste, held in June or July, when the Mayor and the Town Council go up to Burrator Reservoir and enjoy a lunch of grilled lake trout. They meet on the lawn by the head weir, and the procedure is as follows:

> The Party being assembled, a Goblet filled with pure Water taken from the Weir by the Corporation Surveyor is handed by him to the Chairman of the Water Committee, who presents the same to the Mayor and requests him to drink thereof,
>
> 'To the pious Memory of Sir Francis Drake',
>
> and, passing the Cup from one to the other, each drinks and repeats the same words. Another Goblet, being filled with Wine, is then presented by the Chamberlain to the Mayor, who drinks to the toast,
>
> 'May the descendants of him who brought us Water never want Wine'.

Two interesting details concerning the background to the ceremony are worth noting. One is that, although Sir Francis initiated the provision of the water supply, the Corporation of Plymouth footed the bill. And at one time it was necessary for the citizens to make a regular inspection of the reservoir and canal, to make sure that the tin-miners on the moor were not diverting the supply for their own uses.

That other Devon seaport, Bideford, also used to have a water festival, centred around a Beat the Clock Race. Competitors tried to cross the bridge while the clock was striking eight. This race has now been superseded by a Round the Town race, held on the eve of Bideford Regatta. Bideford also has its Manor Court, similar to a Court Leet or Baron Leet, but of comparatively recent origin. It was instituted as late as the 1880s, when the manor became vested in the mayor and corporation, and it serves the purpose of allowing the townsfolk to ventilate their grievances and to suggest ideas for improving the town.

An essential and popular item in any Devon revel in the old days was wrestling, or, in Devon parlance, 'wrasling' or 'wraxling'. It was especially popular near the Cornish border, since a great rivalry existed between the two counties. The rules of Cornish and Devon wrestling were different; Cornish consists mainly of shoulder-play whereas Devon wrestlers relied chiefly on their legs and feet. Cornish wrestlers often wore no shoes, Devon wrestlers had their shoes baked hard, to make them stronger. They were permitted no iron toe-caps or nails. Devon wrestling, unless carefully refereed or played in a tolerant and gentlemanly manner, could easily deteriorate into a kicking-match. They were very tough characters, those wrestlers. One told Mrs Whitcombe in the 1870s, when she asked him if he had ever had any accidents:

'Nothing to speak of – only three ribs broken and a shoulder dislocated.'

Baring-Gould, who devoted a whole chapter to Devonshire wrestlers in his *Devon Characters & Strange Events*, supplies many an interesting detail on techniques and personalities. The Devonshire wrestling shoes, he says, were soaked in bullock's blood and then baked, which made them as hard as iron. The umpires, three in number, were known as 'sticklers'. The ring in which the matches were held was covered with tan.

In spite of the different techniques and rules, Cornish and Devon wrestlers were often matched against each other. Probably the greatest of all the Devonshire men was Abraham Cann, born in 1794. In October 1826 he fought a tremendous duel with James Polkinghorne, the Cornish champion at Tamar Green, Devonport, in the presence of 17,000 spectators. They finished ten rounds, each receiving tremendous punishment. Then Polkinghorne marched off in disgust, following a disputed fall. Cann was adjudged the winner, but the result was rather unsatisfactory. The prize money was £200, but very much more changed hands in bets.

When a more humane age objected to the brutal Devon style of wrestling, with its emphasis on shin-kicking, the public lost interest, but Cornish wrestling still survives.

It would hardly be proper to conclude this chapter without mentioning cider-making, a rural industry which has long held an important part in the life of Devonshire men. There is an old tradition that cider was first made in the reign of Elizabeth I, but Dr W. G. Hoskins has shown that it was part of the regular routine on Devon manors at least as early as the thirteenth century.

The cider-making process followed the pattern common to all the western counties of England. The apples were ground by a great stone wheel revolving in a huge circular stone trough. The resulting pulp was placed between layers of clean straw and pressed in a cider-press. The juice ran out into a flat tub called a 'Kieve', or 'trin', where it was left for three or four days to start fermentation. During this period all the debris and dirt found its way to the surface and was skimmed off. The liquid was then poured into casks to finish its fermentation.

Devon had several local variations. Water was never added to cider proper, but it was sometimes poured over the 'cheese' after the first pressing, holes being made to allow the cheese to absorb it. Pressed a second time, this cheese yielded a thin, sharp liquor, often served up by the quart and gallon to farm labourers, and much appreciated as being thirst-quenching, but only mildly intoxicating. It was not honoured by the name of cider, but was referred to simply as 'beverage'.

Baring-Gould gives the recipe for making sweet cider:

A bucketful of the new cider is put in the cask, then brimstone is lighted in an old iron pot, and a match of paper or canvas is dipped in the melted brimstone and thrust into the cask through the bung-hole which is closed. The fumes of the sulphur fill the vessel, and when the barrel is afterwards filled with cider all fermentation is arrested. Sweet cider, if new, is often rather unpleasant from the taste of the sulphurous acid.

An alternative method is to keep pouring the cider from one hogshead to another, whenever it shows signs of fermenting.

The Devon palate did not, or perhaps does not, much appreciate sweet cider. It prefers its drink 'rough'. It certainly has a much higher alcohol content than sweet cider.

> Then fill up the jug, boys, and let it go round,
> Of drinks not the equal in England is found,
> So pass round the jug, boys, and pull at it free,
> There's nothing like cider, rough cider, for me.

Baring-Gould says that mustard was commonly added to champagne cider, to give it a sting; otherwise, he adds, cider is 'the purest and least adulterated of all drinks'. He does not, however, mention the steaks, horse-shoes and other doubtful ingredients frequently added to the fermenting cider, 'to give it body'.

Many of the apparently exaggerated stories about the former drinking prowess of Devon villagers undoubtedly had their origins in 'beverage' not the 'rough stuff'. S. H. Burton quotes an old man who remembered that on his father's farm the workers drank two quarts each before starting work in the mornings. 'On Sundays a sixty-gallon barrel of cider was tapped for the fourteen men who worked there . . . on wet days, the pub always opened at seven in the morning.' This was at Drewsteignton.

Cider is still made on some Devonshire farms, and many more still possess the necessary equipment. It is often massive and can give rise to speculations as to how it was driven. The power was, in fact, often supplied by a horse, especially for the initial grinding of the apples. Sometimes the animal simply walked round the stone trough, turning the stone wheel as it went; sometimes it was provided with geared equipment which made its task easier.

Pack horses provided the chief means of transport in Devon later than in most other counties; only a comparatively few places were served by coach roads even as late as the early nineteenth century. A writer in 1829 states:

Fifty years ago a pair of wheels was scarcely to be seen on a farm in the county, and at present the use of pack-horses still prevails, though on the decline. . . . Hay, corn, fuel, stones, dung, lime, etc., and the produce of the fields, are all conveyed on horse-back; sledges, or sledge-carts, are also used in harvest time, chiefly drawn by oxen.

Oxen, though slower than horses, were used mainly for pulling heavy loads, and strong beasts were bred for the purpose. They were employed particularly in hauling loads uphill, and farmers living at the foot of formidable Devon hills would keep a team of oxen in readiness to earn a few shillings. For centuries cattle were quadruple-purpose animals, kept for beef, traction-power, milk and cream. The first two qualities were to some extent complementary, and, while beef animals normally yield small quantities of milk, it is usually rich in cream; hence the reputation of Devonshire cream. Later, farmers of the rich pastures of South Devon introduced Channel Island and perhaps some French blood into their native cattle, producing eventually the magnificent South Devon breed, which combines high yields of milk and cream with size.

Quarrying and mining have long played an important role in Devon economy. Mining began in prehistoric times, undoubtedly as tin-streaming, or extracting the ore from the beds of streams. This method was employed on Dartmoor as late as 1730, but shaft-mining was already being practised in the fifteenth century. Some of the earliest extant documents, from the twelfth and thirteenth centuries, refer to the 'ancient customs and liberties' of the tin-miners, and historians have pointed out that the tinners were so well organised before the evolution of the feudal system that they were able to escape and operate outside its strict rules. A tin-miner was a free man, though bound by the regulations of his own Stannary Courts, and he needed to pay little attention to the local feudal lords, being able to trespass where he liked in search of tin. Early in the sixteenth century Richard Strode, MP for Plympton, was convicted by the Stannary Courts and put in Lydford prison, for committing actions prejudicial to the 'ancient customs and liberties' of the tinners. He had tried to get Parliament to regulate mining near the ports of Devon, on the reasonable grounds that the debris resulting from the miners' activities was blocking the harbours. In medieval times the tinners had a strong ally in the Crown, to whom the mineral rights belonged and to whom it was advantageous to support any organisation which could curb the too-powerful barons.

Other minerals mined in Devon at various times include lead, silver, gold, copper, iron, arsenic and wolfram. There was a small coal mine at Bovey Heathfield and another near Bideford. Many ruins of old mine buildings are still to be seen on the moors of North

Devon. China clay is still extracted on a large scale on Dartmoor, and extensive quarrying of stone continues. Other clay is used in a number of flourishing potteries.

Devon's lace-making industry was traditionally centred at Honiton and was popularly supposed to have been introduced by religious refugees from the Low Countries at the time of Elizabeth I, but it probably existed before that date. Queen Victoria's wedding dress was of Honiton lace, made at Beer and Branscombe. Before the provision of general education in 1870, children of lace-making families went to lace-schools, to learn the trade, when they were five to seven years old. The pupils included boys as well as girls, for men often worked at the craft in the evening, or at times when other employment failed.

Dr Hoskins maintains that the lace trade exhibited some of the worst aspects of industrial exploitation. 'The lace-workers toiled at this close work for ten or twelve hours a day and were recognised by the sallow complexions, rickety frames and general appearance of languor and debility. Most of the workers were girls and young women, and after years of this confinement it was not surprising that they could produce only puny and short-lived children.' Baring-Gould, on the other hand, thought that the trade was not injurious to the workers' health and quoted instances of lace-workers living to beyond the age of seventy and more.

A number of Devon towns and villages had weaving mills, dyeing works and associated enterprises, there being plenty of small, swiftly-flowing streams to provide power. Uplyme, which has such a mill, also grew cultivated teazels, for cloth-napping, and stray descendants of the plants still appear in local gardens.

Villagers around Dartmoor used to scrape lichen off the rocks for use in dyeing. Treated with a tin extract and certain other ingredients, some of the lichens produced a brilliant scarlet dye, while others yielded dyes of purple, yellow and reddish-brown.

The whortleberry, an abundant and much-appreciated crop of the moors, is still gathered and enjoyed. Mrs Bray, writing in 1833, describes them as 'delicious when made into tarts and eaten with that luxury of all luxuries, the clouted or, as we call it, scalded cream of our delightful county'.

'Urting, as it was known in Devon, was a long-established tradition, and whole families would assemble to go up to the moors to gather the 'urts. Apparently it was even considered a legitimate reason for children to miss school. At the beginning of an 'urting expedition the pickers would recite;

> The first I pick I eat;
> The second I pick, I throw away;
> The third I pick, I put in my can.

This was considered a charm necessary to ensure a good 'urting.

A country practice so far referred to only obliquely is 'swaling'. The term is commonly used on the moors to describe the burning of gorse and heather, to promote the growth of fresh young vegetation, though unfortunately it is often carried out at seasons when it must harm nesting birds. It is also used to describe the practice of trimming hedge-banks and burning the dross in autumn. And, in fact, one can assume that 'swaling' means any kind of cleaning by fire, for a pig can also be 'swaled', or 'swelled', which means singeing off its bristles, by means of burning straw, after it has been killed – an operation in which I have often assisted. Iris M. Woods, of Dunstone Cottage, Widecombe, wrote in 1967:

those who were children in the first decade of this century describe how they looked forward to this annual ritual. I have been up myself to the ridge behind this cottage on the first Sunday of March (when it happened to be a still, fair day) and have seen the thin spires of smoke rising from every hill and ridge within sight!

10   The Circling Year

IN EXAMINING New Year customs, it is important to remember the calendar change of 1753, when eleven days were 'lost'. The traditional date for wassailing the apple-trees, was the eve of Twelfth Night, which by our present-day reckoning would be 5 January. But to this we have to add the eleven lost days, which takes the wassailing ceremony to 16 January. Old Devon folk were adamant about it:

'It baint no good to go wassailing on Old Christmas Eve,' an old Bampton man told me in 1949. 'Thik Old Twelfth Night be the time for it.'

Nevertheless, it seems that some Devon parishes adopted the new ways. A member of the Devonshire Association saw wassailing near Torquay on 5 January 1849; and another observed it at Ashburton on 5 January 1887. Baring-Gould also gives Old Christmas Eve as the usual date for the ceremony.

Wassailing was a family affair. After drinking mulled cider and eating toast soaked in it, the grandfather of a family led the whole clan out-of-doors to the home orchard and directed the proceedings.

They stood under the biggest or oldest tree, a girl wedged some cider-soaked toast into a fork in the branches. She drank a draught of cider from a pitcher and poured the rest over the tree trunk. A band of sorts then struck up, and everyone sang the Wassailing Song.

After three cheers had been given, any of the men who possessed guns discharged them upwards, through the branches of the tree. The party then went on to the next tree, though in many places it was sufficient to wassail just the one.

There are many versions of the Wassailing Song, though nearly all vary in only minor details. One which I have sung on more than one occasion runs:

> Old Apple Tree, Old Apple Tree,
> We wassail thee and hope that thou wilt bear;
> For the Lord doth know where we shall be
> Till apples come another year.
> For to bear well and to bloom well,
> So merry let us be;
> Let every man take off his hat and shout to thee,
> Old Apple Tree, Old Apple Tree,
> We wassail thee and hope that thou wilt bear
> Hat fulls,
> Cap fulls,
> Three bushel bag fulls,
> And a little heap under the stairs.

Some versions begin 'Here's health to thee, Old Apple Tree', which is appropriate, for 'Wassail' is derived from two Saxon words meaning 'Good Health'. But the ceremony was regarded as more than a toast. It was, in the old days, performed with great earnestness. The family underlined its identity with the orchard by eating and drinking its products and returning symbolic samples to it as an offering. Their lives and the lives of the trees were bound closely together. After all, it was part of their livelihood. Each member of the family had to dip his mug in the cider bowl, swallow some of the cider-soaked toast, and sing the song. Even children were brought out to join in; so were the sick and invalids, unless too ill to clamber out of bed.

If anyone were missing, the family feared that the charm would not be effective.

Before guns became a commonplace possession, the trees were beaten with sticks.

In some districts only the males went into the orchard, and when they returned to the house they found the door barred against them. It was only unfastened when they had guessed what was roasting on the spit – and a most unlikely object was always chosen.

Sometimes, a small boy would climb into the apple tree and sit there, calling, 'Tit, tit, more to eat'. He was then handed bread, cheese and cider.

As far as I am aware, no Devon parish now observes the custom, and has not for a long time. It was seen at Ashburton in 1887 and survived at Molland until about 1870. Both Mrs Bray, in 1833, and Mrs H. P. Whitcombe, writing in 1874, however, use the present tense in referring to wassailing.

A song which I have heard in Devon in the present century, referred to as 'an old Wassailing Song', has a first verse which runs:

> There was an old man,
> And he had an old cow,
> And how to keep her, he didn't know how;
> So he built up a barn,
> To keep that cow warm,
> And a little more cider will do us no harm!
> Harm, my boys, harm!
> Harm, my boys, harm!
> And a little more cider will do us no harm!

Although this song may have occasionally been sung at a wassailing, I doubt whether it properly belongs there. It sounds more like a drinking-song.

Writing in 1959, Iona and Peter Opie say that on New Year's Eve, 'Bread and a piece of coal are put out to ensure health, wealth and happiness to the household when fetched in the next day'. Uplyme used always to have a party for 'singers and ringers' on New Year's Eve, and on New Year's Day a party for the older parishioners, who each received a blanket, a sheet or a piece of cloth.

There were other beliefs connected with New Year's Day: clothes must never be washed then, or someone would be washed out of the house, never to return; paying money on that day is lucky, as it ensures prompt payment of cash due for the rest of the year; and the bees must be given a present, presumably some sugar or honey.

At East Budleigh a curious peal of bells used to mark the passing of the Old Year. Each bell clapper had one of its sides muffled. When the New Year arrived, the mufflers were removed and a full peal was rung.

At midnight on Old Christmas Eve, 5 January, cattle, sheep and horses were supposed to kneel down, facing the east. The belief was recorded around 1900, but is now probably lost.

Plough Monday was the first Monday after Twelfth Night, when the routine work of the countryside began again after the long Christmas break. On this day ploughs were brought out to resume their work in the fields. Our ancestors celebrated this work-a-day occasion with revelry, ceremony and dancing. All the old festivities disappeared in Devonshire long ago but certain ceremonies have been revived in a few places in recent years. On the first Sunday after 6 January a plough is drawn through the west doorway of Exeter cathedral and blessed before the altar. A similar ceremony is performed at Bratton Fleming, where a horse-plough is stored for the rest of the year in a room at the base of the tower. In each instance the service is held in cooperation with local Young Farmers' Clubs.

Shrove-tide and Ash Wednesday, which usually fall in February, mark the beginning of Lent, a sombre period which in medieval times tended to make virtue out of necessity, at a season when provisions were becoming scarce. We know Shrove Tuesday now as Pancake Day, but to old Devon folk it was Lenshard Day, while the preceding day was Collop Monday. A collop is a slice of meat, and it was a tradition to eat them, with eggs and pancakes, as a final treat before the long Lenten fast.

Many Devon villages, among them Gittisham, Clovelly, Molland, Budestown and Bridestow, had a tradition no longer observed except in Gittisham, of children calling at the houses asking for alms. It was, often, associated with 'lensharding', which consisted of throwing broken crockery into the doorway of anyone who refused to contribute. 'Shard' means a piece of broken crockery.

In some villages, including Molland 'lensharding' was performed without a request for money. Clovelly children chased up and down

their cobbled street, rattling tin cans and making as much commotion as possible. They said it was to scare off witches but children
love any excuse to make a noise. Several versions of the verses they
recited were written down. Here is one of the most popular:

> Lent crock, give a pancake,
> Or a fritter for my labour.
> Or a dish of flour, or a piece of bread,
> Or what you please to render.
> I see by the latch,
> There's something to catch;
> I see by the string,
> There's a good dame within.
> Trap, trapping throw,
> Give me my mumps, and I'll go.

A Tavistock version contained a more open threat in the last two
lines, which went:

> At the door goes a stone,
> Come, give and I'm gone.

An Exmoor verse runs:

> Tipety, tipety, tin, give me a pancake,
> And I will come in.
> Tipety, tipety toe, give me a pancake,
> And I will go.

Gittisham children sing a very similar verse, except that nowadays
they ask for money instead of a pancake.

Another Shrove-tide verse begins:

> Shrove-tide is now at hand,
> And we are come a-shroving;
> Pray, dame give us something,
> An apple, or a dumpling,
> Or a piece of crumple cheese
> Of your own making,
> Or a piece of pancake. . . .'

It then concludes as in the Bridestowe version.

A former rector of Molland thought that the crock-throwing custom may have originated in a reminder to the inmates of the house selected that they had something to confess and be shriven of before Lent, though others suggest that this seems unlikely. Edward Capern, the postman-poet of Bideford, thought it served as rough village justice, shaming villagers who had misbehaved in some way. On the other hand, other writers have noted that the crock-throwers used to make a point of visiting the parsonage and the houses of prominent farmers, and one can hardly expect that these people would have been singled out as the chief sinners.

Several places have preserved accounts of the procedure if a crock-throwing culprit were caught. In Exmoor parishes his face was blackened with soot, but he was then given a pancake. In and around Tavistock he was dragged inside and made to twirl round an old shoe hanging in front of the hearth fire, until the fire and the pace became too hot for him. One of the girls of the household was then expected to rescue him, and he, in turn, had to give her a present at the next fair.

Mothering Sunday, traditionally the fourth Sunday in Lent, has in recent years been given a new lease of life by its transformation, largely for commercial reasons, regrettably, into Mother's Day. This is mainly due to the influence of American soldiers stationed in England during the last war. In fact American Mother's Day falls in May, not in Lent, and has no connection with mid-Lent Sunday. Originally the 'Mother' referred to in Mothering Sunday was the Mother Church, not one's physical mother. Medieval villagers used to go in procession to their mother church, in their native village, and the date later came to be kept as a time for family reunions at which a Mothering Cake was always placed on the table. Sarah Hewett gives the rest of the menu for the family feast, as 'a hind quarter of lamb, with mint sauce, a well-boiled suet pudding, seakale and cauliflower, wheat firmity, with home-made wines'.

Lady Day, 25 March, is of course, Quarter Day, and, in the past, many annual farm tenancies ran from that date. Lady Day tenancies were inevitably a complicated arrangement and depended heavily on goodwill between the incoming and outgoing tenants, for they involved both being on the premises together during the previous winter, the outgoing man clearing up his winter fodder, while the newcomer prepared the soil for his coming harvest.

Lady Day was also the occasion for a number of hiring fairs in Devon, as for example, at Holsworthy, South Molton and Okehampton. It was the day when girls and domestic servants in particular signed up with their employers for the coming year.

For some unexplained reason, the custom of crock-throwing at Hartland took place on Good Friday, where it was combined with cock-throwing. In some versions of this brutal sport, stones or sticks were thrown at a cock until it died, but the Hartland custom was rather different. The cock was placed under an earthenware pan, at which cudgels, known as 'kibbits', were thrown until it was broken. The cock, of course, escaped, and everyone chased it. The kibbit-thrower shared the bird with whoever caught it but had to compensate its owner.

Possibly there is a connection here with the old belief that it is lucky to break crockery on Good Friday, for the sharp edges of every shard are supposed to pierce the body of Judas.

There are numerous traditions about lucky and unlucky behaviour on Good Friday. Most countrymen know that Good Friday is the day 'hardained by the Lard for plantin' tetties', as Sid Davis, a Topsham man, told me in about 1948 – or beans or peas or other seeds, for that matter – and many still follow the ancient precept, though probably through convenience (it is a holiday at the proper sowing-season) than from any deep-seated belief. It was said, though it could hardly have been believed, that beans sown on Good Friday would have their shoots appearing above ground by Easter morning. On the other hand, it was considered very unlucky to do washing on Good Friday; indeed, it was regarded as a sin. Nor would fishermen put out to sea on this day. But Good Friday was the appropriate day for moving bee-hives.

Maundy Thursday, the day before Good Friday, is the traditional time for giving and receiving alms. The custom was observed at Exeter cathedral until early in the nineteenth century. 'Peter's Pence' were distributed to children at the door by the north tower, but there was such confusion and clamour that some of the youngsters were able to slip around the cathedral and join the crowd for a second penny. So the custom was altered to a general scramble for pennies, scattered in the graveyard.

At Ideford an almsgiving ceremony took place on Good Friday, in accordance with a charity founded more than three hundred years ago. The recipients lined up and collected their money from the table-like top of the donor's tomb.

Good Friday hot-cross buns were, of course, well-known in Devonshire, and a Good Friday bun, hung from the kitchen rafters for a whole year, would bring luck to the house. Sarah Hewett records the belief that such a bun, placed in a hot oven to dry and then grated and mixed with water, was an efficacious cure for diarrhoea.

> When Good Friday comes, an old woman runs
> With one, or two a penny hot cross buns.
> Whose virtue is, if you'll believe what's said,
> They'll not grow mouldy like the common bread.

On the other hand, Ernest Martin quotes the belief that 'the mouldy portions, removed from time to time and mixed with water, were suitable as curative agents for any complaint or disease, of both human beings or cattle'.

The traditional cry of sellers of buns on Good Friday was:

> Hot Cross buns; Hot Cross buns.
> One a penny, two a penny, Hot Cross buns.

To this William Crossing adds four other lines:

> Smoking hot, piping hot,
> Just come out of the baker's shop;
> One a penny poker; two a penny tongs;
> Three a penny fire-shovel, Hot Cross buns.

There was an old belief, also known in Devon that the sun dances when it rises on Easter morning 'in honour of Christ's rise from the darkness of the grave'. A. R. Wright quotes several interviews with old country people who claimed to have seen it; and anyone who has observed the spring sunrise from the top of a high hill can understand their joy. Apparently, at one time, it was almost obligatory to rise early and see the spectacle. There was also a belief, especially on Dartmoor and Exmoor, that in the centre of the sun's disc, as it rose on Easter morning, one could see the device of a Lamb, or of a Lamb and Flag. Girls used to take smoked glass with them on these excursions, to look at the sun.

April 1st was April Fool's Day, in Devon as elsewhere. It was also known as 'Tail-pipe Day', presumably because it was the custom to pin a card with the words 'Please kick me', or something similar, to the buttocks of a victim. This was recorded from Christow, the informant adding that it was done on the afternoon of April Fool's Day. However the more general version is that such tricks must be played before midday.

Dartmoor had its own spring festival – Bellever Day, when villagers from miles around assembled at Bellever Tor for hare-hunting. The sport lasted for a whole week, soon after Easter, with the Friday as the climax. Says Baring-Gould, writing in 1899:

> All the towns and villages neighbouring on Dartmoor send out carriages, traps, carts, riders; the roads are full of men and woman, ay, and children hurrying to Bellever. . . . Whether a hare be found and coursed that day matters little. It is given up to merriment in the fresh air and sparkling sun. . . .

St Mark's Eve, 24 April, was the traditional date for divination concerning marriage. Sarah Hewett records a Devon tradition in which a girl went to the churchyard at midnight, plucked three tufts of grass from a grave on the south side of the church, and placed them under her pillow. Her dreams would then reveal her future. If her sleep was dreamless she would be 'single and miserable all her life'.

Maypole dancing is still enjoyed at Lustleigh, on the first Saturday in May, and Kingsteignton, now on Spring Bank Holiday Monday, which serves as a reminder that in many instances the old customs have been spread to dates throughout the month, to suit local convenience. At Lustleigh the Town Orchard has been given to the parish as a permanent site for the May Day Festival.

Uplyme's Maypole dancing used to take place on Good Friday, the only holiday of the year for farm workers, but later the festivities were transferred to Whit Tuesday, when they merged with the Club Fête; here the leading part was played by local Friendly Societies, who marched through the streets, headed by a band, to a church service, followed by a dinner in a large marquee.

Combe Martin used to celebrate a curious festival, 'The Hunting of the Earl of Rone'. On the afternoon of Ascension Day the villagers, wearing their best clothes, marched to Lady's Wood to search for the Earl. They were led by a party of men dressed as Grenadiers. After spending some time looking in every unlikely spot they found the Earl lurking in some undergrowth. They fired a volley and then, surrounding the prisoner, set him, face to tail, on a donkey decorated with garlands of flowers and a necklace of 12 sea-biscuits. The Earl and the other chief characters in the procession, the Fool and the Hobby-Horse, wore grotesque masks. The fool carried a broom and a bucket of dirty water. The Hobby-Horse had realistic jaws, that worked mechanically and were known as 'the mapper', perhaps a corruption of 'snapper', for the Horse capered along, snapping at the spectators.

At intervals along the route the Grenadiers, who wore tall paper hats adorned with ribbons, halted and fired a volley, whereupon the Earl fell off his donkey, wounded. The grief-stricken Fool and Hobby-Horse attempted to cure him. For the rest of the time they collected money from the crowd. Anyone refusing to contribute was either sprinkled with dirty water by the Fool, or seized by the Hobby-Horse, or both. The procession made its way to the sea-shore, but was a long time getting there, for, as a nineteenth-century writer points out, 'refreshments were taken en route, and the rate of progress varied inversely as the number of public-houses along the line of march'.

The celebration was said to mark the anniversary of the capture of an Irish refugee, the Earl of Tyrone, who landed nearby and lived for a time in woods near the village, existing on sailors' biscuits, which he wore as a necklace. If the story is correct, the custom would date to the reign of Queen Elizabeth I, when a rebellion in Ireland was led by the Earl of Tyrone. But certain elements in the pageant, including the Fool, the Hobby-Horse and the attempts to cure the fallen Earl, would seem, from analogy with similar practices in other parts of the country, to be very much older. The festival was held regularly until 1837.

Modbury had a spring fair on 4 May which, according to the old calendar, was Old St George's Day. At least, that is when it began, but it traditionally lasted nine days. The start of the Fair was announced on the eve of St George's Day by the town crier, who stood on the old market cross and saw the glove hoisted. Private householders, who wished to sell ale or cider during the fair period, hung a holly bush over the door. In earlier days, when few shops existed in the town, this was said to be the only occasion in the year when it was possible to buy cloth there. The fair was still flourishing in the 1880s.

Mrs Whitcombe, writing in 1874, refers to the 'southern division of the county', where 'the children carry about little dolls, prettily dressed and laid in white boxes – these they call 'May babies'. She gives the date for this tradition as 29 May – Oak Apple Day – but Christina Hole, in 1941, connects the custom with May Day and says that the dolls were then still carried around at Ilfracombe, Bishopsteignton and at Edelesborough, where they sat in a decorated chair, sometimes covered with a white sheet, which was removed while the children sang a song of welcome to the summer. At Bishopsteignton the boys carried short poles, decorated with flowers. The children always expected alms, though they did not usually ask for money.

Sarah Hewett, however, quotes a rhyme, said to have been chanted by children carrying flower-decked dolls around certain un-named villages on May Day. The last lines do contain a request for a reward.

> Round the Maypole, trit, trit, trot;
> See what a Maypole we have got;
>> Fine and gay,
>> Trip away,
> Happy is our New May-day.
> Good morning, merry gentlefolks!
> We wish you a happy May;
> We come to show our May garland,
> Because 'tis the first of May.
>> Come kiss my face,
>> And smell my mace,
>> And give the little children
>> Something!

Baring-Gould briefly mentions a May-Day tradition at Millbrook, where 'boatmen carried a dressed ship about the streets with music'. Another curious and painful custom was observed by the children who beat each other with nettles on 3 May, which was therefore called 'Stinging-nettle Day'. It has been recorded for Bovey Tracey, North Tawton, Torquay and elsewhere.

The custom of Beating the Bounds, once widespread, is still observed, at irregular intervals, at Ipplepen, one recent occasion being 1950. The procession takes ten hours to walk around the parish boundaries, and selected victims are bumped on the appropriate stones.

Exeter used to observe a similar custom, annually, on the Tuesday before Ascension Day. The procession was led by the Mayor and Corporation, the boys of St John's Hospital taking an active part. Ducking in the water featured prominently in the proceedings, especially during the journey by boat. The procession followed the city boundaries; in addition, the several parishes observed their own similar ceremonies. Boys again played the most prominent part, though accompanied by clergy and respectable parishioners. They carried white wands, decorated with coloured tape or ribbons, and splashed with water anyone who did not give them money when asked. The parochial bound-beating was held on Ascension Day itself.

A variation on the ceremony used to be performed in Farway parish, the last recorded occasion being in 1884. At Hornshayne House, in the Coly valley, the boundaries of Farway, Southleigh and Colyton all meet, some rooms being in one parish, some in the others. It is remembered that a small boy was made to crawl along a beam in or near the kitchen – the exact line of the parish boundary.

A bizarre dispute once arose between Farway and Southleigh as to which parish should be responsible for a pauper resident at Hornshayne. Minute examination revealed that, although the boundary line ran through the middle of the attic in which he slept and also through the middle of his bed, he normally slept with his feet in Southleigh and his head in Farway. Farway therefore had to accept responsibility for him.

At Bovey Tracey the first Monday after 3 May was Mayor's Monday, when the parish bounds had to be beaten. A writer in 1882 states that the custom was still observed in that year, when 'the mayor-elect and about forty freeholders drove around the outskirts of the parish, inducing "colts" to kiss the magic stone, pledging allegiance in upholding ancient rights and privileges, and dining together at the Dolphin Hotel'.

Sarah Hewett, writing in 1900, says that Roodmass Day was still observed at Bovey Tracey on the first Monday after 3 May. This, of course, is a Roman Catholic festival. A procession was formed to beat the bounds of the parish, the villagers carrying large garlands of flowers mounted on staves, and decorating their houses with blooms.

Ascension Day usually falls in May. In North Devon a belief existed that water from certain holy wells was particularly efficacious if collected on the morning of Ascension Day, the earlier the better. Some invalids took away water in bottles, to be treasured for use at home throughout the year. Wells at North Molton and Hatherleigh are mentioned in this connection. At Hatherleigh 'young people used to flock to the well, dropping pins into the water and expressing a wish'.

In 1896 a writer in the *Transactions of the Devonshire Association* says she had heard of no fewer than 24 village and town revels in North Devon alone on Whit-Monday, though she adds that they were more fashionable 60 years earlier. She provides some details of the activities:

> On the morning of the revel hats gaudily trimmed with ribbons were hung up in conspicuous places and were sometimes worn in church as an advertisement that wrestling would take place. Trees were fixed on either side of the door of a house to show that it was a bush house, privileged to sell ale during the revel without being licensed. Standings were erected on the village green, where sweets and gingerbread were sold, on the Sunday, and wares of all kinds on the Monday. All classes joined in the games and sports, wrestling, skittles, boxing, running, cock-fighting, climbing the greased pole, football, dancing, and cock-shying. Women ran for gowns, legs of mutton and other prizes; men wrestled for hats and silver spoons; boys climbed a greased pole on which was mounted the prize; and young men gave their young women fairings, usually packets of sweets, made of almonds, sugar and spices, or gingerbread nuts, or Spanish nuts.

St Frankin, a saint apparently unknown elsewhere, has a place in Devon hagiology. May 19th, 20th, and 21st also known as Francimass were reserved for him. Baring-Gould, who heard of him at Chawleigh and Burrington in 1894, thought that his name was an euphemism. He had heard two slightly different versions of the story. One was that a brewer named Frankin, suffering badly because of competition from cider-makers, sold his soul to the Devil, in return for the promise of a frost every year on those three days in May, when it could be guaranteed to kill the apple-blossom. In the other version the brewers of North Devon promised to adulterate their ale in return for the frosts. So when frosts do come at that critical period, it is a sign that the Devil is fulfilling his part of the contract, because the brewers have fulfilled theirs!

Oak Apple Day, 29 May, officially commemorates the escape of Prince Charles, afterwards Charles II, following the Battle of Worcester in 1657, and the Restoration of the monarchy. The festivities have, however, probably become confused with other celebrations. In the early nineteenth century, for instance, 29 May was celebrated in Exeter as 'Lawless Day', without any apparent reference to King Charles or to Oak-Apples.

A writer in 1819 describes a kind of civil war that was waged in the streets throughout the day by rival gangs, who fought each other with cudgels. An essential part of the exercise was to dam the open drains, with any materials available, to form pools or 'bays'. At these stations they held passers-by to ransom, giving three cheers for everyone who paid up and splashing defaulters with muddy water. What money they collected was speedily spent in public-houses, and by evening the proceedings were so riotous that many of the worst offenders were arrested and locked up, to learn later that 'if there is no law on Lawless Day, there is law the next day'.

James Cossins mentions that on 29 May boys and girls wore gilded oak apples and leaves. Torquay people were also observing the custom in 1880, and some carried bunches of nettles to sting those not wearing oak leaves. At Devonport, in about 1850, a boy dressed in evergreens and a tinsel crown, representing King Charles in the oak tree, was the centre of a procession led by a drum and fife band. At Plymouth, the central figure in the parade was a man in a large coop covered with evergreens. His attendants were a crowd of chimney-sweeps, in full regalia, who danced around him. This was Jack-in-the-Green, sometimes confused with the historical figure of Charles II.

The Tiverton Oak-Apple Revel was a lively pageant featuring Charles and his opponent Cromwell. There was no doubt where the town's sympathies lay – with Charles. He was carried through the streets on a throne, dressed like a king, whereas Cromwell was 'the coarsest and most repulsive-looking scoundrel the town could produce . . . naked to the waist . . . and with a long shaggy tail made of a hempen rope much frayed at the end'. He carried a big bag of soot tied to his waist, and he and his attendants daubed anyone they could catch. The two processions met in the middle of the town in a boisterous free-for-all. Any prisoners taken were ransomed, and the money was spent in public-houses. In addition to all this everybody was expected to be up early in the morning, collecting greenery to decorate their houses, and they wore oak sprigs and oak-apples in their buttonholes or on their hats.

Mrs Bray describes much the same custom, including a mock-battle, at Tavistock in 1832. The battle was fought mainly with water and was appearently good-humoured. Houses and people alike were decorated with oak leaves and oak apples, and again there was an emphasis on early rising. It was generally believed, says Mrs Bray, that on that day any person might cut oak boughs wherever he pleased, provided it was done before 6 o'clock in the morning.

She also quotes another tradition in which 29 May is Garland Day. In preparation for it, small boys went around the countryside collecting as many birds' eggs as they could find, a procedure they called 'halfing'. They also begged or stole flowers from every garden in the neighbourhood. They then made garlands composed of two crossed hoops, decorated with flowers, and acting as a frame for the birds' eggs strung across the middle. On Oak Apple Day morning they got up early and dressed in ribands, oak leaves and gilt caps. They paraded the town in small groups, each with a leader, who carried the garland, and accompanied by a band of drums and whistles. The purpose, of course, was to collect alms, which they divided between them. In the afternoon they placed the garlands on a stone or post and threw stones at them, each boy trying to break most eggs. There was one exception to this wholesale vandalism of birds' nests; on no account might a robin's egg be taken.

There do not seem to be many memories in Devonshire of the Midsummer fires that are a feature of folklore in some other counties. The few Midsummer customs I have been able to find are concerned with omens and charms rather than with communal activities. But Miss Dorothy Banks of Tavistock observed in 1967 that: 'Here and in Cornwall bonfires are lit on all high tors on 23 June to commemorate the beacons lit to give warning of the approach of the Armada in 1558.'

Lapford revel was held on the first Sunday after 7 July, the day of St Thomas à Becket, to whom the church is dedicated. It was a tradition at farmhouses to make a 'pestle pie' – a hugh concoction too big for any pie-dish and kept in shape by a frame of iron hoops. One such pie contained 'a ham, a tongue, whole specimens of poultry and game, all previously prepared, seasoned and partly cooked'. Morchard had a similar tradition.

Communal sheep-shearings on Exmoor were occasions for revels, or at least for merry-making. Everyone from neighbouring farms came to lend a hand with the work and afterwards sat down to a good dinner, followed by music and dancing.

Lammas (1 August) was the old Celtic festival of Lugnasad, Christianized to some extent and transformed into 'Loaf-mass', or a festival of the first fruits. Exeter's Lammas Fair is one of the few survivals of fairs and other festivities associated with the season. Ernest Martin quotes an old custom practised by Devonshire farmers which involved taking four pieces of Lammas bread, made from the first corn threshed from the harvest, and crumbling them in the four corners of the barn.

Some of the most valuable information about end-of-harvest customs in Devon comes from Mrs Bray, an eye-witness in 1832 of the ceremony of 'Crying the Neck'. She described it as follows:

When the reaping is finished, towards evening the labourers select some of the best ears of corn from the sheaves; these they tie together, and it is called the *nack*. Sometimes as it was when I witnessed the custom, this nack is decorated with flowers, twisted in with the reed, which gives it a gay and fantastic appearance. The reapers then proceed to a high place, and there they got, to use their own words, to 'holla the hack'. The man who bears this offering stands in the midst, elevates it, whilst all the other labourers form themselves into a circle about him; each holds aloft his hook, and in a moment they all shout, as loud as they possibly can. 'Arnack, arnack, arnack, we haven, we haven, we haven'. This is repeated three times; and the firkin is handed round between each shout.

Mrs Bray makes several ingenious suggestions about the meaning of the words. To me it seems likely that what she heard was simply 'Our nack; we have en', spoken in Devonshire accent. It is interesting, in passing, to note that, at that date, the labourers were harvesting with reap-hooks rather than with scythes.

Mrs Whitcombe has the additional information that, after the shout in the field, the nack, or neck, is taken to the farmhouse and hung in the kitchen till the following harvest. From various oral sources I have gathered that the nack had to be made from the last stalks of corn cut, and that originally they were woven into the form of a doll. This image was placed at the head of the table at the subsequent harvest home supper and was then hung in the kitchen or barn until after Christmas. When ploughing was resumed, presumably on Plough Monday, it was taken out to the field and ploughed under the first furrow.

The custom was evidently widespread in the county and is mentioned by almost every writer on folk-lore and local history, each offering some variation on the general theme. J. R. W. Coxhead says that at Ilfracombe, where the custom ended in the last years of the nineteenth century, the neck was made of 'four plaits of bearded wheat, about as thick as a man's wrist'. It must never be allowed to become wet on the journey to the farmstead; if it did, the man who carried it had to forfeit his drink in the celebrations that followed. The neck was burnt at the end of the following harvest. Ernest Martin records that, before giving the triumphal harvest cry, the man holding the neck would hold it near the ground and stoop as if in obeisance, his comrades doing likewise. In a ceremony that Sarah Hewett saw near Newton Abbot, the 'head-man' waved the neck above his head. After the company had all taken a drink of cider, they went to the farm kitchen and sat down to a generous supper, followed by merrymaking which went on till dawn. In this instance, the neck remained at the kitchen table for a year, after which it was fed to 'the best beast in the stall'. Sarah Hewett heard a harvest verse, shouted as the last corn was cut:

> We-ha-neck! we-ha-neck!
> Well aplowed! Well asowed!
> We've reaped! And we've a-mowed!
> Hurrah! hurrah! hurrah!

Well-a-cut – well abound!
Well-a-zot upon the ground!
We-ha-neck! we-ha-neck!
Hurrah! hurrah! hurrah!

This is very similar to a verse which I have heard quoted in many other parts of the West Country. She also supplies a version which incorporates the name of the farmer who has just finished his harvest. This would seem to me to have some significance, for Mrs Bray says that 'when the weather is fine, different parties of reapers, each stationed on some hill, may be heard for miles around, shouting, as it were, in answer to each other'. There was, indeed, considerable competition to get the harvest finished first, and the harvesters would take pride in letting their neighbours know that their farm had reached the end. A letter written to Alice Gomme, the famous folklorist, by her sister Agnes from Totnes, in August 1891, says:

there will be no chance of getting an old 'neck' as they are always destroyed when the next harvest comes. Mr Turner says the custom has quite gone out. They haven't had anything of the kind for years – but one could easily be made by an old man in the village, who used to make them. The Kirn Babby was a bunch of wheat and it had a kind of frock put on, and just the wheat ears peeping out. They don't know anything further about it.

Following on harvest, sometimes even before harvest is finished, comes Michaelmas (29 September), the traditional end of the farming year, and the date when farm tenancies change hands. Associated with that change were the hiring fairs, when farm and domestic workers sought new employment for the coming year. Sarah Hewett describes how women and girls, who wanted jobs as domestic servants, used to 'repair to the "fair-field" of the district and stand in rows on exhibition', awaiting inspection by potential employers. A pleasure fair followed the business. These fairs were also called 'Giglet Fairs', and in Holsworthy, Okehampton and South Molton the custom was observed until the last decade or so of the nineteenth century. However, this writer associates them with Lady-day and 'the first Saturday after Christmas-day', rather than Michaelmas.

Some of the autumn fairs, Tavistock for example, were known as

Goose Fairs, partly because goose was the chief dish at official functions associated with the event. Geese traditionally went stubbling – that is, picking up the stray grains in the harvest fields, in August and September, and were therefore at their best and plumpest around Michaelmas. Vast droves of geese used to walk from Devon to London, to market, taking weeks to complete the journey. At certain places en route shoemakers used to fashion small shoes of soft leather for the feet of any geese that became lame.

Barnstaple Fair was proclaimed by an announcement from the mayor, after a repast of spiced toast and ale in the council chamber. The occasion was marked by the hoisting of a glove on a decorated pole, as at Honiton and Exeter. Associated with this fair was a stag-hunt on Exmoor, the stag being turned loose on the second day of the fair near the village of Brendon. Brent Goose Fair, at the end of September, was another fair held 'under the glove'.

Bampton Pony fair is held on the last Thursday of October. It is a lively and picturesque occasion, which I have often attended, its main feature being the disposal of the year's crop of Exmoor ponies. Formerly it was held at Simonsbath, but was transferred to Bampton in 1850.

The end of October brings us to Hallowe'en and the bonfire season. It is, of course, the natural time for bonfires. Hedge-trimmings and the vegetative dross and debris of the year have to be disposed of somehow, and fire is a convenient way to do it. In former times it was also the season when surplus animals, which could not be fed in the coming winter, were slaughtered and salted down. The custom probably survives on some farms to the present day, in the practice of killing and curing a pig for home use each autumn.

On the Somerset side of Devon, and more commonly so on the Somerset side of the border, Hallowe'en is sometimes known as Punkie Night, the 'punkies' being turnip, mangold or pumpkin lanterns, hollowed out, a candle burning inside and shining through the grotesquely carved face. They are generally carried in procession by children on either Hallowe'en or 5 November. At Challacombe, Barbrook and Brayford, the custom of throwing 'lenshards' at doors was associated with Bonfire Night instead of Shrovetide. In some parts of Devon poor people used to visit the houses of the rich, begging a gift of fire, which was also accompanied by a small gift of money. This was on Hallowe'en.

On 5 November public or communal, rather than small private bonfires, were the custom, still followed in many places. Ottery St Mary has a particularly spectacular Bonfire Night celebration, during which flaming tar-barrels are carried through the crowd, to bring good luck. Boys perform in the afternoon, adults in the evening. Those who take part are mostly natives of Ottery. Visitors may join in, but generally think it too dangerous. Flames shoot fiercely from one end of the barrel, and, when it begins to disintegrate, showers of sparks, burning fragments of wood, and drops of melted tar rain down on the crowd. The sole protective clothing consists of rough mittens, which are pieces of sacking, soaked in water and stitched together on three sides. Some years ago, at the turn of the century, the police attempted to stop the custom. They arrived in force from Exeter, but the people of Ottery overturned their horse-drawn vehicle and flung it into the river. A particularly large bonfire, associated with a firework display, used to be lit in the Cathedral yard at Exeter.

Things often got out of hand and flaming tar-barrels were kicked about the streets. At their height, in the middle of the nineteenth century, the Exeter celebrations used to last for nearly 24 hours, and people were woken up at four o'clock in the morning by the firing of cannon. Youngsters used to parade the streets carrying guys and asking for money. A service was held in the Cathedral during the afternoon.

On Guy Fawkes day in 1850 an extraordinary procession attacking, apparently, both the Roman Catholic Church and the Oxford Movement, was held in Exeter; the programme calls it 'The Pontifical Procession on the Festival of Saint Guido Fawkes, Exeter'.

The Western Morning News of 16 October 1867 reported:

A few days ago the magistrates at Exeter decided to issue handbills with a view of counselling the public against taking part in the usually disgraceful and dangerous scenes which occur in the Cathedral yard on Guy Fawkes Night. A counter-placard has been posted calling on 'Young Exeter' to rally round the bonfire as usual, in fact to muster strongly on the occasion. Various rumours are afloat as to the effect the notice issued will have on the demonstration, though the whole matter really rests with the citizens themselves.

GOD SAVE THE QUEEN.

NO POPERY! NO POPERY!!

ORDER OF THE GRAND PROCESSION,
For the Evening of Nov. 5th.

Rocket Brigade, to clear the way.

Forty begging bare headed Friars,
With Torches in their Hands to throw a Light on the Darkness of the Scene, and their own Iniquity.

| Officers of the Inquisition, with Instruments of Torture for Heretics. | **The Inquisitor General on an Ass.**
The Pope, Pius the Ninth,
In Full Pontifical Robes, carried in a Chair of State, on Men's Shoulders.
The Cardinal Archbishop of Westminster,
Dr. WISEMAN, in full Robes. | Officers of the Inquisition, with Instruments of Torture for Heretics. |

The BAND playing the "ROGUE'S MARCH."

The Twelve Roman Catholic Bishops of England.

| Monks with Torches. | Bishop of Liverpool.
Bishop of Clifton.
Bishop of Birmingham.
Bishop of Plymouth.
Bishop of Southwark.
Bishop of Hagglestown. | Bishop of Beverly.
Bishop of Salford.
Bishop of Salop.
Bishop of Merioneth.
Bishop of Nottingham.
Bishop of Northampton. | Monks with Torches. |

Romish Priests,
But in the Disguise of Puseyite Clergymen of the Church of England ; as the Procession moves along, they will Chant the following old Song :—

" We stick firm to the loaves and fishes,
And hold fast with very great care ;
It is clear if we give up our LIVINGS,
We cannot yet live upon air."
Sing fal de lal, &c.

" The world no doubt hypocrites call us,
And bid us act honest and fair,
But what can we do with our wives then,
For *they* cannot yet live upon air."
Sing fal de lal, &c.

| Printer's Devils Tormenting. | **Renegade Members from the Church of England,**
With a Fool's Cap on their Head, a Bandage on their Eyes, a Padlock on their Lips, and a Halter about their Necks. | Printer's Devils Tormenting. |

The True and Faithful Citizens of Exeter will then follow and surround the Procession, giving expression to the Religious and Loyal Feelings of their Hearts, by shouting
" THE PROTESTANT CHURCH OF ENGLAND FOR EVER !
" DOWN WITH THE POPE AND POPERY !!
" THE QUEEN SUPREME !!!
" No PUSEYISM !!!!
" No TRAITORS WITHIN THE CHURCH !!!!!"

The Procession will enter the Cathedral Yard about Half-past Eight, and move round the Yard. The Procession will stop at intervals for those who like it, to kiss the Great Toe of the Pope, and then proceed to the Bonfire, where the Pope and Cardinal will be hanged on a Gibbet, and burnt with all the indignity heaped upon them which *their late daring* and impudent, but at the same time contemptible usurpation of power over the British people deserves.

The Bishops and the Inquisitor General, will then be kicked round the Bonfire, and then kicked into it, the Band playing GOD SAVE THE QUEEN, and the people singing—

" Frustrate their Popish tricks,
" Confound their politics,
" GOD SAVE THE QUEEN !"

Brixham has a local legend that William of Orange, hearing the bells of the parish Church ringing out at sea on 5 November 1688, and thinking it was to welcome him, landed. But in fact they had always been rung on that day since the discovery of the Gunpowder Plot in 1605.

Bideford used to elect a mock mayor, 'The Mayor of Shamickshire', on 9 November. Another man, dressed as a woman, was appointed to be his wife, and the pair were carried round to the town's public houses, where they made a series of speeches for as long as they were capable. A good deal of horse-play, including blazing tar-barrels, seems often to have been a feature of the evening.

Later in the month, on the fourth Thursday of November, Moretonhampstead held a feast in honour of St Andrew, to whom its church is dedicated. The celebrations followed the usual Devonshire pattern, with races, sports (including wrestling), sideshows and stalls. It was customary for the wealthier homes to keep open house and to serve a dish similar to Morchard pestle-pie. It was called Gammon Pie, but was a huge affair containing legs of pork, whole fowls and generous quantities of other ingredients.

A prominent feature of the Christmas celebrations in Devon was the Ashen Faggot. It seems to have been regarded as a substitute for the Yule Log and was used in a number of party activities. The faggot consisted of a mass of ash twigs and small branches, bound together with as many withies as possible. At Christmas it was hauled into the house with considerable ceremony, and pushed into position on the hearth, in the great chimney-place which is such a feature of Devon farm and manor houses. As it burnt, the withies snapped one by one. Each was the signal for the host to call for another round of cider, which increased the conviviality as the evening wore on.

As usual the custom showed slight variations from place to place. In one widespread version, the young people in the party each chose a bond, and the owner of the bond which snapped first would be the first to marry in the coming year. Sometimes the ashen faggot was bound with chains, which must have reduced the opportunities for both drinking and divination. In another version, the faggot was bound with nine bonds. As they snapped and more cider circulated, anyone who opted out of the drinking bout was expected to pay for the next nine drinks. Some of the faggots were very large – as much as seven or eight feet long, and weighed a hundredweight or two.

The traditional reason for using ash is said to be that Mary and Joseph lit a fire of ash twigs to keep their baby warm at the first Christmas. The ash was, however, long considered a sacred tree and often used in charms and healing. When the old open fireplaces began to be superseded by smaller grates and stoves, the tradition still lingered to the extent of cutting ash logs at the appropriate time – which was, incidentally, Christmas Eve. A utilitarian reason which underlies the use of ash is, of course, that the wood will burn well when it is green. From some reminiscences, one can gather that the wood for the Ashen faggot had indeed to be cut green when the faggot was made, on Christmas Eve or just before.

The Ashen Faggot was a local substitute for the Yule Log, and in parts of the county there was also a substitute for mistletoe, a small furze bush 'dipped in water, powdered with flour and studded all over with holly berries'. It was termed a 'kissing bush'.

At Exeter, in the 1820s, or thereabouts, church choirs apparently spent most of the night before Christmas parading around the town and singing carols outside the houses of the principal citizens. Cups of tea and coffee sustained them through the small cold hours; stronger beverages and bowls of soup were also supplied by appreciative householders. They finished about six o'clock in the morning and made their way to the Cathedral, where the doors were opened at 6.30 and morning service began at seven. The choir boys sang in the Minstrels' Gallery by candlelight.

Christmas Mumming Plays are known to have been performed at Exeter, Tiverton, Stoke Gabriel, Bow, Broad Clyst, Ashburton, Dartington, Silverton, Bovey Tracey and Sidmouth, but few details have been preserved.

11   Charms, Cures and Traditional Beliefs

CLAIMS TO FORETELL the future will always attract an audience. That divination by various methods should feature largely in the folklore of Devon, as of other counties, is not surprising.

On Dartmoor, near Deanscombe, is an old mine-working called Clakeywell Pool, where it is said that, on certain nights, you could hear the name of the next person in the parish who was going to die announced in a loud voice.

The church porch also played an important part in divination. There used to be a widespread belief that anyone who waited there at midnight on Midsummer Eve would see the souls of parishioners going into the church. Those that failed to come out would die during the coming year. If any watcher fell asleep, he, too would die before the year was out.

Mrs Bray mentions two brothers from Tavistock, who peeped through the keyhole of the local church at midnight on Midsummer Eve, to see the souls of those who were to die. 'Their imagination was so worked up that they fancied they saw themselves in this funereal procession.' Both died soon afterwards.

At Bridestowe villagers assembled at the church gate. One young man, told by his friends that his spirit had entered the church and had not returned, died soon afterwards at harvest time, following a very minor and brief illness. It seems likely that fright had something to do with his death.

Girls or boys wanting to know whom they were going to marry went to the church porch at half-past midnight on St Valentine's Eve, with a handful of hempseed. On the stroke of half-past twelve they started homewards, sowing hempseed on either side and repeating:

> Hempseed I sow, hempseed I sow,
> She/he that will my true love be,
> Come, rake this hemp seed after me.

A wraith of their lover then appeared, wrapped in a winding-sheet, and raked up the hempseed. The custom has long been discontinued, which is just as well. Anyone rash enough to try it might be arrested on suspicion of possessing cannabis!

Valentine's Day was a significant date for lovers. If a girl peeped through the keyhole of her front door at first light and saw a cock and hen together, it meant that she would be married before the end of the year. On St Valentine's Eve a girl could take the alphabet, each letter written on a small separate piece of paper, and place them face downwards in a bowl of water. A pair of shoes were put on the floor in front of the bowl in the form of the letter T. This verse was then recited:

> I place my shoes like the letter T,
> In hopes my true love I shall see,
> In his apparel and his array,
> As he is now and every day.

The charm was repeated three times, the shoes being moved each time. In the morning some of the letters would be found turned over, face upwards; these supplied the initials of the boy's name. The same divination could also be tried on Midsummer Eve.

Girls would also pick yarrow from a man's grave and place it under their pillows, murmuring:

> Yarrow, sweet yarrow, the first I have found,
> And in the name of Jesus I pluck it from the ground.

They would then hope to dream of their lovers. When the first new moon after Midsummer appeared, a girl would address it:

> All hail, new moon, all hail to thee!
> I prithee, new moon, reveal to me
> This night who shall my true love be
> Who he is and what he wears,
> And what he does all months and years.

Here is a charm involving the new moon, which predates the arrival of tights! A girl who removed one stocking, when she saw the first new moon of the year, and then ran across a field, found between her big toe and the next a hair the same colour as her lover's.

If a rose were plucked on Midsummer Day, packed away and left undisturbed, it was said to be as fresh as ever on Christmas Day. If the girl who had picked it then wore the flower to church, her lover would come and take it from her.

To learn one's future fate, an empty room was prepared by placing various objects in it. On Midsummer Eve, at midnight, the man who wanted to know his future was led blindfolded into the room. The first article he touched provided a clue. A basin of water meant that he was in danger of drowning; a ring that he would be married; and so on.

A girl who hoped to see the spirit of her future husband went to bed before midnight, took off her left garter and tied it round her right stocking, saying:

> This knot I knit, to know the thing I know not yet,
> That I may see the man that shall my husband be,
> How he goes, and what he wears,
> And what he does all days and years.

The man would then appear to her in her dreams.

To bring back an unfaithful lover, a girl would take the clean blade-bone of a lamb and, using a white ribbon, tie it as high as possible in the chimney of her bedroom. With a penknife borrowed from a bachelor, she would then stab it on nine consecutive nights, each time in a different place, saying meanwhile:

> Tis not this bone I means to stick,
> But my lover's heart I means to prick,
> Wishing him neither rest nor sleep
> Till unto me he comes to speak.

At the end of the nine days the lover would return, probably nursing a cut finger or some other wound, which he wanted bound up.

Country people usually know the method of divination by the Bible, which involves opening the Book at random, and trying to find some clue to the future in the first words that meet the eye. It was a method popular in Devon, and one which I have seen practised more than once. Sometimes the Bible might be used in casting of a horoscope. The seeker read the 49th chapter of *Genesis*, which summarises the characters of the sons of Jacob, and picked the one which he thought suited him best.

An extraordinary variety of articles have been used for divination in Devonshire. Four-leaved clovers and even-leaved ash leaves were regarded as effective in revealing a girl's true love, if the right charm (of which the are several versions) were repeated. At noon on Midsummer Day a hen's egg broken into a tumbler will, on careful examination, provide a clue to the social position or occupation of a future husband.

Girls used to collect crab-apples and lay them out on the loft floor to form the initials of their lovers. Later, at dawn on Old Michaelmas Day, they would examine them again, and the most faithful young man would be he whose apples were in the best condition.

Divining by apple-peel is a well-known device. The girl peeled a large apple without breaking the rind, stood in the centre of a room, and threw the peel with her right hand over her left shoulder. As it fell on the floor, it formed the initial of her future husband's name. This was supposed to be effective only on the feast of Saints Simeon and Jude (28 October), and there was an appropriate rhyme, which I had heard, but have forgotten, to recite during the ceremony.

Another apple charm involved holding the fruit in the right hand, while combing one's hair with the left and looking in a mirror. The lover was then supposed to appear – to the sharp-sighted or the imaginative – looking over the girl's shoulder into the mirror.

Hazel nuts were also used in divination. At a party each girl put a hazel nut on the bar of a grate. The first nut to catch fire indicated the first girl to marry. If a nut cracked before blazing, its owner would be jilted. If it smouldered, the girl would have an unhappy life, perhaps even a short one, and would never marry. If the nut jumped off the bar, it meant that she would travel instead of marrying.

If a girl were lucky enough to marry, all sorts of customs and traditions surrounded the wedding ceremony. To begin with, the bride could carry a small packet of bread and cheese, to give to the first woman or girl she met on leaving the church. She could also take a small clove of garlic in her pocket, and a sprig or two of rue and rosemary in her bouquet, to bring good luck in her married life. It was unlucky if the newly-wed couple saw a toad or frog on their way from the church, or if a cat, dog or hare passed between them (though for a hare to do so would be a most unlikely event). A well-known rhyme describes the best day of the week to have a wedding:

> Monday for wealth;
> Tuesday for health;
> Wednesday's the best day of all;
> Thursday for crosses;
> Friday for losses;
> Saturday no luck at all.

Mrs Sarah Orledge, of Exeter, who recited this for me in about 1948, added,

> The best day is Sunday.

At Lynton, young men used to prevent the bride and groom from leaving the churchyard by fastening lengths of rope, decorated with flowers, across the gate. The bridegroom had to scatter a handful of coins, for which the young men scrambled, allowing the rope to fall.

Mrs Orledge told me, in the late 1940s, that Tuesday and Wednesday were considered the luckiest days of the week; Friday the unluckiest. The only lucky time on Thursday was the hour before sunrise.

She said that certain actions are lucky or unlucky on certain days of the week. For instance, it is unlucky to turn a feather-bed or cut one's nails on a Sunday, or to move house on a Friday. It is very lucky, though, to be born on a Sunday. Children weaned on Good Friday always do well. Good Friday, as we have seen, is a traditional day for sowing and planting, but the first three days of March – the 'blind days – are so unlucky that no seed should be sown then. Sarah Hewitt compiled a list of 'Evil Days', when no new enterprise should be undertaken:

January 3, 4, 5, 9, 11; February 13, 17, 19; March 13, 15, 16; April 5, 14; May 8, 14; June 6; July 16, 19; August 8, 16; September 1, 15, 16; October 16; November 15, 16; December 6, 7, 11.

A white horse is considered to be lucky, if the proper formalities are observed on seeing it, according to old Jack Christow, born at Barnstaple, whom I knew in the 1930s. For instance, one has to spit three times, standing at each attempt where the spittle fell on the previous occasion. Or you can mark the sole of your shoe with a white cross. On the first day of the month, say 'White Rabbit'. Walking under a ladder, or seeing an ambulance, are considered unlucky by children, but any evil influence may be avoided by holding one's collar until a four-legged animal appears.

Many charms and traditional beliefs had a medical purpose. Wart cures were, and still are, numerous in every county. Here is one recorded for Devon, set to rough verse.

> Take an eel and cut off the head.
> Rub the warts with the blood of the head.
> Then bury the head in the ground.
> When the head is rotten the warts fall off.

The necessity of burying something – such as a beef-steak or, in this instance, an eel's head – is a common feature of wart cures; and it is probable that warts will disappear naturally, in about the time that it takes for meat to decompose in the soil.

Another wart cure involves taking from a running stream small stones equal to the number of warts. Put them in a clean white bag and throw onto the highway. The warts will be transferred to whoever picks up the bag. Probably the most efficacious part of the cure, however, is to wash the warts in strong vinegar for seven consecutive mornings. Mrs Orledge knew this one.

Theo Brown, the Devonshire folklorist, wrote in 1962 that she had heard an interesting case of wart-charming from Mrs D. K. Brackenbury of the Ring of Bells, North Bovey. It concerns her mare 'Double Brown'.

We bought her at Exeter horse sales in February 1956, when skeleton-thin and covered on her under-sides with large warts. Under her near forearm there was a large bunch of the bleeding variety, and she stood in a pool of blood. I could not let her go to the butchers, and bought her under the hammer for 35 guineas. Mr V. S. advised me to dress the warts daily with acri-flavine emulsion (which I did, but only those under her arm). Then Mr Chudley of Greenawell Farm told me that he had had animals cured of warts by an old man from Westcott (whose name I cannot remember).

When Mrs Brackenbury visited Chagford, the old man was out:

I told Mr Chudley, who had a word with the old man, who, in turn, said it did not matter, as he could cure them by 'remote control', so to speak. I continued to dress the warts under the mare's arm, which gradually peeled off and cleared up – there is not a vestige of a scar there now – but what is even more remarkable, so also did all the other warts from under her belly, between her thighs, etc., which I had not touched at all with the dressing.

Warts are infectious and one cannot help thinking that the acriflavine, together with careful attention, played a part.

Curing cramp is more difficult, but a cramp ring could be made from three nails or screws from a coffin, dug up out of a churchyard. Some people still carry a cork in their pocket, and tuck it into the foot of the bed at night to ease rheumatism, a related complaint.

A potato in the pocket is another cure for rheumatism. This is probably still used by Devon villagers. To be entirely effective, it must first be put there, unknown to the wearer, by a member of the opposite sex.

Whooping cough could be relieved, it was said, by putting a slice of new bread into the mouth of a donkey, and passing the afflicted child three times over and under the animal's body.

Toothache was traditionally cured by carrying in one's pocket a tooth bitten from a skull. Writing on 8 January 1833, Mrs Bray said:

> Only this very day, had I not been too lazy to stir from my room, I might have had the gratification of seeing a scramble after old teeth in a skull. For Miss Elizabeth Greco ... asked me if I knew what was going on in the churchyard, so many persons, old and young, were thronging to it. Scarcely had she spoken when Mary Colling came running in and said if I wanted to see an old custom she had told me of I had only to go to the churchyard, for several skulls having, in making a grave, been dug near the remains of Orgar's tomb, there was going on such a scene as she had never before witnessed; men and women tugging with their mouths at every tooth they could find left to cure them. . . .

She adds that toothache was a very common complaint around Tavistock, 'Where it is common to see *young* women with not a sound front tooth in their heads; and many a handsome face is thus spoilt and looks old before its time.' She attributes it to the drinking of the very acid local cider.

Another cure was a mixture of two quarts of rat's broth (presumably made by stewing rats), one ounce of camphor, and one ounce of essence of cloves – a teaspoonful to be taken three times a day. A third method was to cut one's finger and toe nails, wrap the parings in tissue paper, and insert the package in a slit made in the bark of an ash tree before sunrise. This was said to cure toothache for life!

Toads seem to have been a remedy for a wide range of ailments. They were useful creatures to the white witch. The contents of the creature's head were inserted into a leather pouch one inch square, which is placed inside a white silk bag. This was laid on the stomach of a patient in bed with a skin disease. On the third day the invalid would be sick, after which the bag was buried, and, as it decayed, the person recovered.

Another technique was to burn several large toads in a vessel in which their ashes stood no risk of contamination from any other substance. The ashes were then stored in a wide-mouthed jar, closely corked and kept dry. One teaspoonful taken in milk for nine mornings when the moon was waxing was said to cure dropsy.

Toads reduced to a 'brown crisp mass' and then pounded to powder, produced a substance used as snuff and said to cure nose-bleeding! Toad ashes, prepared according to a minutely-described ritual, were also used to cure bleeding in other parts of the body, if sewn into a small silk bag and placed on the heart.

One recipe quoted by Sarah Hewett is for the fine old Devon malady, 'zweemyheadedness'. The head is washed with plenty of old rum (the remains, presumably, of what caused the zweemyheadedness in the first place), and the back and face with sour wine. Flannel is worn next to the skin, and a packet of salt carried in the left-hand pocket.

To cure 'thrush', the head of a live duck has to be placed in the child's mouth, so that it inhales the creature's breath. Or three rushes from a swiftly-flowing stream were passed through the child's mouth, one by one, and thrown into the rivulet. The 'thrush' was then carried away with the rushes. The second of these cures was probably less alarming for the child. To prevent a recurrence, the 8th Psalm had to be read over the patient three times a day, three days a week, for the next three weeks. Here we see a powerful combination of the Holy Scriptures and the traditional importance of the number three, especially three times three.

Baring-Gould describes a more drastic remedy. He says that the clerk of Lydford church used to carry children suffering from 'thrush' up the church tower, and hold them over the battlements of each of the pinnacles in turn, while he recited the Lord's Prayer. This was one of the ways by which he augmented his income.

Mrs H. P. Whitcombe records an instance, in 1854, of a young woman, subject to fits, who attended church service accompanied by 30 young men.

Service over, she sat in the church porch, and, as the young men passed out, each of them dropped a penny in her lap, until the thirtieth came, who took up the 29 pence and substituted half-a-crown. With this coin in her hand she walked three times round the Communion table; and afterwards she had the half-crown made into a ring; by the wearing of which she believed she would recover her health.

The young woman must have been very popular, if she could persuade 30 men to co-operate with her in the experiment.

Mrs Whitcombe adds that a sexton had been bribed to allow a patient to enter a church at midnight; he crept three times under the Communion-table to effect a cure. And she quotes a letter from a Tavistock parishioner, who wrote to the vicar, Mr Bray, in 1835, for permission to borrow the churchyard key, so that he could go at midnight 'to cut off three bits of lead about the size of a half-farthing, each from three different shuts (spouts), for the cure of fits'.

She gives, too, an account of a woman, 'respectably attired and accompanied by an elderly gentleman', who, in 1855, was admitted to the cemetery at Plymouth. The woman, who had a goitre, rubbed her neck three times each way on either side of the grave of the last corpse buried there.

To cure ague, when a sufferer feels that an attack is imminent, he should go to the nearest crossroads at midnight, on five nights, and there bury a new-laid egg.

Many cures require the proper words to be repeated at the proper time. A cure for scalds and burns, which several writers on Devon folk-lore quote, and which I myself have heard, runs:

> Three wise men came out of the east,
> One brought fire and two brought frost.
> Out fire! In frost!
> In the name of the Father, Son and Holy Ghost.

Another version substitutes 'angels' for 'wise men'.
A rhyme recited to cure a sprain was:

> Bone to bone, and vein to vein,
> And vein turn to thy rest again.

It was said to have been recited by Jesus to cure his horse, when it tripped and sprained its leg, as He was riding to Jerusalem.

To staunch a flow of blood the following rhyme was said to be effective:

> Jesus was born in Bethlehem,
> Baptised in river Jordan, when
> The water was wild in the wood,
> The person was just and good;
> God spake, and the water stood;
> And so shall now thy blood –
> In the name of the Father, Son and Holy Ghost, Amen.

The request for permission to cut lead from the rainwater spouts of a church to cure fits illustrates the importance traditionally attached to the church and its furnishings. It was believed almost within living memory that gratings from stone statues of saints, scattered at the entrance to pigsties and cattle shippons, would ward off disease. And in Lydford it was thought that a heart made of lead, cut from the frames of church windows, would cure a woman of sore breasts. She had to wear it as an amulet.

May dew was a pleasanter remedy and much easier to obtain. It had to be collected in the early morning from a churchyard and was said to be a cure for tuberculosis or consumption, as it used to be called, and was also much in demand as a cosmetic.

Death was only too commonplace in the countryside before the days of the National Health Service, and those who lived out the life span of seventy years were not numerous. There was a natural preoccupation with death, and many charms and traditional beliefs relate to it. To induce the end to come easily, all boxes and locks in the house where the person was dying had to be unfastened. Also, the bed was moved so that no beam was immediately overhead, to impede the passing spirit. It was held that a person must not be allowed to die on a mattress of goose-feathers and a plate of salt placed on the breast of a corpse was supposed to help the soul on its journey.

To be the first buried in a newly consecrated churchyard was thought extremely unlucky. Sometimes a dog was buried there first, or a stranger. Many years ago, at Bovey Tracey, the local people refused to use a new churchyard for a long time, until a stranger had been interred there. On the other hand, to be buried in a grave with the corpse of a still-born child was thought very lucky. Such a grave was often held open, or was re-opened, to take the next corpse in the parish.

The prophetic pool of North Tawton is a pit in the grounds of Bath House, usually dry but occasionally, especially in dry weather, filled with water from an erratic little spring. One version of its legend says that it becomes full 'before the death of any great prince or other strange accident', but another associates its filling with death or disaster to the local family of de Bath.

The White Bird of the Oxenhams belongs to the Oxenham family of Zeal Monachorum; one, John Oxenham, accompanied Sir Francis Drake on a voyage to the Spanish Main in 1572, and was the first Englishman to launch a ship on the Pacific. According to the legend, just before an Oxenham is to die, a white bird, or, in some versions, a white-breasted bird, is seen hovering nearby.

The story seems to begin with a Margaret Oxenham, who lived at some remote time (for all the versions that I have seen start with 'Once upon a time'), and was heiress to considerable property. She had decided to marry a neighbouring landowner, Bertram, when, in an accident, he received a blow on the head which made him an imbecile. At first inconsolable, she was eventually courted by another knight, Sir John of Roxamcave. On the wedding morning, as she was making her preparations, a white bird appeared and hovered over her. Later, as she stood at the altar by the side of her groom, the mad Bertram rushed in and stabbed her.

Apart from this tragedy, the tradition seems to be based on a rare tract entitled, *A True Relation of an Apparition in the likenesse of a Bird with a white breast, that appeared hovering over the Death-Beds of some of the children of Mr. James Oxenham, of Sale Monachorum, Devon, Gent.* published in 1635. In it the chief source seems to be a letter, dated 1632, in which a Mr James Howell supplies the inscription he saw on 'a huge Marble' in a stone-cutters' yard by St Dunstan's in Fleet Street, London. The inscription recorded that the bird with the white breast had been seen fluttering around four members of the Oxenham family, namely a John Oxenham, his little son James, his sister Mary and his mother Elizabeth.

Baring-Gould criticized this tradition. The marble, he points out, has never been found, and was never erected in the local church of

South Tawton. The names and approximate dates of the persons mentioned do not tally with those of the Oxenham family as shown by records of the seventeenth century. He is inclined to think that the whole story was a fabrication by James Howell, imprisoned in the Fleet for debt and endeavouring to raise enough cash to buy his way out. However, once the legend became known it was difficult to arrest it, and there are subsequent references to dying Oxenhams seeing the bird of ill-omen in 1743, and 1892, and at other dates.

A robin entering any house, and showing no anxiety to leave, but sitting and crying 'weep, weep', is a sure presage of death. Magpies in Devon are mostly bad omens, and to see four at a time means death. The notion of telling the bees of a death in the household is very old and is known in most English counties, but in Devon it was thought necessary to turn round the bee-hives, so that they faced in the opposite direction, on the day of the funeral.

Two old Devon charms may strike us as having intriguing possibilities:

'Anoint your eyes for three days with the combined juices of the herbs dill, vervain and St John's wort, and the spirits of the air will become visible to you.'

And this sinister one told me by Mrs Orledge:

'Sew into a garment which is worn next to the skin a long thin herring-bone. As the bone dries up, or withers, so will the person wearing it gradually pine away and die.'

It would seem to be a recipe for getting rid of unwanted husbands.

12   The World of Nature

THE TRADITION of the penned Cuckoo, so widespread in Somerset, is apparently not known in Devon. The bird is generally associated with good luck charms. People would say:

For good luck, run three times in a circle, with the sun, on first hearing the cuckoo in spring.

Or, run as fast as possible to the nearest gate and sit on it. Otherwise you will become lazy and feel no inclination to do any work until the cuckoo comes again, the following spring. We can surmise that many people have been neglecting to sit on the top of five-barred gates in the April sunshine!

To hear the first cry of the cuckoo on one's right was lucky; on the left unlucky.

> When the cuckoo comes to the bare thorn,
> Sell your cow and buy your corn;
> But when he comes to the full bit,
> Sell your corn and buy you sheep.

The 'bare thorn' implies a backward spring, with little grass for livestock in April, when the cuckoo arrives; hence the advice is sound.

Rhymes about the cuckoo's call, beginning in April and ending, as a rule, in June, are commonplace, but this Devonshire version contains a warning:

> He who in July the cuckoo's voice doth hear
> Will die before he comes another year.

The fact that ravens have a birthday is not so well known. The date was emphatically said by Jack Christow and other old Devon countrymen to be Good Friday.

It was popularly believed that on Easter Eve rabbits laid eggs. And if the left leg were removed from one of these creatures, snared in a churchyard at midnight on Easter Eve, it would bring good luck to its possessor. The belief that cocks lay eggs is also widespread, and I have often been shown 'cocks' eggs', which are the very small eggs produced by hens at the beginning or end of the laying period.

It is, of course, unlucky to kill a robin, or a swallow, and to take their eggs results in one's little finger growing crooked.

Devon has several curious beliefs about adders. On Dartmoor, where they are often numerous, a farmer told Mrs Bray that he always carried an ash stick. When he saw an adder, he drew a circle around it with his stick. The adder, he said, would never cross the circle; it would rather go through a fire. This man said that a collar of woven ash twigs, placed around the neck of an animal which had been bitten by an adder, would effect a cure. Baring-Gould remembered how a moorman healed a dog attacked by an adder; he held the animal's head over a cauldron in which elder-flowers were being boiled.

As elsewhere, snake skin was held to have certain curative properties and to be particularly useful in extracting thorns. It was used as a repellent, rather than an attraction, and was applied to the opposite side of the body to the wound. Thus, to remove a thorn embedded in the front of one's finger, the snake's skin was applied to the back. If applied to the front, it could force the thorn right through the finger. Jack Christow used to keep a snake's skin tucked in the peak of his cap – for luck, he said.

The smooth mistletoe is regarded as an exceptionally unlucky plant in Devon, and there was a tradition that in ancient times farmers were forbidden to allow mistletoe to grow in their orchards. Sarah Hewett quotes an instance of an orchard, half in Devon and half in Somerset, where mistletoe grew profusely on trees in the Somerset half, but refused to grow in Devon, despite attempts to cultivate it.

Even the cheerful primrose could be unlucky in certain circumstances. Sarah Hewett once saw a small girl severely punished for bringing a bunch into a farmhouse in early spring. Her mother was reacting to an old tradition that the number of chicken reared that season would be equal to the number of primroses in the bunch.

A handful of fleabane burnt each day during summer will keep house-flies out of the house, and St John's wort, provided it was gathered on St John's Day or on a Friday, was a protection against thunderbolts, fire and evil spirits. The flowers and leaves were dried and placed in a jar hung by a window. Or they could be placed around the neck, to ward off mental illness or as a love charm.

In times past a number of Devon villages had 'Dancing Trees', around which the villagers danced and held revels on festival days. Baring-Gould mentions several still in existence in his time, though they tended to be very old and decayed. One, of which he gives a detailed account, was the Meavy Oak:

This tree till within this century was, on the village festival, surrounded with poles, a platform was erected above the tree, the top of which was kept clipped flat, like a table, and a set of stairs erected, by means of which the platform could be reached. On the top a table and chairs were placed, and feasting took place.

He offers the additional information that it was also known as the Gospel Oak, because preaching used to take place from the steps of the cross erected under its shadow. The cross, he considered, had been placed there to provide Christian significance for a spot already regarded as sacred.

There was a similar flat-topped tree near Dunsford, on the road between Exeter and Okehampton. It was said locally that the Fulford family, of Great Fulford, held their lands on condition that they dined once a year on top of the tree; the occasion was also marked by a dance around the tree for all their tenants.

Trebursaye, near Launceston, used to have an oak, and dancing was held regularly on top of it. The custom was apparently discontinued when a woman fell off and broke her neck. Stories of her ghost soon multiplied. Horses as well as people apparently were scared by seeing it dancing on the tree. Eventually the vicar of Launceston was called in to exorcise the phantom.

Another Dancing Tree near Lifton had a tradition of dances held on its top. It was always supposed to be the first tree in the neighbourhood to come into leaf. When it fell down, its name was perpetuated by the Royal Oak Inn, nearby.

The Cross Tree at Moretonhampstead was a pollarded elm, its branches trained horizontally to form a kind of platform. On special occasions a more substantial floor was raised above it and dancing took place. An eyewitness of a celebration there on 28 August 1801, wrote:

The Cross Tree floored and seated round, with a platform, railed on each side, from the top of an adjoining wall to the tree, and a flight of steps in the garden for the company to ascend. After passing the platform they enter under a grand arch made of boughs. There is sufficient room for thirty persons to sit around, and six couples to dance, besides the orchestra.

This tree was seriously damaged by a gale on 1 October 1891, but its stump was still vigorous at the turn of the century. It was evidently not as old as some of the other dancing trees, for it had managed to force its way through the masonry at the base of a medieval village cross.

A curious legend was attached to a group of trees in Tewin, Herts, churchyard. There were nine of them – six ash and three sycamore – all splitting into fragments the tomb of a Lady Anne Grimstone. It was said that to her dying day she denied the resurrection of the body and might as well believe that nine trees would spring from her body.

Sarah Hewett mentions a thorn bush which, like the famous Glastonbury Thorn, blooms at Christmas, in the grounds of Clooneaven House, Lynmouth.

Cats, as well as being associated with witches, often feature in weather lore:

When the cat in February lies in the sun,
She will creep under the grate in March.

An old cat playing like a kitten is a reliable sign of rain. There is
a strange tradition that May kittens will never thrive, which seems
nonsense, for May, with warm summer weather ahead, would appear
to be the best month of the year for any animal to be born. Devon
people said, however, that they should be drowned immediately, to
avoid bad luck and disaster.

It is similarly unlucky to have a baby and a kitten in the house
at the same time, or for a cat to sit on a baby's cot or cradle, as it
would draw the baby's breath. Treading on a cat's tail was also
unlucky (at least, for the cat!).

Most countrymen can predict approaching rain or storms by
watching the behaviour of rooks. When the birds linger around the
rookery or return home at mid-day, rough weather is coming; if they
go far afield, the weather will be fine.

A strange omen, that could hardly apply in most counties other
than Devon, is: 'If the deer rise up dry and lie down dry on St
Bullion's Day (4 July), it is a sign that there will be a good goose
harvest.'

Signs of rain, from the evidence of birds, include:

Swallows, martins and other larger creatures, such as herons, flying
low;
peacocks calling;
rooks making more noise than usual;
ducks quacking loudly.

Clover stalks standing upright, the flowers of African marigold,
pimpernel and sorrel closing, and the flowers of the cinquefoil
opening, are held to be signs of rain.

Much Devon weather lore is more or less identical with that in
other counties and follows the dictates of observation and common
sense: 'If wind in daytime shift from north to south-west or south,
rain is pretty sure to follow; if, on the other hand, it shift from south
or south-west to north, the weather will probably clear up.'

Now that we can see weather maps daily on television, we can
appreciate that these observations sum up pretty accurately the

behaviour of the winds around depressions and anti-cyclones. When, after a wet and windy day, the wind dies down at sunset, Devon folk say that the wind has gone to sleep with the sun, and so predict finer weather. This too is usually correct. Those sayings which try to predict the weather for the coming year from the weather on a certain day are naturally less accurate. They include:

If Christmas Day falls on a Monday there will be a hard winter and a year of storms and gales; if New Year's Day is on a Saturday there will follow a hot summer, a late harvest and good garden crops; good weather on St Paul's Day (26 January) means good weather all the year; a storm on 2 February betokens an early spring, but a fine, clear day means that spring will be late; pleasant, productive years follow rain in February or a frost-free day on 10 March; thunder on 1 April brings good crops of corn and hay; fogs in April foretell a poor wheat crop.

Several sayings mention the advantages of a cold May and the dangers of a wet one, though this seems against common sense, for plenty of rain during the growing season is surely what is needed. Nevertheless:

> A cold May is kindly, and fills the barns kindly;

but

> For a warm, wet May
> The parsons do pray.
> For then death-fees
> Do come their way.

The tradition of 40 days of rain after St Swithin's (15 July) is extended in Devon from the 15th to 1 July. A hot summer is held to predict a very cold January, and a warm October foretells a cold February. 'For every fog in October, a snow in winter'. And October gives a foretaste of the weather for the following March.

There is, of course much weather lore attached to the moon. A new moon 'with the old one in her arms' betokens wet weather. So does a new moon 'on her back'. 'A Saturday's new moon once in seven years is once too soon', for it inevitably brings much rain. Most seeds should be sown when the moon is waxing.

Countrymen living on Dartmoor near the river Dart would, according to Baring-Gould, observe, 'Us shall have bad weather mister, I hear the Broadstones a-crying'. The Broadstones are granite boulders in the river bed, and the crying comes from the sound of the wind in the tortuous glen. The observation is probably accurate.

Notes

1 *The Devil in Devon* (pages 16-27)

THE DEVIL'S LIMEKILN, Kevin Crossley-Holland, *Pieces of Land,* 1972, 226; Jack Hurley, *Legends of Exmoor,* 1973, 41.

THE DEVIL'S CAUSEWAY, J. R. W. Coxhead, *The Devil in Devon,* 1967, 7.

DUNKERY HILL, Jack Hurley, *Legends of Exmoor,* 1973, 43

THE VALLEY OF ROCKS, Kingsley Palmer, *Oral Folk-Tales of Wessex,* 1973, 108.

THE DEVIL'S FRYING-PAN, S. Baring-Gould, *A Book of the West,* 1899, 159.

DEVIL'S TOR, S. Baring-Gould, *A Book of the West,* 1899, 171.

HEL TOR, J. R. W. Coxhead, *The Devil in Devon,* 1967, 8-9.

THE DEVIL AT BRENT TOR, Mrs Bray, *Traditions, etc., of Devonshire,* 1838, Vol 2, 281-285.

MOVING CHURCH BUILDING STONES, Rev. G. S. Tyack, *Lore and Legend of the English Church,* 1899, 21; J. R. W. Coxhead, *The Devil in Devon,* 1967, 9.

THE DEVIL'S STONE, J. R. W. Coxhead, *The Devil in Devon,* 1967, 8.

DEVIL'S BOULDER AT SHEBBEAR, J. R. W. Coxhead, *The Devil in Devon*, 1967, 7; J. R. W. Coxhead, *Old Devon Customs*, 1953, 15-16.

THE DEVIL AT EAST WORLINGTON, J. R. W. Coxhead, *The Devil in Devon*, 1967, 7.

THE DEVIL AND BIDEFORD BRIDGE, J. R. W. Coxhead, *The Devil in Devon*, 1967, 9.

THE DEVIL AND SIR FRANCIS DRAKE, J. R. W. Coxhead, *The Devil in Devon*, 1967, 9; S. Baring-Gould, *A Book of the West*, 1899, 359.

THE DEVIL AT LUSTLEIGH CHURCH, J. R. W. Coxhead, *The Devil in Devon*, 1967, 10; S. Baring-Gould, *A Book of Dartmoor*, 1900, 173-4.

THE DEVIL AT TORQUAY, Mrs H. P. Whitcombe, *Bygone Days in Devonshire & Cornwall*, 1874, 99-102.

THE WILD HUNT, or YETH HOUNDS, Mrs H. P. Whitcombe, *Bygone Days in Devonshire & Cornwall*, 1874, 49-51; *Choice Notes from Notes & Queries*, 1859, 169-70.

THE DEVIL AT SHAUGH BRIDGE, S. H. Burton, *Devon Villages*, 1973, 129.

THE DEVIL'S HOOF-MARKS, J. R. W. Coxhead, *The Devil in Devon*, 1967, 12; also Personal Communications (JWS of Taunton, in the 1950s).

THE DEVIL CAUSES STORM AT WIDECOMBE, J. R. W. Coxhead, *The Devil in Devon*, 1967, 10; S. H. Burton, *Devon Villages*, 1973, 137; Mrs H. P. Whitcombe, *Bygone Days in Devonshire & Cornwall*, 1874, 51-3.

THE DEVIL AND BISHOP BRONESCOMBE, J. R. W. Coxhead, *The Devil in Devon*, 1967, 10; also, 31-2; S. Baring-Gould, *A Book of Dartmoor*, 1900, 139-40.

THE DEVIL AND ST DUNSTAN, Mrs H. P. Whitcombe, *Bygone Days in Devonshire & Cornwall*, 1874, 127-8.

THE DEVIL AND THE BREWER, S. Baring-Gould, *Devonshire Characters*, First Series, 6.

THE DEVIL AT DAWLISH, Sarah Hewett, *Nummits & Crummits*, 1900, 177-9; Mrs H. P. Whitcombe, *Bygone Days in Devonshire and Cornwall*, 1874, 90-4.

THE DEVIL AT UPLYME, Uplyme Women's Institute, *The Story of Uplyme*, 1970, 27.

THE DEVIL GOES COURTING AT MARWOOD, J. R. W. Coxhead, *Devon Traditions and Fairy Tales*, 1959, 33-5.

THE DEVIL GOES COURTING AT BRIDGERULE, J. R. W. Coxhead, *The*

Devil in Devon, 1967, 18-9.

THE DEVIL AND THE DEAD MAN'S SKIN, *Choice Notes from Notes and Queries,* 1859, 170.

THE DEVIL AND JOSEPH GOULD, J. R. W. Coxhead, *The Devil in Devon,* 1967, 26-8.

THE DEVIL'S DOOR, personal communications.

THE DEVIL AT TAVISTOCK, Mrs Bray, *Traditions, etc., of Devonshire,* 1838, Vol 2, 281-5.

THE DEVIL SHOT BY A FARMER, J. R. W. Coxhead, *The Devil in Devon,* 1967, 13.

THE DEVIL AT TOPSHAM, J. R. W. Coxhead, *The Devil in Devon,* 1967, 13.

THE DEVIL AT POUNDSGATE, S. H. Burton, *Devon Villages,* 1973, 135.

THE DEVIL AT PONSWORTHY, S. H. Burton, *Devon Villages,* 1973, 135.

THE DEVIL SPITTING ON BLACKBERRIES; personal communications (numerous – still widely quoted).

2 *Pixies and Fairies* (pages 28-40)

PIXIES, GENERAL NOTES, Mrs Bray, *Traditions, etc. of Devonshire,* 1838, Vol 1, 156-7; 172-92; Mrs H. P. Whitcombe, *Bygone Days in Devonshire & Cornwall,* 1874, 44-9; J. R. W. Coxhead, *Devon Traditions and Fairy Tales,* 1959, 48-53; personal communications.

REWARDING PIXIES, Mrs Bray, *Traditions, etc., of Devonshire,* 1838, Vol 1, 175-6; J. R. W. Coxhead, *Devon Traditions & Fairy Tales,* 1959, 58-60; W. Crossing, *Tales of Dartmoor Pixies,* 1890, 62-6.

PIXY THRESHERS, J. R. W. Coxhead, *Devon Traditions & Fairy Tales,* 1959, 56-58; W. Crossing, *Tales of Dartmoor Pixies,* 1890, 60-62.

CHILD TAKEN BY PIXIES, Mrs Bray, *Traditions, etc., of Devonshire,* 1838, Vol 1, 176-7.

FAIRY OINTMENT, Mrs Bray, *Traditions, etc., of Devonshire,* 1838, Vol I, 184-8; Katharine Briggs & Ruth Tongue, *Folktales of England,* 1965, 38-9; S. Baring-Gould, *A Book of the West,* Vol 1, 1899, 188-93.

PIXIE-LED, J. R. W. Coxhead, *The Devil in Devon,* 1967, 17-8; Mrs Bray, *Traditions, etc., of Devonshire,* 1838, Vol 1, 168-9, 182-3; J. R. W. Coxhead, *Devon Traditions & Fairy Tales,* 1959, 50-3; Katharine Briggs, *The Fairies in Tradition & Literature,* 1967, 137-8; S. Baring-Gould, *A Book of Dartmoor,* 1900, 245-6; Jack Hurley, *Legends of Exmoor,* 1973, 35.

JOHN FITZ AND HIS WELL, Mrs H. P. Whitcombe, *Bygone Days in Devonshire & Cornwall*, 1874, 67; R. C. Hope, *The Legendary Lore of the Holy Wells of England*, 1893, 63 and 66.

PIXY ASSOCIATIONS WITH PLACES, Jack Hurley, *Legends of Exmoor*, 1973, 32 and 35; S. H. Burton, *Devon Villages*, 1973, 117; Sarah Hewett, *Nummits and Crummits*, 1900, 38-9; Mrs Bray, *Traditions, etc., of Devonshire*, 1838, Vol I, 172-92; Mrs H. P. Whitcombe, *Bygone Days in Devonshire & Cornwall*, 1874, 67-8, 83-4; 114; W. Crossing, *Tales of the Dartmoor Pixies*, 1890, 1-98.

TOM WHITE OF HUCCABY, W. Crossing, *Tales of the Dartmoor Pixies*, 1890, 44-9; J. R. W. Coxhead, *Devon Traditions & Fairy Tales*, 1959; 53-5;

PIXIES AND THE TULIP GARDEN, Mrs Bray, *Traditions, etc., of Devonshire*, 1838, Vol 1, 190-2.

KITTY JAY, S. H. Burton, *Devon Villages*, 1973, 123.

THE PLOUGHMAN'S BREAKFAST, W. Crossing, *Tales of the Dartmoor Pixies*, 1890, 71-3.

HELP BY PIXIES, Katharine Briggs, *The Fairies in Tradition & Literature*, 1967, 137-8.

THE PIXIES & THE LAZY SERVANT, Mrs Bray, *Traditions, etc., of Devonshire*, 1838, Vol 1, 188-90.

SACRIFICING TO THE PIXIES, S. Baring-Gould, *A Book of Dartmoor*, 1900, 208.

MINERS AND PIXIES, Mrs Bray, *Traditions, etc., of Devonshire*, 1838, Vol III, 256.

PIXY RIDERS, W. Crossing, *Tales of the Dartmoor Pixies*, 1890, 73-4.

'A CRITICAL PLACE FOR CHILDREN', Mrs Bray, *Traditions, etc., of Devonshire*, 1838, Vol III, 102.

THE FOX AND THE PIXIES, J. R. W. Coxhead, *The Devil in Devon*, 1967, 29-31.

3   *Witches* (pages 41-51)

LAST EXECUTIONS FOR WITCHCRAFT, J. R. W. Coxhead, *Devon Traditions & Fairy Tales*, 1959, 104; Christina Hole, *A Mirror of Witchcraft*, 1965, 144-5; Ernest W. Martin, *Heritage of the West*, 1938, 153-4; J. R. W. Coxhead, *Legends of Devon*, 1945, 126-143.

TYPES OF WITCHES, Sarah Hewett, *Nummits & Crummits*, 1900, 63-5.

A PARSON-WIZARD, S. Baring-Gould, *A Book of the West*, Vol 1, 1899, 244-5.

OLD BAKER, Christina Hole, *A Mirror of Witchcraft*, 1965, 251-2; Mrs H. P. Whitcombe, *Bygone Days in Devonshire & Cornwall*, 1874; 9-10.

WITCHCRAFT AT ASHREIGNEY, Paul Karkeek, *Report & Transactions of the Devonshire Association*, Vol XIV, 1882, 390-4.

THE WITCH OF MEMBURY, Paul Karkeek, *Report & Transactions of the Devonshire Association*, Vol XIV, 1882, 387-90; also; Vol IX, 172; J. R. W. Coxhead, *Devon Traditions & Fairy Tales*, 1959, 155-62.

A WITCH OF EXETER, J. R. W. Coxhead, *Devon Traditions & Fairy Tales* 1959, 149.

BREAKING A WITCH'S POWER, Christina Hole, *A Mirror of Witchcraft*, 1957, 244.

ALICE TREVISARD, Christina Hole, *Witchcraft in England*, 1945, 11-12.

WITCH TURNING INTO HARE, Mrs Bray, *Traditions, etc., of Devonshire* Vol II, 276-8; Christina Hole, *Witchcraft in England*, 1945, 57.

A WITCH AT CRANMERE POOL, Mrs Bray, *Traditions, etc., of Devonshire*, 1838, Vol I, 261.

MORE WITCHES INTO HARES, J. R. W. Coxhead, *Devon Traditions & Fairy Tales*, 1959, 105.

MOLL STANCOMBE, J. R. W. Coxhead, *Devon Traditions & Fairy Tales*, 1959, 107-8.

THE WITCH OF VIXEN TOR, J. R. W. Coxhead, *Devon Traditions & Fairy Tales*, 1959, 71-5.

THE WITCH OF DALWOOD, J. R. W. Coxhead, *The Devil in Devon*, 1967, 53-5

THE WITCH OF AXMOUTH, J. R. W. Coxhead, *Legends of Devon*, 1954, 163-5.

WITCHCRAFT AT CLYST ST. LAWRENCE, J. R. W. Coxhead, *Devon Traditions & Fairy Tales*, 1959, 112-5.

MORE NINETEENTH-CENTURY WITCHES, S. Baring-Gould, *A Book of the West*, 1899, 111-3.

STONE AT HUNTERS LODGE, Mrs H. P. Whitcombe, *Bygone Days in Devonshire & Cornwall*, 1874, 83.

4   *Ghosts* (pages 52-62)

WILLIAM III AND MARY IN SOUTH DEVON, Christina Hole, *Haunted*

England, 1940, 67; Jack Hallam, *The Haunted Inns of England,* 1972, 46.

JUDGE JEFFREYS AT LYDFORD, Mrs H. P. Whitcombe, *Bygone Days in Devonshire & Cornwall,* 1874, 35; S. H. Burton, *Devon Villages,* 1973, 142.

LADY HOWARD OF FITZFORD, S. Baring-Gould, *A Book of the West,* Vol 1, 1899, 277-84; Mrs H. P. Whitcombe, *Bygone Days in Devonshire & Cornwall,* 1874, 66-7.

GHOST OF SQUIRE BOONE, J. R. W. Coxhead, *The Devil in Devon,* 1967, 42-5.

MADAME GOULD OF LEW TRENCHARD, Christina Hole, *Haunted England,* 1940, 117-20.

PARSON FROUDE OF RACKENFORD, S. H. Burton, *Devon Villages,* 1973, 155.

THE PARSON OF LUFFINCOTT, S. H. Burton, *Devon Villages,* 1973, 165.

PARSON GHOST OF UPLYME, Uplyme Women's Institute, *Story of Uplyme,* 1956, 26.

THE GHOSTS OF CRANMERE POOL, J. R. W. Coxhead, *Devon Traditions & Fairy Tales,* 1959, 41-43; *Choice Notes,* 1859, 170-1; Mrs H. P. Whitcombe, *Bygone Days in Devonshire & Cornwall,* 1874, 57-8; R. C. Hope, *The Legendary Lore of the Holy Wells of England,* 1893, 63; S. Baring-Gould, *A Book of the West,* Vol 1, 1899, 214.

THE GHOST OF COFFINSWELL, S. Baring-Gould, *A Book of the West,* Vol 1, 1899, 303.

STEPHEN'S GRAVE AT PETER TAVY, S. H. Burton, *Devon Villages,* 1973, 140; Mrs H. P. Whitcombe, *Bygone Days in Devonshire & Cornwall,* 1874, 102.

THE GHOST OF A SEDGMOOR VICTIM, J. R. W. Coxhead, *Devon Traditions & Fairy Tales,* 1959, 91-2.

MURDERED PEDLARS, Mrs H. P. Whitcombe, *Bygone Days in Devonshire & Cornwall,* 1874, 113-4; 123.

SIR WILLIAM TRACEY AND SIR ROBERT CHICHESTER, Mrs H. P. Whitcombe, *Bygone Days in Devonshire & Cornwall,* 1874, 125-6.

THE TREASURE OF DOWN HOUSE, TAVISTOCK, Mrs Bray, *Traditions, etc. of Devonshire,* 1838, Vol II, 298-300; also J. R. W. Coxhead, *Devon Traditions and Fairy Tales,* 1959, 39-41.

THE TREASURE OF TROW HILL, J. R. W. Coxhead, *Devon Traditions & Fairy Tales,* 1959, 95-6.

THE TREASURE OF CHETTISCOMBE, Mrs H. P. Whitcombe, *Bygone*

Days in Devon & Cornwall, 1874, 112.

GHOSTS AT SPREYTON, S. H. Burton, *Devon Villages,* 1973, 122.

GHOSTS AT DEVON INNS, Jack Hallam, *The Haunted Inns of England,* 1972, 46-53.

THE WEAVER'S GHOST, Mrs H. P. Whitcombe, *Bygone Days in Devonshire & Cornwall,* 1874, 102-4; R. C. Hope, *The Legendary Lore of the Holy Wells of England,* 1893, 64.

POLTERGEIST AT SAMPFORD PEVERELL, S. Baring-Gould, *A Book of the West,* Vol. I, 1899, 108.

OTTERY ST. MARY'S EFFIGY, Mrs H. P. Whitcombe, *Bygone Days in Devonshire & Cornwall,* 1874, 82-3.

SPIRIT GUIDANCE AT EXETER, Christina Hole, *Haunted England,* 1940, 132-4.

THE INNKEEPER'S DAUGHTER, and THE ONE-LEGGED FOOTMAN, Mrs Bray, *Traditions, etc., of Devonshire,* 1838, Vol III, 61-65; 88-89.

BLACK DOG ON DARTMOOR, Sarah Hewett, *Nummits and Crummits,* 1900, 39-41. See Theo Brown, 'The Black Dog'. *Folklore,* Sept. 1958. Vol LXIX, 175-192.

BLACK DOG OF YEOLMBRIDGE: *Notes & Queries,* December 10th, 1870, Vol VI, 4th series.

BLACK DOG OF UPLYME, Uplyme Women's Institute, *The Story of Uplyme,* 1956, 26; Kingsley Palmer, *Oral Folk-Tales of Wessex,* 1973, 126; J. R. W. Coxhead, *Devon Traditions & Fairy Tales,* 1959, 94-95; Jack Hallam, *The Haunted Inns of England,* 1972, 52-53.

BLACK DOG OF PONSWORTHY, S. H. Burton, *Devon Villages,* 1973, 135.

THE WILD HUNT, S. Baring-Gould, *A Book of the West,* Vol I, 1899, 184; J. R W. Coxhead, *The Devil in Devon,* 1967, 40-2; Mrs H. P. Whitcombe, *Bygone Days in Devonshire & Cornwall,* 1874, 49-51.

THE HAIRY HANDS, S. H. Burton, *Devon Villages,* 1973, 125.

THE SPECTRAL BLACK HEN, J. R. W. Coxhead, *The Devil in Devon,* 1967, 39-40.

TAMAR, TORRIDGE & TAVY, Mrs H. P. Whitcombe, *Bygone Days in Devonshire & Cornwall,* 1874, 96-7; J. R. W. Coxhead, *Devon Traditions & Fairy Tales,* 1959, 69-71.

EARTH GNOMES AT FERNWORTHY, J. R. W. Coxhead, *Devon Traditions & Fairy Tales,* 1959, 75-6.

OLD CROCKERN, S. Baring-Gould, *A Book of the West,* 1899, 182-3.

THE GIANT OF GRABBIST, Ed. K. M. Briggs & R. L. Tongue, *Folktales of England*, 1965, 68-70; *The Fairies in Tradition & Literature*, K. M. Briggs, 1967, 63.

GIANTS AT PLYMOUTH, Mrs H. P. Whitcombe, *Bygone Days in Devonshire & Cornwall*, 1874, 73-4; J. R. W. Coxhead, *Devon Traditions & Fairy Tales*, 1959, 77-81.

GIANT'S GRAVE AT KENFORD, Mrs H. P. Whitcombe, *Bygones Days in Devon & Cornwall*, 1874, 107; S. H. Burton, *A West Country Anthology*, 1975, 142-3.

ORDULF, J. R. W. Coxhead, *Devon Traditions & Fairy Tales*, 1959, 69-71; Mrs Bray, *Traditions, etc., of Devonshire*, 1838, Vol II, 48-52; Mrs H. P. Whitcombe, *Bygone Days in Devonshire & Cornwall*, 1874, 60-1.

DRAGON BY THE EXE, Mrs H. P. Whitcombe, *Bygone Days in Devonshire & Cornwall*, 1874, 96-7; S. H. Burton, *A West Country Anthology*, 1975, 128-9; Personal communication, early 1950s.

6   *Churches, Saints and More Treasure* (pages 66-71)

ST BRANNOC AT BRAUNTON, Derek Parker, *The West Country*, 1973, 169; Kingsley Palmer, *Oral Folk-Tales of Wessex*, 1973, 47.

CELTIC DEDICATIONS, W. G. Hoskins, *Devon*, 1954, 39-41; W. G. Hoskins, *Devon & Its People*, 1959, 219-22, and 312.

SAXON SAINTS, W. G. Hoskins, *Devon & Its People*, 1959, 41-44.

THE PRAYER BOOK REBELLION, W. G. Hoskins, *Devon*, 1954, 233-4; Derek Parker, *The West Country*, 1973, 180.

TREASURE AT TAVISTOCK, Mrs Bray, *Traditions, etc., of Devonshire*, 1838, Vol II, 295-6; Mrs H. P. Whitcombe, *Bygone Days in Devonshire & Cornwall*, 1874, 61-2.

THE RADFORD TREASURE, J. R. W. Coxhead, *Devil in Devon*, 1967, 65-6.

THE TREASURE IN THE CELLAR, J. R. W. Coxhead, *Devil in Devon*, 1967, 66-68.

JOHN CANN'S TREASURE, S. Baring-Gould, *A Book of the West*, Vol I, 1899, 245.

THE RIFLING OF BROKEN BARROW, S. H. Burton, *Exmoor*, 1974, 118; J. R. W. Coxhead, *The Devil in Devon*, 1967, 19-20.

7   *Local Heroes and Rogues* (pages 72-98)

SIR FRANCIS DRAKE, Mrs Bray, *Traditions, etc., of Devonshire*, Vol II, 1838, 169-75; J. R. W. Coxhead, *Devon Traditions & Fairy Tales*, 1959, 15-19; W. G. Hoskins, *Devon & Its People*, 1959, 106-11; Derek Parker, *The West Country*, 1973, 121; Kingsley Palmer, *Oral Folk-Tales of Wessex*, 1973, 25; Mrs H. P. Whitcombe, *Bygone Days in Devonshire & Cornwall*, 1874, 70-3; Christina Hole, *Haunted England*, 1940, 139-40.

ARTHUR AND KING ALFRED, S. H. Burton, *Exmoor*, 1974, 94-5.

JOSEPH OF ARIMATHEA, Jack Hurley, *Legends of Exmoor*, 1973, 46-7.

ROBERT GIFFARD, J. R. W. Coxhead, *Devon Traditions & Fairy Tales*, 1959, 38-9.

SIR PETER CAREW, J. R. W. Coxhead, *The Devil in Devon*, 1967, 59-63; *Transactions of the Devonshire Association*, Vol 32, 1888, 481.

THE HORSE-SHOES OF HACCOMBE, J. R. W. Coxhead, *Devon Traditions & Fairy Tales*, 1959, 81-3.

SIR WILLIAM COFFIN AND THE PRIEST, J. R. W. Coxhead, *The Devil in Devon*, 1967, 15-16.

SQUIRE BIDLAKE, S. Baring-Gould, *Devonshire Characters*, 1908, 219-23; J. R. W. Coxhead, *The Devil in Devon*, 1967, 34-5.

JOHN WESLEY, W. G. Hoskins, *Devon and Its People*, 1959, 126-9.

PARSON JACK RUSSELL, S. Baring-Gould, *A Book of the West*, 1899, Vol I, 104-7.

PETER ORLANDO HUTCHINSON, John Bland, *Odd and Unusual England*, 1974, 28-9.

EDWARD CAPERN, S. Baring-Gould, *Devonshire Characters*, 1908, 325-331; S. H. Burton, *Devon Villages*, 1973, 172-3.

THE WATERCRESS WOMAN, Mrs Bray, *Traditions, etc., of Devonshire*, 1838, Vol II, 251-4.

THE DOONES, J. R. W. Coxhead, *Devon Traditions & Fairy Tales*, 1959, 21-8.

THE GREGGS OF CLOVELL, S. H. Burton, *Devon Villages*, 1973, 169-70.

THE GUBBINSES OF LYDFORD, S. H. Burton, *Devon Villages*, 1973, 142.

THE CHERITONS, Sarah Hewett, *Nummits and Crummits*, 1900, 159-64.

THE KING OF THE BEGGARS, Ernest W. Martin, *Heritage of the West*, 1938, 127-38; S. Baring-Gould, *A Book of the West*, Vol I, 1899, 116-8; Sarah Hewett, *Nummits & Crummits*, 1900, 149-52.

MENDICANT IMPOSTORS, Mrs Bray, *Traditions, etc., of Devonshire,* 1838, Vol: III, 158-63.

THE BRAMPFYLDES OF POLTIMORE, J. R. W. Coxhead, *Devon Traditions & Fairy Tales,* 1959, 88-90.

SQUIRE NORTHMORE & THE PRESS GANG, J. R. W. Coxhead, *The Devil in Devon,* 1967, 33-4.

SIR JOHN FITZ, S. Baring-Gould, *A Book of the West,* Vol I, 1899, 277-80; Mrs Bray, *Traditions, etc., of Devonshire,* Vol II, 1838, 322-4; Mrs H. P. Whitcombe, *Bygone Days in Devonshire & Cornwall,* 1874, 64-5.

SHILSTON UPCOTT, J. R. W. Coxhead, *Devon Traditions & Fairy Tales,* 1959, 30-3.

CRUEL COPPINGER, J. R. W. Coxhead, *The Devil in Devon,* 1967, 21-4; TOM FAGGUS, Jack Hurley, *Legends of Exmoor,* 1973, 58-62.

NICHOLAS MASON, Mrs Bray, *Traditions, etc., of Devonshire,* 1838, Vol III, 288-91.

ELFRIDA, William of Malmesbury, *Chronicle of the Kings of England,* c. 1135, 3d. 1847, 159-61; S. Baring-Gould, *A Book of the West,* Vol I, 1899, 268-70; Mrs Bray, *Traditions, etc., of Devonshire,* 1838, Vol II, 20-31.

EULALIA PAGE, S. Baring-Gould, *A Book of the West,* Vol I, 1899, 273-7.

PRINCESS CARABOU, Sarah Hewett, *Nummits & Crummits,* 1900, 137-49.

JOANNA SOUTHCOTT, Sarah Hewett, *Nummits & Crummits,* 1900, 153-59; S. Baring-Gould, *Devonshire Characters,* 1st Series, 1908, 390-404; personal communications.

THE OLD TESTAMENT FARMER, Mrs Bray, *Traditions, etc., of Devonshire,* 1838, Vol II, 255-7.

THE BIGAMOUS DUCHESS OF KINGSTON, S. Baring-Gould, *A Book of Dartmoor,* 1900, 214-5.

VARWELL OF BRIXHAM, *A Book of the West,* Vol I, 1899, 293-4.

THE LORD OF DYRWOOD, S. H. Burton, *A West Country Anthology,* 1975, 126, quoting Thomas Westcote, *A View of Devonshire in 1630.*

DOLLY TREBBLE, S. Baring-Gould, *A Book of Dartmoor,* 1900, 196-8.

LADY DARKE, S. Baring-Gould, *A Book of Dartmoor,* 1900, 183-9.

LADY EDGCUMBE, Mrs H. P. Whitcombe, *Bygone Days in Devonshire & Cornwall,* 1874, 74.

OLD MOTHER HUBBARD, Derek Parker, *The West Country,* 1973, 134; S. H. Burton, *Devon Villages,* 1973, 102.

8   *Legends and Memories* (pages 99-117)

SEVEN CHILDREN AT A BIRTH, S. H. Burton, *A West Country Anthology*, 1975, 110-11, quoting Thomas Westcote, *A View of Devonshire In 1630*, S. Baring-Gould, *A Book of the West*, Vol I, 101-3.

THE RAVENS AND THE BABY, J. R. W. Coxhead, *The Devil in Devon*, 1967, 39, quoting *Transactions of the Devonshire Association*, Vol 90, 242.

THE SHEEP WHICH HANGED A MAN, Mrs H. P. Whitcombe, *Bygone Days in Devonshire & Cornwall*, 1874, 124.

CHILDE'S BURIAL, Mrs Bray, *Traditions, etc., of Devonshire*, 1838, Vol II, 53-5; S. Baring-Gould, *A Book of the West*, Vol I, 1899, 371-2; Mrs H. P. Whitcombe, *Bygone Days in Devonshire & Cornwall*, 1874, Vol II, 55-7; S. Baring-Gould, *A Book of Dartmoor*, 1900, 202-3; J. R. W. Coxhead, *Devon Traditions & Fairy Tales*, 1959, 36-8; Theo Brown, 'The Dartmoor Legend of Mr Childe', *Folklore*, 1954, Vol 65, 103-109.

THE NORTH WYKE DISPUTE, S. Baring-Gould *A Book of Dartmoor*, 1900, 151-4.

CHOLERA VICTIMS AT SHEEPSTOR, Mrs Bray, *Traditions, etc., of Devonshire*, 1838, Vol III, 110-2.

THE TREASURE OF BERRY POMEROY, J. R. W. Coxhead, *The Devil in Devon*, 1967, 46-7, quoting *Transactions of the Devonshire Association*, Vol XI, 1879, 346-7.

DR CLIFFORD'S BAG OF GOLD, J. R. W. Coxhead, *The Devil in Devon*, 1967, 37-8.

ROUNDHEAD CUPIDITY, J. R. W. Coxhead, *The Devil in Devon*, 1967, 36-7.

CHARLES II AT CHARDSTOCK, J. R. W. Coxhead, *The Devil in Devon*, 1967, 55-6.

ATHELSTAN & ANLAF AT AXMINSTER, S. Baring-Gould, *A Book of the West*, Vol I, 1899, 45-8.

CROMWELL AT BOVEY TRACEY, J. R. W. Coxhead, *The Devil in Devon*, 1967, 35-6.

VESPASIAN AND WILLIAM THE CONQUEROR AT EXETER, W. G. Hoskins, *Devon and its People*, 1959, 20 & 46-7.

EXETER NOT IN DEVON, S. H. Burton, *A West County Anthology*, 1975, 146, quoting Cecil Torr, *Small Talk at Wreybridge*, 1921.

BOROUGHS IN DEVON, W. G. Hoskins, *Devon*, 1954, 58.

BRADNICH V. EXETER, S. H. Burton, *A West County Anthology*, 1975. 129, quoting Thomas Westcote, *A View of Devonshire in 1630;* Mrs H. P. Whitcombe, *Bygone Days in Devonshire & Cornwall*, 1874, 107-8.

DEVON BEYOND THE TAMAR, S. H. Burton, *Devon Villages*, 1973, 144.

RING-IN-THE-MERE, S. Baring-Gould, *A Book of the West*, Vol I, 1899, 58-9; Mrs H. P. Whitcombe, *Bygone Days in Devonshire & Cornwall*, 1874, 81.

ORIGINS OF BARNSTAPLE, S. Baring-Gould, *A Book of the West*, Vol I, 1899, 122-3

ST. BRANOCK, Mrs H. P. Whitcombe, *Bygone Days in Devonshire & Cornwall*, 1874, 123.

ST. NECTAN AT CLOVELLY, S. Baring-Gould, *A Book of the West*, Vol I, 1899, 151.

FOUNDATION OF TAVISTOCK, S. Baring-Gould, *A Book of the West*, Vol I, 1899, 266-7.

BIDEFORD BRIDGE, S. Baring-Gould, *A Book of the West*, Vol I, 1899, 140; Mrs H. P. Whitcombe, *Bygone Days in Devon & Cornwall*, 1874, 117-8.

DARTMOOR IN LYDFORD PARISH, S. H. Burton, *Devon Villages*, 1973, 142 and 136.

THE BLACK DEATH IN DEVON, W. G. Hoskins, *Devon*, 1954, 169-2; W. G. Hoskins, *Devon & Its People*, 1959; 67-70.

'THE POTATO-MARKET', Mrs Bray, *Traditions, etc., of Devonshire*, 1838, Vol I, 160; Kingsley Palmer, *Oral Folk-Tales of Wessex*, 1973, 42.

TIN-MINING AND STANNARY LAW, Robert R. Pennington, *Stannary Law*, 1973, 1-195.

FIRES AT TIVERTON, S. H. Burton, *A West Country Anthology*, 1975, 120-2, quoting Thomas Westcote, *A View of Devonshire in 1630*, and Samuel Smith, *The Late Dreadful Fire at Tiverton*, 1732; Ernest W. Martin, *Heritage of the West*, 1938, 170-3.

FIRES AT HONITON & SOUTH MOLTON, Ernest W. Martin, *Heritage of the West*, 1938, 165-72.

EDDYSTONE LIGHTHOUSE. S. Baring-Gould, *A Book of the West*, 1899, Vol I, 363-5.

HURRICANE AT WIDECOMBE, Mrs Bray, *Traditions, etc., of Devonshire*, 1838, Vol I, 310-4.

WHIRLWIND AT TAVISTOCK, Mrs Bray, *Traditions, etc., of Devonshire*, 1838, Vol III, 268-70.

1947 SNOWSTORM, *Doidge's Western Counties Annual*, 1948, 139-49.

SMUGGLING AT CAWSAND, S. Baring-Gould, *A Book of the West*, Vol I, 1899, 366-7.

SMUGGLERS AT BRIXHAM, J. R. W. Coxhead, *Devon Traditions & Fairy Tales*, 1959, 83-5.

SMUGGLERS AT BLACKBOROUGH, J. R. W. Coxhead, *Devon Traditions & Fairy Tales*, 1959, 92-4.

SMUGGLER'S LEAP, J. R. W. Coxhead, *The Devil in Devon*, 1967, 24.

WRECKERS' WINDOW AT SHALDON, John Bland, *Odd and Unusual England*, 1974, 128.

THE EVIL PRIEST OF TEIGNMOUTH, Mrs H. P. Whitcombe, *Bygone Days in Devon & Cornwall*, 1874, 94.

THE IRON CAGE OF MARY TAVY, S. H. Burton, *Devon Villages*, 1973, 141.

THE DARTMOUTH PRISONERS OF WAR, S. H. Burton, *A West Country Anthology*, 1975, 170-1, quoting Thomas Westcote, *A View of Devonshire in 1630*.

TREACHERY ON LUNDY, Mrs H. P. Whitcombe, *Bygone Days in Devon & Cornwall*, 1874, 121-2.

HUGUENOTS IN DEVON, S. Baring-Gould, *A Book of the West*, Vol I, 1899, 126-7.

PRINCETOWN PRISON BUILT FOR FRENCH PRISONERS, W. G. Hoskins, *Devon and its People*, 1959, 140-3.

9 Devonshire Life and Tradition (pages 118-134)

THE ANCIENT FORESTS OF DARTMOOR AND EXMOOR, S. Baring-Gould, *A Book of the West*, Vol I, 1899, 177-81; W. G. Hoskins, *Devon*, 1954, 244; 262-9.

SQUATTERS, S. Baring-Gould, *A Book of the West*, Vol I, 1899, 197; S. Baring-Gould, *A Book of Dartmoor*, 1900, 201; S. H. Burton, *Devon Villages*, 1973, 136.

COB AND COTTAGES, S. Baring-Gould, *A Book of the West*, Vol I, 1899, 79-80; S. H. Burton, *A West Country Anthology*, 1975, 114, quoting Count L. Magalotti, *The Travels of Cosmo III*, 1669; Mrs Bray, *Traditions, etc., of Devonshire*, 1838, Vol II, 139; Sidney H. Heath, in *Doidge's Western Counties Annual*, 1948, 125-6; Personal Communications from E. Devon villagers in the 1950s: W. G. Hoskins, *Devon*, 1954, 268.

OLD MORETONHAMPSTEAD, S. H. Burton, *Devon Villages*, 1973, 115.

DRYSTONE WALLING, S. H. Burton, *A West Country Anthology*, 1975, 157-8, quoting William Crossing, *The Dartmoor Worker*, 1903; also Personal Communications.

SALTING DOWN A CORPSE, Mrs Bray, *Traditions, etc., of Devonshire*, 1838, Vol I, 27-33; S. H. Burton, *Devon Villages*, 1973, 124.

FUNERAL CUSTOMS, Mrs Bray, *Traditions, etc., of Devonshire*, 1838, Vol II, 127; S. Baring-Gould, *A Book of Dartmoor*, 1900, 172. S. Baring-Gould, *A Book of the West*, Vol I, 1899, 39; also 14-5.

BELL-RINGING, Mrs Bray, *Traditions, etc., of Devonshire*, 1838, Vol II, 127; S. H. Burton, *Devon Villages*, 1973, 131; also personal communications; Mrs H. P. Whitcombe, *Bygone Days in Devonshire & Cornwall*, 1874, 32-3.

CHURCH ALES, S. H. Burton, *Devon Villages*, 1973, 40 & 100; Personal Communications from E. S. of Kingsbridge, 1948; Mrs H. P. Whitcombe, *Bygone Days in Devonshire & Cornwall*, 1874, 38.

PURITAN PROHIBITION OF CHURCH ALES, W. G. Hoskins, *Devon*, 1954, 252.

ALE-TASTERS AND COURT LEETS, J. S. A. in *Report & Transactions of the Devonshire Association*, Vol 14, 1882, 181-5; Margaret Gascoigne, *Discovering English Customs & Traditions*, 1969, 18.

LYDFORD'S REPUTATION, Mrs H. P. Whitcombe, *Bygone Days in Devonshire & Cornwall*, 1874, 39-40; S. Baring-Gould, *A Book of Dartmoor*, 1900, 131.

NO COWS IN CHURCHYARDS, G. S. Tyzack, *Lore & Legend of the English Church*, 1900, 57-8.

GLOVES AT FAIRS, Christina Hole, *English Custom & Usage*, 1941-2, 92-3; Mrs H. P. Whitcombe, *Bygone Days in Devonshire & Cornwall*, 1874, 39; S. H. Burton, *Devon Villages*, 1973, 131.

PAIGNTON PUDDING, Mrs H. P. Whitcombe, *Bygone Days in Devonshire & Cornwall*, 1874, 39; Margaret Gascoigne, *Discovering English Customs & Traditions*, 1969, 19.

HOLNE RAM FEAST, S. H. Burton, *Devon Villages*, 1973, 133; Robert Burnard in *Transactions of the Devonshire Association*, Vol 28, 1896, 99-102.

KINGSTEIGNTON RAM FEAST, A. R. Wright, *British Calendar Customs*, Vol I, 1936, 169.

THE PLYMOUTH 'FISHING FEAST', Mrs H. P. Whitcombe, *Bygone Days in Devonshire & Cornwall*, 1874, 35-8; Christina Hole, *English Custom*

& *Usage*, 1941-2, 104; Margaret Gascoigne, *Discovering English Customs & Traditions*, 1969, 19; personal communications.

TRADITIONAL RACES AT BIDEFORD, Margaret Gascoigne, *Discovering English Customs & Traditions*, 1969, 18; personal communications.

WRESTLING, Mrs H. P. Whitcombe, *Bygone Days in Devonshire & Cornwall*, 1874, 29; S. H. Burton, *A West Country Anthology*, 1975, 174-6; S. Baring-Gould, *Devonshire Characters and Strange Events*, 1908, 110-124.

CIDER, W. G. Hoskins, *Devon*, 1954, 94-5; S. Baring-Gould, *A Book of the West*, Vol I, 1899, 83-95; S. H. Burton, *Devon Villages*, 1973, 113; personal communications from E. Devon villagers in the 1950s.

HORSES AND OXEN, W. G. Hoskins, *Devon*, 1954, 150-1; S. H. Burton, *A West Country Anthology*, 1975, 157, quoting Moore, *History of Devonshire*, 1829, Vol I, 426; personal observations.

TIN-MINING, W. G. Hoskins, *Devon*, 1954, 130-5; R. P. Pennington, *Stannary Law*, 1973, passim; S. H. Burton, *The West Country*, 1972, 226-9; Derek Parker, *The West Country*, 1973, 122-3.

OTHER MINERALS, W. G. Hoskins, *Devon*, 1954, 135-40; Walter Minchinton, *Devon at Work*, 1974, 42-59.

LACE-MAKING, W. G. Hoskins, *Devon*, 1954, 141-2; S. Baring-Gould, *A Book of the West*, Vol I, 1899, 51-8.

WEAVING AND TEAZELS, Uplyme W.I., *The Story of Uplyme*, 1956, 13-6.

LICHENS FOR DYES, S. Baring-Gould, *A Book of Dartmoor*, 1900, 249-51.

PICKING WHORTLEBERRIES, Mrs Bray, *Traditions, etc. of Devonshire*, 1838, Vol I, 317; R. W. Patten, *Exmoor Custom and Song*, 1974, 14-15; S. H. Burton, *A West Country Anthology*, 1975, 161-2, quoting William Crossing, *The Dartmoor Worker*, 1903.

SWALING, Personal observations and communications. Also Iris M. Woods of Dunstone Cottage, Widecombe, in a letter to the Survey of English Folklore written in 1967.

10   *The Circling Year* (pages 135-157)

WASSAILING APPLE-TREES, Personal observations and communications; *Gentlemen's Magazine*, Vol 61, 1791, 403; *Transactions of the*

Devonshire Association, Vol 6, 1873, 266-7; also Vol 8, 1876, 49-50; Sarah Hewett, *The Peasant Speech of Devon*, 1892, 26-7; *Folk-Lore*, Vol 6, 1895, 93; *Devon Notes & Queries*, Vol 2, 1903, 206; A. R. Wright, *British Calendar Customs*, 1938, Vol 2, 60-5; Mrs Bray, *Traditions, etc., of Devonshire*, 1838, Vol I, 335; Mrs H. P. Whitcombe, *Bygone Days in Devonshire & Cornwall*, 1874, 26-7; S. Baring-Gould, *A Book of the West*, Vol I, 1899, 89; J. R. W. Coxhead, *Old Devon Customs*, 1953, 9-11; R. W. Patten, *Exmoor Custom & Song*, 1974, 6-8.

NEW YEAR BELIEFS AND CUSTOMS, Iona and Peter Opie, *Lore & Language of School Children*, 1959, 291; A. R. Wright, *British Calendar Customs*, Vol 2, 46 and 19; 1938.

PLOUGH MONDAY, Margaret Gascoigne, *Discovering English Customs & Traditions*, 1969, 18-9; R.W. Patten, *Exmoor Custom & Song*, 1974, 23.

COLLOP MONDAY AND SHROVE TUESDAY CUSTOMS, Mrs H. P. Whitcombe, *Bygone Days in Devonshire & Cornwall*, 1874, 25-6; R. W. Patten, *Exmoor Custom & Song*, 1974, 8-9; Margaret Gascoigne, *Discovering English Customs & Traditions*, 1969, 19; S. H. Burton, *Devon Villages*, 1973, 169; A. R. Wright, *British Calendar Customs*, Vol I, 1936, 4-6; *Transactions of the Devonshire Association*, Vol 17, 1885, 123-4; *Western Antiquary*, Vol I, 1881, 183; personal communications.

MOTHERING DAY, Sarah Hewett, *Nummits & Crummits*, 1900, 87-88.

LADY DAY, Personal communications from E. Devon; Sarah Hewett, *The Peasant Speech of Devon*, 1892, 82.

COCK-THROWING AT HARTLAND, R. P. Chope, *The Dialect of Hartland*, 1891, 35.

BREAKING CROCKERY ON GOOD FRIDAY, Sarah Hewett, *Nummits & Crummits*, 1900, 50.

GOOD FRIDAY SUPERSTITIONS, A. R. Wright, *British Calendar Customs*, Vol I, 1938, 80, 81, 84; R. W. Patten, *Exmoor Custom & Song*, 1974, 10; personal communications and observations, 1948.

MAUNDY THURSDAY, James Cossins, *Reminiscences of Exeter Fifty Years Since*, 1878, 36.

THE HUNTING OF THE EARL OF RONE, Mrs H. P. Whitcombe, *Bygone Days in Devonshire & Cornwall*, 1874, 33-34; George Tugwell, *The North Devon Scenery Book*, 1863, 109-13; R. W. Patten, *Exmoor Custom & Song*, 1974, 12-3.

BEATING THE BOUNDS, Margaret Gascoigne, *Discovering English Customs & Traditions*, 1969, 19; James Cossins, *Reminiscences of Exeter*

Fifty Years Since, 1878, 10-2; J. R. W. Coxhead, *The Devil in Devon*, 1967, 52-3.

GOOD FRIDAY DOLE AT IDEFORD, Sarah Hewett, *Nummits & Crummits*, 1900, 93.

GOOD FRIDAY BUNS, Sarah Hewett, *Nummits & Crummits*, 1900, 77; Ernest W. Martin, *Heritage of the West*, 1938, 28; personal observations and communications; William Crossing, *Folk Rhymes of Devon*, 1911, 142.

GLOVES ON EASTER EVE, A. E. Stothard, *The Borders of the Tamar and the Tavy* 1879, 118-9.

SUNRISE ON EASTER DAY, A. R. Wright, *British Calendar Customs*, Vol I, 1938, 96-8; Ernest W. Martin, *Heritage of the West*, 1938, 30-32; R. W. Patten, *Exmoor Custom & Song*, 1974, 10.

APRIL FOOL'S DAY, *Transactions of the Devonshire Association*, Vol 83, 1951, 75-6; R. W. Patten, *Exmoor Custom & Song*, 1974, 10; Personal observations.

BELIEVER DAY, S. Baring-Gould, *A Book of the West*, Vol I, 1899, 204-5.

ST MARK'S EVE, Sarah Hewett, *Nummits & Crummits*, 1900, 33.

MAY DAY FESTIVITIES, Margaret Gascoigne, *Discovering English Traditions & Customs*, 1969, 19; Uplyme W.I., *The Story of Uplyme*, 1956, 11; R. W. Patten, *Exmoor Custom & Song*, 1974, 11-13; S. H. Burton, *Devon Villages*, 1973, 181, R. N. Worth, *History of Devonshire*, 1886, 242; *Western Antiquary*, Vol I, 1882, 140; Mrs Bray, *Traditions, etc., of Devonshire*, Vol I, 1838, 323-328; S. Baring-Gould, *A Book of the West*, Vol I, 1899, 206-7; Mrs H. P. Whitcombe, *Bygone Days in Devonshire & Cornwall*, 1874, 30; Christina Hole, *English Customs and Usage*, 1941, 76-7; Ernest W. Martin, *Heritage of the West*, 1938, 37-8; Sarah Hewett, *Nummits & Crummits*, 1900, 91; S. Baring-Gould, *A Book of the West*, Vol I, 1899, 367; *Transactions of the Devonshire Association*, Vol 12, 1880, 105; A. R. Wright, *British Calendar Customs*, Vol I, 1938, 246.

ROODMAS DAY, Sarah Hewett, *Nummits and Crummits*, 1900, 92-3.

ASCENSION DAY, A. R. Wright, *British Calendar Customs*, Vol I, 1938, 140; *Transactions of the Devonshire Association*, Vol 40, 1908, 190-2; R. C. Hope, *The Legendary Lore of the Holy Wells of England*, 1893, 63-4.

WHITMONDAY REVELS, Miss H. Saunders, *Transactions of the Devonshire Association*, Vol 28, 1896, 346, 348.

ST FRANKIN'S DAY, S. Baring-Gould, *A Book of the West*, Vol I, 1899,

84, *Transactions of the Devonshire Association*, Vol 27, 1895, 64.
LAWLESS DAY IN EXETER, J. R. W. Coxhead, *Old Devon Customs*, 1953, 20-1.
OAK APPLE DAY, James Cossins, *Reminiscences of Exeter Fifty Years Since 1878*, 34; W. Pengelly, *Transactions of the Devonshire Association*, Vol 12, 1880, 108; *Western Antiquary*, Vol I, 1879, 57; also Vol I, 1882, 71; Sarah Hewett, *Nummits and Crummits*, 1900, 93-5; Mrs Bray, *Traditions, etc., of Devonshire*, 1838, Vol II, 288-91; A. R. Wright, *British Calendar Customs*, 1938, Vol 2, 270; Letter from Dorothy Banks of Tavistock, dated 21 September 1967, to Survey of English Folklore.
PESTLE PIES, *Transactions of the Devonshire Association*, Vol 28, 1896, 346 and 348; S. Baring-Gould, *A Book of the West*, Vol I, 1899, 42.
SHEEP-SHEARING FESTIVITIES, R. W. Patten, *Exmoor Custom & Song*, 1974, 24-5; personal communications.
LAMMAS FAIRS & CUSTOMS, Christina Hole, *English Custom & Usage*, 1941, 92-3; Ernest W. Martin, *Heritage of the West*, 1938, 60-1; personal communications, per R. N. of Chagford.
CRYING THE NACK AND HARVEST HOME FEASTS, Mrs Bray, *Traditions, etc., of Devonshire*, 1838, Vol I, 329-31; Mrs H. P. Whitcombe, *Bygone Days in Devonshire & Cornwall*, 1874, 27-8; personal communications; Sarah Hewett, *Nummits &. Crummits*, 1900, 96-9; Ernest W. Martin, *Heritage of the West*, 1938, 68-9; J. R. W. Coxhead, *Old Devon Customs*, 1953, 12-3; Manuscript letter to Alice Gomme from her sister Agnes, dated 25 August, 1891, in the Gomme papers, Survey of English Folklore.
HIRING FAIRS, Sarah Hewett, *Nummits & Crummits*, 1900, 98-9; personal communications; Mrs H. P. Whitcombe, *Bygone Days in Devonshire & Cornwall*, 1874, 34.
HAMPTON PONY FAIR, S. Baring-Gould, *A Book of the West*, Vol I, 1899, 118-9; personal observations.
HALLOWE'EN & GUY FAWKES, personal observations and communications; R. W. Patten, *Exmoor Custom & Song*, 1974, 16-24; A. E. Stothard, *The Borders of the Tamar & the Tavy*, 1879, 291; A. R. Wright, *British Calendar Customs*, Vol 3, 1938, 146, 148; James Cossing, *Reminiscences of Exeter Fifty Years Since*, 1878, 70-2.
OTTERY ST MARY; Venetia Newall, 'Two English Fire Festivals in Relation to their Contemporary Social Setting', *Western Folklore*, October 1972, Vol 31, 264-74.

GUY FAWKES AT EXETER, *The Western Morning News*, 16 October 1867.

BRIXHAM BELLS, Guide Book to Brixham Parish Church, published September 1948.

THE MAYOR OF SHAMICKSHIRE, R. Chope, *The Dialect of Hartland*, 1891, 19.

MORETONHAMPSTEAD FEAST, A. R. Wright, *British Calendar Customs*, Vol 3, 1938, 191.

THE ASHEN FAGGOT, *Transactions of the Devonshire Association*, Vol 6, 1873, 208-209; Vol 11, 1879, 107-8; Sarah Hewett, *Nummits & Crummits*, 1900, 92 and 82; J. R. W. Coxhead, *Old Devon Customs*, 1953, 5-9; R. W. Patten, *Exmoor Custom & Song*, 1974, 22; Ernest W. Martin, *Heritage of the West*, 1938, 78-9; Anon, *Echoes of Exmoor*, 1923, 46-54; A. R. Wright, *British Calendar Customs*, Vol 3, 1938, 213-14; Mrs H. P. Whitcombe, *Bygone Days in Devonshire & Cornwall*, 1874, 42-3; personal communications, per S. V. of Barnstaple and others.

THE KISSING BUSH, R. P. Chope, *The Dialect of Hartland*, 1891, 53.

CHRISTMAS AT EXETER, James Cossins, *Reminiscences of Exeter Fifty Years Since*, 1878, 72-3.

CHRISTMAS MUMMING PLAYS, Theo Brown, 'The Mummers' Play in Devon and Newfoundland', *Folklore*, Vol 63, 30-5; E. C. Cawte, Alex Helm and N. Peacock, *English Ritual Drama*, 1967, 43-4: Edmund Chambers, *The English Folk Play*, 1933, 237; for fragments of the Bovey Tracy play see R. J. E. Tiddy, *The Mummers Play*, 1923, 157-158. He notes that at the end of the performance 'Rule Britannia' was sung.

11   Charms, Cures and Traditional Beliefs (pages 158-170)

SEEING SPIRITS ON MIDSUMMER EVE, *Transactions of the Devonshire Association*, Vol 9, 1877, 90; A. R. Wright, *British Calendar Customs*, Vol 3, 1940, 19; Mrs Bray, *Traditions, etc., of Devonshire*, 1838, Vol II, 127-8; S. Baring-Gould, *A Book of Dartmoor*, 1900, 231.

ST JOHN'S EVE AT BRIDESTOWE, Ernest W. Martin, *Heritage of the West*, 1938, 42-3.

FORETELLING A MARRIAGE, A. R. Wright, *British Calendar Customs*, Vol 2, 1938, 152-4; Mrs H. P. Whitcombe, *Bygone Days in Devonshire*

& *Cornwall*, 1874; 22-4; personal communications.

WEDDING CUSTOMS, Sarah Hewett, *Nummits & Crummits*, 1900, 22-4, 101; personal communications.

LUCK, GOOD AND BAD, Sarah Hewett, *Nummits & Crummits*, 1900, 49-60; Mrs H. P. Whitcombe, *Bygone Days in Devonshire & Cornwall*, 1874, 6; personal communications from Mrs Sarah Orledge of Exeter, 1940; Iona & Peter Opie, *The Lore & Language of School-Children*, 1959, 206-7, 211, 216, 300.

CURES, A. R. Wright, *British Calendar Customs*, 1938, Vol 1, 82; Vol 2, 206; Mrs H. P. Whitcombe, *Bygone Days in Devonshire & Cornwall*, 1874, 14-20; Sarah Hewett, *Nummits & Crummits*, 1900, 65-81; S. Baring-Gould, *A Book of Dartmoor*, 1900, 126; *Choice Notes*, 1859, 173; personal communications; Rev. G. S. Tyack, *Lore & Legend of the English Church*, 1899, 124; Mrs Bray, *Traditions, etc., of Devonshire*, 1838, Vol II, 291-4; Theo Brown, 'Living Images', *Folklore*, 1962, Vol 73, 36-9; Theo Brown, 'Post Reformation Folklore in Devon', *Folklore*, 1961, Vol 72, 391-2.

DEATH CUSTOMS & TRADITIONS, Mrs Bray, *Traditions, etc., of Devonshire*, 1838, Vol II, 291-5; Sarah Hewett, *Nummits & Crummits*, 1900, 13-5, 25; Mrs H. P. Whitcombe, *Bygone Days in Devonshire & Cornwall*, 1874, 40-2; *Choice Notes*, 1859, 172; Rev. G. S. Tyack, *Lore & Legend of the English Church*, 1899, 81, 83.

THE WHITE BIRD OF THE OXENHAMS, S. Baring-Gould, *A Book of the West*, Vol 1, 1899, 217-22; Sarah Hewett, *Nummits & Crummits*, 1900, 15-9; Mrs H. P. Whitcombe, *Bygone Days in Devonshire & Cornwall*, 1874, 109-11; S. H. Burton, *Devon Villages*, 1973, 119; Richard Cotton, *The Oxenham Omen*, in *Transactions of the Devonshire Association*, Vol 14, 1882, 221-46.

A PROPHETIC POOL, R. C. Hope, *The Legendary Lore of the Holy Wells of England*, 1893, 66; Mrs H. P. Whitcombe, *Bygone Days in Devonshire & Cornwall*, 1874, 114.

TWO INTRIGUING CHARMS, Sarah Hewett, *Nummits & Crummits*, 1900, 80 and 82.

12   *The World of Nature* (pages 171-177)

CUCKOO TRADITIONS, Sarah Hewett, *Nummits & Crummits*, 1900, 52, 110, 112.

THE RAVEN'S BIRTHDAY, Ernest W. Martin, *Heritage of the West,* 1938, 28.

RABBITS ON EASTER EVE, Ernest W. Martin, *Heritage of the West,* 1938, 30.

COCKS' EGGS, personal observations.

ADDERS AND SNAKE SKINS, Mrs Bray, *Traditions, etc., of Devonshire,* 1838, Vol I, 95; S. Baring-Gould, *A Book of the West,* Vol I, 1899, 182; *Choice Notes,* 1859, 169.

MISTLETOE, PRIMROSES AND OTHER PLANTS, Sarah Hewett, *Nummits & Crummits* 1900, 36, 57, 66, 75, 79, 119; personal communications.

DANCING TREES, S. Baring-Gould, *A Book of the West,* Vol 1, 1899, 226-32.

THE LYNMOUTH THORN, Sarah Hewett, *Nummits & Crummits,* 1900, 37.

CAT TRADITIONS, Sarah Hewett, *Nummits & Crummits,* 1900, 53, 54, 108; Mrs H. P. Whitcombe, *Bygone Days in Devonshire & Cornwall,* 1874, 6.

ROOKS & THE WEATHER, R. Inwards, *Weather Lore,* 1950, 190; personal observations.

BIRDS AND THE WEATHER, Sarah Hewett, *Nummits & Crummits,* 1900, 118-9; personal observations.

WEATHER LORE, R. Inwards, *Weather Lore,* 1950, 108, 109, 122, 190; Sarah Hewett, *Nummits & Crummits,* 1900, 105-20; S. Baring-Gould, *A Book of the West,* Vol 1, 1899, 197.

Folk Museums

Ashburton:
Local antiquities, weapons, costumes, lace, implements, lepidoptera, bygones.

Barnstaple:
North Devon Athenaeum, the Square.
Local geological specimens, local antiquities.
St. Anne's Chapel Museum, St. Peter's Churchyard, High Street (open summer only).
Local antiquities.

Bicton:
Bicton Countryside Museum.
Bicton Gardens, East Budleigh.
Countryside items, including farm machinery, crafts, etc. (open March to October).

Bideford:
Museum, Municipal Buildings.
Local pottery, shipwrights' tools, geological specimens.

Exeter:
Guildhall, High Street.
City regalia.
Royal Albert Memorial Museum, Queen Street.
Silver, paintings, glass, costume, natural history, anthropology.
Rougemont House Museum.
Archaeology and local history.

Honiton:
Allhallows Public Museum, High Street.
Lace, Devon kitchen, fossils, ancient implements.

Kingsbridge:
Cookworthy Museum, Fore Street.
Story of China Clay, Victorian kitchen, rural life, costumes, local history, shipbuilding tools, trade.

Morwellham Quay:
    Industrial archaeolog
Plymouth:
    City Museum, Drake Circus.
    Local and natural history, art.
    Elizabethan House.
    Period furnished.
    Buckland Abbey.
    Drake relics, ship models, folk gallery.
Salcombe:
    Sharpitor (National Trust).
    Local history, trade, crafts, agricultural bygones, natural history, shipbuilding.
South Molton:
    Museum, Town Hall.
    Local history, documents, bygones.
Torquay:
    Natural History Society Museum, Babbacombe Road.
    Caves, natural history, local folk culture.
Topsham:
    Museum, The Strand.
    History of the port and trade of Topsham.
Totnes:
    The Elizabethan House, Fore Street.
    Period furniture and costumes, local tools, toys and domestic items, archaeology, documents.

Bibliography

ANON. *Choice Notes from Notes & Queries*, 1859
BARING-GOULD, Rev. S.
  A Book of the West, 1899
  A Book of Dartmoor, 1900
  Devonshire Characters & Strange Events, 1908
BLAND, JOHN *Odd & Unusual England*, 1974
BRAY, MRS. *Traditions, etc., of Devonshire*, 1838, 3 vols
BRIGGS, KATHARINE *The Fairies in Tradition & Literature*, 1967
BRIGGS, K. M. and TONGUE, R. L., ed. *Folktales of England*, 1965
BURTON, S. H.
  Devon Villages, 1973
  Exmoor, 1974
  A West Country Anthology, 1975
CAWTE, E. C. HELM, ALEX and PEACOCK, N. *English Ritual Drama*, 1967
CHAMBERS, EDMUND *The English Folk Play*, 1933
CHOPE, R. P. *The Dialect of Hartland*, 1891
COSSINS, JAMES *Reminiscences of Exeter 50 Years Since*, 1878
COXHEAD, J. R. W.
  Old Devon Customs, 1953
  Legends of Devon, 1954
  Devon Traditions & Fairy Tales, 1959
  The Devil in Devon, 1967
CROSSING, W.
  Tales of the Dartmoor Pixies, 1890
  The Dartmoor Worker, 1903
  Folk Rhymes of Devon, 1911
CROSSLEY-HOLLAND, KEVIN *Pieces of Land*, 1972
Devonshire Association, Reports & Transaction of, various dates
Folklore, various dates
GASCOIGNE, MARGARET, *Discovering English Customs & Traditions*, 1969

Gentlemen's Magazine, Vol 61 1791

INWARDS, R. *Weather Lore,* 1950

HALLAM, JACK *The Haunted Inns of England,* 1972

HEWETT, SARAH
 The Peasant Speech of Devon, 1892
 Nummits & Crummits, 1900

HOLE, CHRISTINA
 Haunted England, 1940
 English Custom & Usage, 1941-2
 Witchcraft in England, 1945
 A Mirror of Witchcraft, 1965

HOPE, R. C. *The Legendary Lore of the Holy Wells of England,* 1893

HOSKINS, W. G.
 Devon, 1954
 Devon & Its People, 1954

HURLEY, JACK *Legends of Exmoor,* 1973

MAGALOTTI, COUNT L. *The Travels of Cosmo III,* 1669

MARTIN, ERNEST W. *Heritage of the West,* 1938

MOORE, — *History of Devonshire,* 1829

OPIE, IONA and PETER *Lore & Language of School Children,* 1959

PALMER, KINGSLEY *Oral Folk Tales of Wessex,* 1973

PARKER, DEREK *The West Country,* 1973

PATTEN, R. W. *Exmoor Custom & Song,* 1974

STOTHARD, A. E. *The Border of the Tamar & the Tavy,* 1879

TIDDY, R. J. E. *The Mummers' Play,* 1923

TORR, CECIL *Small Talk at Wreybridge,* 1921

PENNINGTON, ROBERT R. *Stannary Law,* 1973

TYZACK, REV. G. S. *Lore & Legend of the English Church,* 1899

UPLYME WOMEN'S INSTITUTE *The Story of Uplyme,* 1970

Western Antiquary, Vol. 1, 1881

Western Folklore, Vol. 31, 1972

WESTCOTE, THOMAS, *A View of Devonshire in 1630*

WHITCOMBE, MRS. H. P. *Bygone Days in Devonshire & Cornwall,* 1874

WILLIAM OF MALMESBURY *Chronicle of the Kings of England,* c. 1135,
 ed. 1847

WRIGHT, A. R.
 British Calendar Customs, 1936
 British Calendar Cures, 1938

Index of Tale Types

Folktales are classified on an international system based on their plots, devised by Antti Aarne and Stith Thompson in *The Types of the Folktale*, 1961, with numbers preceded by AT. Local legends were partly classified by R Th. Christiansen in *The Migratory Legends*, 1958; his system was expanded by K. M. Briggs in *A Dictionary of British Folktales*, 1970-1. These numbers are preceded by ML, and the latter are also asterisked.

Motif Index

Motifs, which are elements recurring within the plots of several folktales (e.g. 'cruel stepmother' in both 'Snow White' and 'Cinderella') have been classified thematically in Stith Thompson's *Motif Index of Folk Literature*, 1966, and E. Baughman's *Type and Motif Index of the Folktales of England and North America*.

General Index